THE
YEARS
BETWEEN

THE
YEARS
BETWEEN

MY EXPERIENCES IN BRITISH COLUMBIA
REFLECTING A CENTURY OF CHANGE

Fay Pettapiece

Published in 2022 by Kinetics Design, KDbooks.ca
ISBN 978-1-988360-80-5 (paperback)
ISBN 978-1-988360-81-2 (ebook)

Editor and project manager: Eloise Lewis, LifeTales, www.lifetales.ca

Cover and interior design, typesetting, online publishing, and printing
by Daniel Crack, Kinetics Design, KDbooks.ca
www.linkedin.com/in/kdbooks/

To my family

for their support in writing this book

and in life.

Contents

"In the modern world we have invented ways of speeding up inventions, and people's lives change so fast that a person is born into one kind of world, grows up in another, and by the time his children are growing up, lives in still a different world."

– Margaret Mead

Preface

I walked four miles to school with cougars lurking nearby. I gathered oysters, clams and crabs from our ever-giving shores, picked wild raspberries, blackberries and huckleberries from our dense forests, churned butter from our cow's milk and lived without electricity or running water.

I was not a pioneer, but my grandmother was. At 13 years old, my grandmother arrived in Vancouver in the 1890s, when Granville Street was a skid road flanked by towering fir and cedar trees, and then spent most of her life in Bella Coola, a remote community on the north coast of British Columbia, and where, as a 10-year-old, I had the good fortune of spending a summer.

My early life, which took place in various locales throughout British Columbia, sometimes imitated pioneer life.

The First Nations have a long history in British Columbia, but it is not a written history. Theirs comes through stories handed down through generations. My purpose in writing this book is to likewise share my stories and show my descendants, and perhaps those new to Canada, what life was like in Canada years ago. Life was not easy, and the differences between then and now are monumental.

While the pioneer days were extremely challenging, when I was born in Vancouver in 1931, life was very basic, with none of the modern conveniences we now take for granted. Most people were poor, but they were kind and helped each other when they could. There was almost no crime, and doors were rarely locked as no one would think of stealing from anyone else. We made our own fun, like dancing to a wind-up gramophone, which usually wound down before the music ended, or playing hopscotch on the street. As children, we were happy, while our parents struggled to feed, clothe and care for us.

This book is comprised of a series of anecdotes I have written over the years. Although in general chronological order, many of the stories stand alone. I have attempted to incorporate some of the fascinating historical details of the transitional years between the pioneer days of our ancestors in Western Canada and life as we know it in the 21st century. My life adventures are a reflection of the changes we have experienced in the years between.

1

My Childhood

CITY LIFE

My First Marriage

Nineteen thirty-six. It was the year that the roof of the Vancouver Forum collapsed due to the weight of snow; it was the year that I picked off all the heads of the next-door neighbour's flowers; and it was the year of my first marriage. I was five years old.

Billy and I were the youngest children on the block. The older ones, aged eight to 12, were usually good to us, giving us sleigh rides in the winter and taking us to the beach in the summer. They did, however, regard us a little like dolls, and one slow May afternoon, they decided that it would be fun to have a wedding ceremony, with the two of us as the bride and groom.

My mother, Flora, often dressed me in blue. At that time, all little girls wore dresses, not pants, when they went out to play, so I had a blue dress on. Billy was sent home to put on something more elegant — a pair of black pants and a white shirt.

A six-foot-long old lace curtain became a veil and was somehow attached to my unruly straight hair. Someone handed me a bouquet made up of local flowers: dandelions, buttercups and bleeding hearts.

Grass served as the greenery. My eight-year-old bridesmaid, also in blue, had found a battered straw hat complete with a tired pink rose. She carried a bouquet similar to mine. Billy stood stalwartly and seriously beside me. The 10-year-old preacher wore an oversized jacket with short pants, and he solemnly held in front of him a large brown book open somewhere near the middle.

The ceremony commenced and was over almost as soon as it began, as no one was entirely certain of what was said at a wedding except "Do you take this man?" and "Do you take this woman?" Billy and I followed all instructions, which really only meant saying "I do" at the right time. A ring was produced and put on my finger, and we were married.

We had mud pies and imaginary tea at the reception and then we put the props away, returned the ring and went to our respective homes for dinner.

When we went out to play the next day, I announced to the group that my family was moving. I wasn't sure where, but it would happen very soon. Everyone took the news calmly and we began our usual games of Anti-I-Over (a ball game) and Kick the Can. My family was, in fact, moving to another part of Vancouver, only two miles away, but at that time, few people had cars and streetcars cost money. I might as well have been travelling to another part of the world.

Later that day, when everyone had gone home, the doorbell rang and Billy appeared at the door, tears streaming down his face and a small suitcase in his hand. He didn't want to leave his family — five, after all, is a rather early age to leave the nest — but his wife was moving and he knew he was supposed to stay with his wife. Fortunately, our parents knew each other and were able to give a satisfactory explanation as to why he didn't have to move with me, and a very relieved Billy returned home to his mother and father.

Franklin Street

Following my childhood "marriage" to Billy, our family moved to Franklin Street, in Vancouver's east end, not far from Hastings Park. The house was a large, brown-shingled edifice, circa 1912. In the front yard stood a sturdy holly tree with branches at suitable intervals for climbing and a large purple rhododendron, which almost covered the small amount of grass on the other side of the walkway. The steps led to a spacious front porch and a carved doorway that framed a six-foot bevelled mirror.

Our house on Franklin Street

The day we moved in, my father, Harry, climbed the stairs carrying a box in his arms and our large cat perched on his shoulders. Suddenly, the cat spotted his reflection in the mirror and, with claws in full traction, ripped down my father's back and flew down the street, never to be seen again — a wise decision on his part, as my father was not noted for his patience or forgiveness. The house, although it sounds grand, was not. But it was large, and the rent was $25 a month. We lived on the main floor with a living room, dining room, kitchen, pantry and two bedrooms. We kept one of the upstairs rooms for my mother's half-brother, George, who came to town occasionally. Uncle George logged in various parts of the province and came to town during snow and fire season and at Christmas. He paid us five dollars a month.

The rest of the upstairs was rented to a family of three for $10 a month. They had a kitchen, dining room, two bedrooms and a large room with bay windows overlooking the backyard. The only bathroom in the house was upstairs. Toilet and bath were in separate rooms and were shared by both families plus whoever happened to be staying in the upstairs room. Strangely, no one seemed to have a problem with this arrangement. Maybe we all had better bladders in those days, and we certainly spent much less time grooming ourselves.

It was our job to stoke the furnace and pay for all the wood and coal required, which was brought by East Indians (which was the term used then), who seemed to have the monopoly on fuel delivery. I have clear recollections of those men in turbans, their skin blackened from carrying bags of coal on their backs. The coal was sent down a chute into a corner of the dark basement. The wood was dumped in a pile outside and my father, with minimal help from me, stacked it beside the house to protect it from the ever-present winter Vancouver rain.

It turned out that I was living on a girls' block. No boys lived on it and none were allowed. There were some boys who lived on the street below that ran perpendicular to ours, but if one ever ventured up the street, he was met by a phalanx of girls and sent back to the little shack area that made up that section of the district. The boys lived in squalid conditions, and, in retrospect, we could have been kinder, but children are not always kind, and we were no exception.

A few years later, all the people in the shacks moved out in unison. Maybe they found jobs, but I think the government moved them. As soon as they were gone, we went down to see what the shacks were like. What we found appalled us. One or two rooms with bare floors or no floors at all, open gaps in the walls, no bathrooms (there was a ravine behind the shacks) and dilapidated in every way. I guess, for a brief time, we felt some remorse for our behaviour, but it was short-lived. For those on the east side of the city, the depression years were not happy ones.

I didn't have a doll, or any other toys, for that matter. My father smoked — the roll-your-own variety — and he considered it his right, as it was his only indulgence. One evening, however, he headed for the store with 20 cents in his pocket, enough to buy tobacco and cigarette paper; but he didn't go to the store. He walked to Hastings Park and went straight to the arcade. He found the bingo booth and paid 10 cents for a card. He played, but no Bingo. He looked at his remaining 10 cents. He could still buy a little tobacco, but he decided to put down those last cents and … BINGO! He said, "I'll have that doll on the top shelf," and returned home with a huge doll dressed in a pink bonnet, pink dress and white shoes tucked under his arm. He was not embarrassed, and I could see the happiness on his face when he handed it to me. It was almost as big as I was! I'm not sure when it was put away, or lost, or given away, or thrown out, but I do wish I had kept it as a tangible part of a wonderful memory of my dad.

These were lean years, but Dad got a job at the *Vancouver Sun* newspaper, so we were able to buy food and pay the rent. There were many in Vancouver on relief, hungry and desperate. My father instructed my mother to supply a meal to whoever came looking for food, even if there was nothing extra or not even enough for us. Many times, I would come home from school to find a thin, tattered man siting on our porch, eating what might have been his only meal of the day or even the week. Sometimes they chopped a little wood or raked a few leaves to pay for their meal. Sometimes these men, or men like them, were found on the streets of Vancouver, collapsed and dying of starvation.

• • •

At five, I was the youngest on the street. Betty, my best friend, was a year older, and the others ranged in age up to 12. And then there was Moira — the beautiful Moira — who was going to university. She had wavy black hair, green eyes and a smile that lit up the day. She certainly lit up my day, and I would wait for her to come home from university just to get a smile and a hello. To be honest, I did not know what university was, but if Moira was going there, I wanted to go there too.

One day, I announced that when I got older, I would go to university. My father shook his head and said, "Don't be silly. Girls are not supposed to go to university; they're not smart enough." He would repeat this remark over the next 12 years.

Well, it was September and time to begin school. Unfortunately, I lived on the "wrong" side of the street, which, I soon realized, was the "right" side of the street. The children in all odd-numbered houses went to MacDonald School and those from the even-numbered houses went to Hastings School. Betty and all the other girls were odd, and I was even, which meant that not only could I not go to school with my best friend, but I also had to walk the eight long blocks alone, four times a day, as everyone had to go home for lunch. There were three classes of each grade, neatly divided into high, medium and low IQ levels. I don't know how they could really establish a six-year-old's IQ level. My teacher was a stern old lady (of about 35) with pleated hair. She whipped us all into shape and gave us our bathroom orders and cues — one or two fingers raised as the situation demanded, so that she and everyone else in class knew what we were up to in the bathroom.

Hastings turned out to be a somewhat advanced school. Once we were in the second grade, we moved from homeroom to geography, arithmetic and gym, with different teachers. We had our own lockers and were expected to take care of our own gym strip, have the proper books with us for each class and, generally, be responsible for ourselves. Some education pundits may think that this was too heavy a load for a seven-year-old, but I liked the concept and think that it was an early positive step towards independence and responsibility.

At that time, children were allowed much more independence and freedom than they have these days, both inside the school and out. The dark factions of our society were not apparent. Murders and kidnappings were unheard of, and even destitute people would not think of invading a house. We had permission to grow.

The Upstairs Room

People who travel the world often comment that the poorest people they encounter are often the most generous and willing to share what they have with friends and strangers alike. During the depression years, while many people were very poor, they were also willing to share with neighbours, friends and down-and-out hobos who called at their door looking for a meal. The terms "one-upmanship" or "keeping up with the Joneses" did not exist and people were not running to the store every day to buy a new radio or lamp just because they could afford it. There was no buying on credit.

During the time we lived on Franklin Street, we shared our house with many long- and short-term visitors. As mentioned, my Uncle George was seldom in town, but his room was often occupied by the many people passing through our lives.

When Blondie came to town, life took on a new excitement. For me, it meant ice cream by the carton! Blondie was a handsome, kind Icelandic logger who headed straight for the beer parlours when he came to town. He usually arrived at the house by way of my father finding him stumbling around or unconscious on the street and somehow loading him onto the streetcar (my father was not a big man, so this was not easily accomplished) and hauling him home. Dad worked at the *Vancouver Sun*, which was in downtown Vancouver's east side, where there were plenty of cheap restaurants, like White Lunch, and beer parlours where loggers, freshly released from the confinement of camps, made it a priority to visit to get loaded.

After a day or two of recovery in the upstairs room, Blondie, who was plagued with stomach ulcers, would emerge and hand me a large sum of money (at least two dollars) to go and buy ice cream. His head had stopped throbbing, which had intensified the severe pain in his stomach. He believed that ice cream would put out the fire. This was my cue to collect Betty and run to the Garden Dairy, where they sold every ice cream flavour in the world. We bought a huge amount of our favourite (peach, at the time) and brought it home to Blondie, who would eat one small dish and leave the rest for us! In 1938, you could buy a lot of ice cream for two dollars and, as there was no refrigeration, it had to be eaten all at once.

After a reasonable length of recovery and more trips to the Garden Dairy on my part, Blondie headed back to the woods where alcohol was limited (only as much as one could carry in, and that lasted only a day or two), and we looked forward to his next visit in about six months.

My maternal grandmother, Emma Gledhill, came to stay in the upstairs room too. She lived in Bella Coola, a remote village on the north coast of B.C. with few amenities. Bella Coola had a hospital, of sorts (my mother had been born there), but not one that did major surgeries, so she came when she needed an abdominal operation. When she recovered, she was, as far as I was concerned, a sweet and gentle addition to the family. My father complained that she always argued with him, but in retrospect, I realize that it was difficult not to argue with my father. Grandma Emma was of Austrian parentage but was born in the Bohemian part of Czechoslovakia. She was artistic and played the zither. She played and sang and taught me the German words to her songs, which I much preferred to English, probably because it sounded different and exotic to me.

Unusual smells often emanated from our house when Grandma was there. One day, arriving home from school, I was met with an odd odour floating up from the basement. When I asked about it, my questions were more or less ignored, so I let it pass. The next day, neither I nor the horrible stench could be ignored. I was sure the basement toilet had erupted, not once, but several times. Finally, I learned Grandma was making sauerkraut — by the crock full. Then I found out that people actually ate it — and liked it! It was completely beyond my comprehension, and I complained about it every day until the fermentation was complete and the only reminder of what had been festering in the crocks was the faint smell of vinegar. To my horror, my grandmother ate some of it every single day.

On another occasion, my mother and father were going out for the evening — a rare occurrence in itself — and Grandma was to look after me. As usual, I had a cold. Grandma waited until my parents were out the door to begin preparations for my cold cure. She peeled and chopped a whole head of garlic, then fried it in butter and heaped it on pieces of toast. Being a picky eater, I was dubious, but I trusted my grandmother and munched on the garlic-laden toast. I loved it and demanded more. She complied. My parents came home and staggered as the air, heavy with garlic, assaulted their senses. My grandmother was in trouble. It took two days to get the air in the house back to normal and about a week to get the garlicky B.O. out of my pores. My cold miraculously disappeared, but we were never allowed to use that cure again.

Grandma was with us for about six months. It was a sad day for me when she boarded the boat to go back to Bella Coola, leaving the upstairs room empty once again.

My mother's brother, George, was ten years older than her. He was a logger who came around every six months, when the camps closed for fire season, Christmas or snow. Uncle George, like many loggers, was a gentle man who loved children. He said very little, smiled a lot and called me "Sunshine." No doubt he had little to say, as I'm sure logging camp conversation was not always appropriate to bring into family life. He sustained a few injuries in the woods, including a serious one, when a log rolled on him, smashing his arm and hand. He stayed with us for three or four months, as his arm healed in a cast with his fingers spread over an ingenious grid and held in place by gut string pulled through a hole in each fingernail and attached to a flat board. He regained almost full use of his hand, although he could not make a tight fist. He went back to work at the camp as if nothing happened. The old loggers were indeed tough people.

But it was never long before the upstairs room was again occupied.

Next was Rena. She and her husband, Horace, were having marital problems and she wanted to leave him. He was a large, loud, belligerent man who smoked smelly cigars, and Rena came to stay in our upstairs room to get away from him. Although Horace threatened my father many times, Dad, who was a very slim five-foot-seven, was not intimidated by anyone, large or small.

For a while, there was a good deal of tension in the household, but Horace did not follow through with his threats to kill my dad, the divorce was finalized and things quieted down. Rena stayed and found another boyfriend — a wealthy one. Frank owned a garage, a car dealership and a Duesenberg, which was a luxury car that went 100 miles an hour. Few of them were made. It was exciting to me

— not because it was a Duesenberg, but because it was a car. We did not own one, of course, and any car was exciting. Frank used to sit me on his lap and let me steer. The best part of it all is that I can still impress some people, to this day, when I say, "I drove a Duesenberg." Rena turned out to be an ungrateful, manipulative and unpleasant person, but more on that later.

My mother's half-sister, Dona, who was 10 years younger than my mother, came to stay in the upstairs room for a few days when she was 19. She was pretty and nice, and I wanted to be near her as much as I could. In fact, one night I was allowed to go up to the room and sleep with her in the old brass bed. The consequences of this are as follows.

At school, a new activity had been added to our classroom routine. At 11:45 each day, we were allowed to stand up in front of the class to tell a joke, discuss a current event or talk about something of interest that had happened that week. I had heard a new joke from the girls on my street, and this seemed to be the ideal time to share it with the class. In my clearest voice and with perfect diction (I had practiced), I asked, "What did the diaper say to the baby?" No one knew, so I gave the answer: "Drop it kid, I've got you covered."

Everyone loved the joke, except one very important person: the teacher. Her face turned red, her pleated hair stood up and she began to yell. "How could you have such a dirty mind? Where have you learned such filth?" and worst of all, "Because of this performance, current events will never be allowed in this classroom again." In fact, I was pretty sure that *I* wouldn't be allowed in the classroom again. I went home for lunch, although I knew I was so bad and so unworthy I didn't deserve any. I felt terrible, ill, in fact. I couldn't tell my mother about the incident and risk another scolding, and I certainly did not want to go back to school and have everyone in the class furious with me because the best part of the day had been cancelled.

Suddenly, my mother looked at me closely and said, "You can't go back to school today." Had she heard? Had the teacher phoned? "You have the measles," she explained. "You have to go straight to the upstairs room, get into bed and close the curtains. You cannot have any light in your eyes for several days." Under normal circumstances, this would have been severe punishment, but, as it was, it became the perfect escape. She probably always wondered why I complied so easily with such a penalty, but I was happy to be saved from a fate I did not wish to contemplate.

How this all came about goes back to the night I had slept in the upstairs room with Dona. She was unknowingly in the contagious stage of measles, but because she had left the next day and people were not able to communicate quickly back then, we were unaware of her measles until days later. So I spent a week in the upstairs room, happily serving out my sentence. Justifiably, the teacher also suffered some punishment. When I did not return to school that day or the next, or for two weeks, she believed that she had offended me deeply and broken my spirit. She felt great remorse. She reinstated current events and I was able to return, somewhat triumphant, to my Grade 3 classroom.

The upstairs room allowed me to experience several cameos of people in different stages of life. We shared our home with these people and they shared a part of their lives with us.

East End Adventures

At seven years old, one might say I was living on the edge. I lived three houses up from Lakewood Street, which is the street that divided those of us who lived in decent, but not elegant houses from the shacks the boys lived in and the foundry, as well as other industrial buildings. We never went beyond Lakewood. We went up the hill to the blind man's home, which sat in the middle of a lovely park and had a beautiful high granite wall on one side. A talented pianist named Ronnie Adams, who sometimes played on the local radio stations, lived there. We often saw him walking around the grounds, white cane in hand. We continued up to the playground where there were swings, a shallow pool and teeter-totters. In the summer, young people often ran programs for the small children in the area. Farther up was an attractive wooden Anglican church, complete with a rosette window, and farther still was my school. This was the limit for Betty and me to roam and we were content with that.

One day, however, we did wander below Lakewood Street. It

was December, and I had just been told some upsetting news. Even though my father had a job, we did not have enough money to buy a Christmas tree. Not even a small one. Everyone else had one, or was going to have one, and we weren't. Betty, of course, was the recipient of my frustration as I stormed around in despair. And then I began to walk … right across Lakewood, past the foundry, past the iron works and almost to the ports and the sugar refinery, loyal Betty trailing me all the way. Finally, having rid myself of the anger and the hopelessness I had been feeling, I stopped. But where were we? Realizing that I was the one to have gotten us into this situation, my mood took a different turn as I tried to remember streets or landmarks that would help to lead us home. The unfamiliar streets were mostly dead ends, leading to shipyards and grain elevators. Finally, we found Franklin Street and began our journey home.

We had walked about two blocks when a large truck came around the corner. It was piled high with Christmas trees. I looked longingly at the huge stack of trees and wished fervently that one would fall off. Then I noticed that one on the top was beginning to slide and, as the truck hit a bump in the road, down came the tree. What luck! I briefly considered calling out to the driver, but the thought quickly passed and we dove on that tree as though it was going to escape. Then we began dragging it — one, two, five, eight blocks — until we were finally home. We proudly presented the tree to my mother, who declared that it was the most beautiful tree she had ever seen, in spite of the one bare side that lost every needle and some of the branches during its long journey on hard pavement. It was erected that evening with the bare side placed discreetly against the wall.

Now all that was left to do was decorate it. But with what? We had no decorations. My grandmother, who was living with us at the time, came to the rescue. As we were used to having to "make do" and be creative, we embarked on crafting homemade decorations. First, we popped corn and strung it on long threads, alternating with cranberries Then we combined a thick syrup and popcorn to make snowballs, which we hung on the tree. Then we cut silver paper into various shapes and used long strips of coloured paper to form chains of various lengths. When all the decorations were on the tree, in my eyes, it was the most beautiful thing in the world. My only present that year was a colouring book, but I was happy with that and my wonderful tree.

• • •

With Christmas and New Year's celebrations over, it was time to go back to school. In Vancouver, January is rainy, cold and wet. My mother, deciding that she had a fragile child, was determined to protect me from the cold and bundled me in every conceivable form of clothing she could think of — all of which I despised. There were the horrible rubbers that pulled over the tops of shoes. Then there were the much-despised cotton stockings, which bagged everywhere and were attached to an uncomfortable garter belt that refused to stay in place. I was always pulling at myself to get it straightened enough so that my heels did not become my toes — not a sophisticated movement. Then came the mitts — idiot mitts, actually, as they were connected by a long line that slid through the sleeves of my coat and hung stupidly out of the sleeves when the coat was not in use. The mitts and scarf were usually hand-knit by my grandmother from whatever wool she could scrounge and were an array of mismatched colours. The hat, made by my mother, topped off the ensemble. It was round with a flat top, in a rusty shade of brown.

I hated all this extra clothing and would have been happy with a coat or sweater, as I usually lost or misplaced one or two of the accessories and would receive a severe scolding on my return home. The old adage "you would lose your head if it wasn't tacked on" was a much-used cliché in our house. The final blow came the day my mother handed me a large, black, ugly umbrella. I wanted nothing to do with it, but my protestations were to no avail. I stormed out of the house looking like a coat rack on which someone had carelessly thrown a bunch of unwanted clothes, and, in addition, I had the responsibility of having to look after yet another ugly and unwanted accoutrement.

On my way home from school with most of my accessories (no hat, no scarf), I was passing the blind man's home when I looked at the long granite wall bordering the property and the street. The top was easily accessible on the Franklin Street end but as Templeton Street sloped down, the wall became about eight feet high at the bottom. I looked at the black umbrella I was clutching in my hand and then at the towering wall and decided that this might be a good day to try my hand at flying. I could jump off the wall and even if the outspread umbrella did not float me safely down, there was a nice patch of grass between the wall and the street that I could land on.

I climbed the wall and worked my way to the high end. I looked down. It was very high to a seven-year-old. But, I reasoned, since I was small and the umbrella was large, I should have a nice flight. I took off and the umbrella sustained me for a few seconds, enough to get me over the grass, then it inverted and down I went onto the hard pavement. I was stunned and everything hurt, especially my legs. This may have been the moment I developed my fear of heights. After the initial shock, I slowly began to move. Nothing seemed to be broken and I got up and dragged myself home. I was met at home by an exasperated mother, but at least I did not get scolded for forgetting my hat and scarf, and I never had to take an umbrella to school again.

Buddy

Buddy came to live with us when he was six weeks old. He was a happy, lively German shepherd and he immediately settled right in with our family. It wasn't long before we realized that he was not only a beautiful little dog but also very intelligent. He was easily trained to bring his dish for dinner, which must have been difficult for him to pick up and carry, since it was a round, enamel bowl. He also did all the other doggie tricks like fetch the paper, sit up, roll over and give a paw. He loved playing with all the girls on the street, and everyone loved Buddy.

He quickly grew into a handsome dog, still playful and always willing to please.

One day, we learned that Buddy had a few tricks of his own, born of natural instinct. Shepherds are, after all, guard dogs. My mother had ordered a 100-pound sack of potatoes to be delivered to our house on a Saturday. Suddenly, she realized that we were going to be away for the day (an unusual occurrence). At that time, doors were rarely locked, so she told the delivery man the door would be open and to leave the potatoes in the basement, and the two dollars she owed him would be on the work bench. We left at about nine in the morning and the man arrived, potatoes on his back, about two hours later. He opened the door, placed his potatoes on the floor and picked up his money. As he turned to go, he heard a low growl. At the door, blocking his exit, sat Buddy. If the man moved towards the door, Buddy's teeth were bared, accompanied by the warning growl. The man sat down on his potatoes and remained there, almost motionless, until five o'clock, when we returned home. We were somewhat amused by the incident but sorry for the man too. He had probably worked for several months to plant, grow, dig, clean and pack his potatoes and then deliver them. He had lost an entire day and, perhaps, several customers. Unfortunately for Buddy, his desire to protect his owners caused him to come to a possibly less than pleasant end.

The following summer, we were all out on the street playing our usual games with Buddy. A few in the group of girls decided to try something new. They each grabbed the edge of the blanket and told me to sit in the middle (I was the smallest and youngest). Together, they tossed me in the air as I yelled and laughed. Buddy, afraid that they were hurting me, rushed up and bit one of the girls. It was more of a nip than a bite, but blood was drawn. The girl's parents did not threaten us, but my father instantly decided that Buddy must go. I cried, pleaded and cajoled, but to no avail. We could not risk a lawsuit if he did it again, and indeed he might, in defence of his family.

Dad had heard of a fisherman who was having a problem with gear being stolen from his boat. It was explained to me that Buddy was a working dog and this would be the ideal job for him. I reluctantly agreed, as there was really no choice, and Buddy was given to the fisherman. Initially, all went well and there were no more thefts. Then I heard that there was a problem. When the boats were rafted together at the wharf, if his boat was tied to the wharf, Buddy would let the other fisherman get to their boats, but he wouldn't let them off! They were trapped until his owner returned.

I never did learn what happened to him in the end. He may have been given to another person or family, and I have always hoped so, but knowing the times and the expendability of animals, I suspect he did not survive very long. A waste of a wonderful dog.

Memories of the War

Some childhood memories are ephemeral and vague, while others are lasting and leave a deep impression that is carried into adulthood. I have many memories of when I was eight. Maybe I was reaching a stage of awareness or perhaps something new was happening to the world — my world. There was some kind of war starting. I knew because people were talking about it a lot.

Nursery rhyme clock that my neighbour gave me as a child. It has stayed in my family, to be enjoyed by my children and grandchildren

My friend Betty's father was a petty officer in the navy and was now being looked upon as a very important person on our street. And Mrs. Wickman, our next-door neighbour, was worried because, although she was English and on our side, her husband was German, and he was going to have to stay out of sight for the rest of the war. As a matter of fact, I don't remember seeing him after war was declared, so maybe he really did stay hidden away in a corner of their house or in the basement, or maybe he had a night job. Maybe he gardened at night too, because their yard had a lovely lawn and flowers in contrast to ours, which was full of couch grass, a few potatoes and some raspberry canes. Although I never got beyond the kitchen door, I think the Wickman's house was neat inside and out. They had no children, so I suppose that somewhat explains all the tidiness. She was a short, heavy-set woman who seemed rather austere. I didn't think she liked me very much, until one day she gave me a beautiful clock. Post-depression, there were few gifts and those received were fully appreciated. She probably had thought carefully about who the recipient would be. The clock had an enamel face with brightly coloured nursery rhyme characters on it. See-Saw Margery Daw, Mary Mary Quite Contrary and Peter Peter Pumpkin Eater were all in little sections around the periphery of the clock. It also had a pendulum and a key to wind it up to last for seven days. I loved that clock and kept it for my children and grandchildren, who now have it. I doubt that any one of them ever had the pleasure from it that I did. I wish I could tell Mrs. Wickman how much enjoyment I got from her gift.

Jim's store was on the corner of Templeton and Hastings streets, just two blocks away. Betty and I were regular customers. Jim was Japanese and his store looked like every other Japanese corner store, with cigarette ads plastered on the exterior — Sweet Caporal, Players, Black Cat — along with other ads for Orange Crush, Coca-Cola, O'Henry and Coffee Crisp bars. Did he get paid by the companies to do that? Inside, the store was quite dark, with oiled floors, a Coca-Cola cooler with ice, a section of very tired vegetables, some shelves of canned goods and, most important, a large glass display case of one-cent candy. We thought he had the best selection of penny candy anywhere, and whenever we could find a penny we would hurry up to Jim's and spend 10 or 15 minutes deciding what candy was going to give us the most satisfaction, value and flavour for our investment. Jim would stand patiently as we decided on one, and just as he would reach for it, we would change our minds. Sometimes I bought a candy but would often save up five pennies and buy ice cream in a cylinder, wrapped in waxed paper and plunked into a cone. I don't know how he could have made much of a living from the store, but in those days, everyone was poor, and he must have made enough to survive. He was always cheerful and kind to us.

In 1940, a little girl from Newcastle upon Tyne arrived on my street. Wilma was on the "even side" and could go to Hastings School — my school — and was even in my class. I rushed home to tell my parents that a new girl in my class had just "evaporated" from England. She talked a little funny, of course, but that made her fascinating. She had a Yorkshire accent and many interesting expressions, some of which required explanation, like "hoist with his own petard," and she was smart. She had beaten me in a spelling bee and although I was not happy about it, I had to respect her for it, considering that I thought her English needed some improvement.

She told me about the mysteries of England and the wonderful food, like "bread and drippin.'" She told me it was the absolute best food in the world, and I really must get my mother to make some. As I was the world's pickiest eater, I went home and demanded bread and drippin'. My mother warned me that I would not like it, but I persisted, so one day, bread and drippin' appeared on my plate. As I ate it, I began to suspect that Wilma had less than exotic tastes than I had hoped.

Wilma had several brothers and sisters and her family was quite poor. I don't know why she was the only one from her family to come to Canada. She lived with a nice young couple who had no children and who, I think, really wanted to adopt her. Whether they did or not remains one of the many unknowns in my life, as we would soon be on the move again and I lost track of both her and Betty.

• • •

On Sundays, we listened to the radio as the conversations of the evacuated children speaking to their parents in England were broadcast on CBC. In the beginning, the conversations were quite formal.

"How do you like Canada, dear?"

"Oh, it's lovely, Mummy."

As time went on, the answers became "Oh, it's swell," along with other coarse words that crept into their vocabulary, like "super" and "hubba-hubba," which were met with gasps on the other end of the phone line.

I'm sure there were many worried parents questioning the wisdom of sending their children to this uncouth country. And, of course, they did stop sending them when the German U-boats became thick in the Atlantic and one of the ships, the SS *City of Benares*, was sunk on September 15, 1940, causing the loss of 77 children.

Something else very bad happened too. A year later, there was a huge bombing raid in a place called Pearl Harbor. It was some place in the United States, and the United States was close to us. Everyone was upset. It was the Japanese who had done this. How could Jim (our kind storekeeper) and his friends and countrymen do such a thing? He was so kind and gentle. Weren't all Japanese like Jim? But Jim hadn't done it. He was still in his store, patiently waiting for us to choose our penny candy. Of course, Jim was not going to be at his store for long. Almost immediately, all Japanese were removed from the 100-mile wide strip along the West Coast, designated as a protected area. We told Jim we didn't want him to go. "I don't want to go," he quietly responded, "but I have to."

I ran home, objecting to my parents, and they said, "It's the law. All Japanese must go."

Within days, the store was boarded up and all Japanese were incarcerated in Hastings Park, living in deplorable conditions, before they were sent to various locations in the interior of the province to live in more deplorable conditions. Someone got the store for little, if any, money, but I never went there again, partly because I could not bear to go without my friend Jim being there, and partly because we were moving again — on Christmas Eve, 1941.

COUNTRY LIFE

Pitt Meadows

Dad quit his job at the *Vancouver Sun*. Three years was a long time for him to be at any one job, and he had met a fellow who owned a fishing boat, who said he could join him for the summer to fish the local waters and share in the catch. My mother was probably not pleased with this new scheme.

We had had a small but steady income for three years, were able to buy a radio as tall as I was, a sofa and two lamps. When the Raleigh or Watkins man came to the door with his suitcase full of interesting bottles and wonderful-smelling packages, we could afford to buy the odd bit of lavender soap or a special cleaning cream. When the Chinese vegetable man came by with a yoke over his shoulders and two huge baskets full of fresh fruit and vegetables slung from them, we could buy a little from him too. The dairy delivery wagon, pulled by two huge Clydesdale horses, with what I thought were horns but were part of the harness, came by every day, leaving their customary deposits up and down the streets. That was Vancouver in 1939, and life was good.

After he'd left the *Vancouver Sun*, Dad didn't have much money, but he had had a wonderful summer. He learned how to fish, manage all the gear and navigate the convoluted coast with chart and compass. It also spawned a dream: to own his own boat and ply the waters every summer in search of salmon, which at that time was quite plentiful.

When he returned after the season, he didn't have a job. Jobs at that time were more elusive than the salmon. Dad was intelligent, but he didn't have a lot of staying power, and he did not like having people in authority telling him what to do. Much to everyone's relief, he got a lab job with Canada Packers, and a few months later, with a dairy. Frank, our tenant Rena's boyfriend, had a friend named Charlie who owned the dairy, and Dad got a job in production. Again, things were going along quite well when Frank came along with a proposal. He had just bought a gas station, store and lunch counter in Pitt Meadows, in the Fraser Valley, and he suggested that Dad, Mom and Rena be partners in the business. Most likely it was a make-work project for Rena.

Pitt Meadows was a small dairy community about 30 miles east of Vancouver surrounded by the Pitt, Alouette and Fraser Rivers. It was, of course, prone to flooding, so there were dykes along the Fraser and perhaps along the other two rivers as well. In the middle was a huge peat bog and everything was wet-wet-wet. I can hardly remember a day without rain.

We arrived at our new place on Christmas Eve. The first things to come into view were two shiny red gas pumps topped with purple and yellow liquids enclosed in glass cylinders and a handle below. Bottles of oil with silver tops stood in a rack at the front door. As we ventured inside, I saw a long mahogany counter with stools in front. There were cans of vegetables, bottles of ketchup and various grocery items lining the shelves. Against one wall stood a huge Wurlitzer jukebox with its Art Deco design of red and green back-lit plastic and a multitude of knobs and buttons. To the right there was a doorway to our living quarters: a small living room, a tiny bedroom for me and a slightly larger one for my mother and father. The kitchen was fairly large, as it had to service not only our family but also the lunch counter section of the business. There was a wood and coal stove but no running water. The drinking water was delivered in a milk can once a week, and the wash water for cooking, dishes, clothes and ourselves was caught in a rain barrel at the back door. A door on the left side of the store lunch counter area led to a long porch-like room where Rena lived — when she was there.

Frank had bought the business with the idea that Rena and my mother would run the store and lunch counter, and my father would look after the gas station. Although it was a good plan in theory, it was doomed to fail, and my first night there was a preview of the life we would live for the next year and a half.

Shortly after we arrived, I had to go to the bathroom. There wasn't one! I was told to go to the outhouse. What was that? I looked out the back door and saw what looked like a huge lake with a long wharf running out to a tiny building in the distance. I was not going out there, it was pitch black and pouring rain. I would fall off the wharf and drown, and no one would ever find me. Being physically urged out the door, I began to scream and cry. Finally, someone took me by the hand and led me to the outhouse all the while trying to allay my fears by telling me that the water on either side was only a few inches deep. I was not convinced. Water everywhere and not one drop of it useable! With that over with, I went to bed, but I was cold. The walls had just been plastered and were still wet and were, no doubt, giving off tons of cold moisture — far too much for the stove two rooms away to overcome. No one thought of Christmas or Santa Claus that night.

We did have Christmas dinner though. A young, pretty lady came into the store on Christmas Day. She was troubled because she had a turkey and didn't know how to cook it. She had come from a privileged family and didn't know how to cook anything. She was not cut out to be a farm wife. After some discussion, a happy resolution was found. My mother would cook Christmas dinner, including the turkey with stuffing, and we would have Christmas dinner together. She and her husband had a farm across the highway and theirs was a house in progress, but it was warm, the food was good and Christmas did not completely pass us by that year.

• • •

The school bus came at 7:30 a.m. and I was one of the first on board. We rumbled for miles around the peat bog, picking up soggy children along the way. At 8:15, we arrived at a one-room school at Dyke One where we had to get off and wait, in the rain, until the bus returned a half hour later with another group of children and take us all together to our one-room school near Dyke Two. I have no idea why he didn't just drive us straight to Dyke Two then continue on to pick up the second group of children, instead of making us stand in the rain for half an hour. We were able to get into this school, but it was still cold, as the janitor did not arrive until 9:00 to start the fire in the pot-bellied stove. As anyone who has ever been in a room with a pot-bellied stove knows, once it gets going, it throws a tremendous amount of heat — but not very far. If you were sitting near the stove you fried, but if you were at the back of the room, you were still cold.

At about 10:30, when the stove was in full swing and glowing red, the ripe aroma of manure, cooking in the heat, filled the room. Before school the boys from the farms had either done the milking or walked through generous piles of fresh manure, which stuck steadfastly to their gum boots. The teacher implored them to wash their boots before coming to school, but with no running water, it was difficult to do and get to school on time. At the end of the day, the transportation scenario was reversed, and I arrived home, cold and wet, at 5 p.m. I then had dinner, did school work or read and went to bed, trying to sleep through the eternal sound of the Wurlitzer crying out "You Are My Sunshine" at least 20 times a night, sometimes interspersed with

"The Rose of San Antone." After six hours of sleep, I was up and off to school again.

The teacher's name was Miss Lemon, and it suited her usually sour personality quite well. One day, after I had been at the school for a few months, our family was to go to Vancouver (our first trip since moving to Pitt Meadows) and we were going to have a steam bath. I guess, these days, it's called a spa. I had been having regular baths in a large galvanized tub on the kitchen floor, but this would be special — and warm. I told Miss Lemon that I would be away for a day as I was going into Vancouver for a bath! I was probably the cleanest child in the classroom even before the steam bath, but when I returned the next day, we had a half-hour lecture on bathing and how she considered anyone who didn't bathe at least once a week very dirty. I didn't think I needed the lecture, and I'm sure, in the case of the boys in the gum boots, it fell on deaf ears.

Dreariness Continued

Life continued drearily in Pitt Meadows, and it is difficult to recall much happiness in the year and a half we resided there. The ride to school was long and dreary, the schoolyard was gravel with no playground equipment of any kind and the school housed three grades taught by one teacher. There was no indoor bathroom, only an outhouse. This was a far cry from my somewhat sophisticated school in Vancouver, which was equipped with lockers, a gymnasium, indoor bathrooms and three classes of each grade. When I first arrived in Pitt Meadows, there were Japanese children in the classroom. The Japanese from the coast had already been transported to the interior or the prairies, but these children were happily living on their berry farms (and there were many) in the Fraser Valley. I remember particularly well a Japanese boy of about 10. He laughed a lot and was usually the centre of whatever fun was taking place in or outside of the classroom. Then, one day, he and all the other Japanese children came to school — and they were not laughing. They had been told they must leave. The next day they were gone. We never saw them again. It is interesting to reflect on how quickly governments can react when they really want to.

Life at home wasn't much better. Both my mother and father were working long hours, from eight in the morning until 10 at night, so they had little time for me. And Rena, when she was there, had taken a particular dislike to me and never missed an opportunity to let me know how stupid and unimportant I was.

Two things did keep me busy after school. One was pumping the gas up into the tall cylinders using the long levers at the bottom of the pumps. It was exciting to see the brightly coloured liquid splash into the long glass containers, but it was hard work for a small, wiry 10-year-old.

The other job was filling the oil bottles, which were neatly stacked on a rack near the pumps. I liked this job and would take the glass bottles topped with shiny metal cone covers into the shed where there were three types of oil — 20-grade, 30-grade and 40-grade — held in large iron barrels on their sides. Each one had a spigot. I loved to hold the bottles under the spigot and watch the amber green oil ooze into the bottles. I was proud of myself too, as I never spilled a drop and made sure that the bottles were filled right to the top. For this, I received 25 cents a week.

As I mentioned earlier, we collected all wash water in a rain barrel. This water was used for washing the many dishes, which accumulated from the lunch counter meals, our clothes and ourselves. We never ran out of water, as rain filled our barrel almost daily. One day, I looked into the barrel and discovered large numbers of tiny, wiggly larvae of some kind. Oh yes, I knew — we had learned about mosquito larvae at school. We had also learned that oil plugged up their breathing mechanisms. Well, I had the knowledge and, of course, access to three barrels of oil. I started with a cupful of 40-grade and poured it into the water barrel. Then, in case that was too thick, I went back to the shed for some 20-grade and, just to be sure, added a third cup, with 30-grade.

It takes little imagination to envision what happened next. My mother came out to get water for dishes to discover the barrel was covered with green slime. My father was summoned, and he understood immediately what had occurred. He uttered many oaths, among them something about a goddamned kid, and angrily dumped the barrel. Not noted for being a "details man," he did not bother to clean the barrel, so when it filled up again with rainwater, there was still an oily green surface on the water, making it unusable. This time, the barrel was cleaned with soap and rinsed with precious drinking water. I was wounded by their lack of appreciation and declared that it wasn't really a problem as the rain barrel would be full in a day. It wasn't. It was the first time I remember being in Pitt Meadows when it did not rain for a week. I did point out that due to my higher education and knowledge I had solved the mosquito problem, but no one was impressed, particularly Rena. It had given her yet another excuse to tell me how stupid I was. Science, I realized, was not going to be my long suit, as my one flight into experimentation had ended in failure and shame. One could say it was a low point in my career as a scientist.

And so it went. Summer was coming and the question was, what to do with Fay? My parents were working 14-hour days, Rena was seldom there to help, there were no children around and we were stuck on the Lougheed Highway with no car and nowhere to go. It was finally decided that I would spend the month of August with my grandmother in Bella Coola. I was excited. I loved my grandmother, and a two-day boat trip sounded like adventure to me. But there was still July to get through. The Kennedys had a dairy farm nearby and were about to begin haying. Would I like to help their three young people put up the hay? Would I?! Horses and hay wagons and young people … what more could a 10-year-old desire? Pitchfork in hand, I climbed up onto the hayrack and was told to spread the hay as others threw it on the wagon. They told me I did my job very well, although I did notice that the 17-year-old often jumped up to help me. After a long day and many accolades for my good work, I was given a reward: a day-old bantam chick.

I carried my prize home, held gently in my hands. I made a nest for it in a cardboard box and filled it with chick amenities: a hot-water bottle, water and food. It stayed by my bed all night. In the morning, I realized that all was not well. The chick was sick and falling over when it tried to walk. I picked up the box and ran to my father for advice. He probably knew less about chickens than someone from Greenland, but to appease me and keep me busy while it died, he said, "Just hold it in your hands and keep moving it to keep the circulation going.

Sometimes they just need a little warmth and movement." I did this all day, and at night settled it comfortably in a nest on top of a hot water bottle. Amazingly, the chick was better the next day and better still the following day. I, of course, became the mother. I would use a stone to scratch the gravel and call it over, and it would come running over to gobble up whatever was there. No one was more amazed than my father when the chick lived. He never said a word about his cure being a shot in the dark, but to me, he was the great chicken expert.

Word got to the Kennedys about the chick's near-death experience and recovery due to my diligence and care. Two days later, another chick appeared; this one was a few days older and at least knew a little about how to eat. Not knowing whether they were boys or girls, I called the first one Banty and the second one Bunty. They were very tame, especially Banty, who always came running when I called. Bunty was a little more tentative, not having bonded to me in the same way that Banty had, but she came too, making sure not to miss anything.

For the entire month, they had my undivided attention (except for pumping gas and filling oil bottles) as we scratched for food or sat on my lap to be petted. At night, they were put into a secure cage in the oil shed until morning, when they were let out and began scratching again. When August came and it was time to leave for Bella Coola, I had some misgivings, as I wasn't sure how capable my parents were of caring for my two precious chicks. They assured me they would take good care of them, and I left on my much-anticipated adventure.

The SS *Cardena* to Bella Coola

From 1889 to 1959, the fleet of 50 Union Steamships boats, with their black and red funnels and company flag, plied the waters of British Columbia, connecting the north to the south. It was, in fact, the only highway, as roads into many remote villages, towns and lumber camps had not yet been built, due to the inhospitable terrain, deep inlets and high mountains. The coastal people were tied to the sea. Boat day, usually once a week, was met with great anticipation as it meant contact with the outside world. It also meant goods, mail and sometimes visitors or workers entering their small world. Woodward's stores, which had a very large food section, even by today's standards, sent huge orders of groceries to individual families, as well as to logging camps, mining camps and fish canneries, which had proliferated up the West Coast from Vancouver to Prince Rupert.

It was a two-day trip on the passenger freighter, SS *Cardena* to get to Bella Coola. However, the boat stopped in Bella Coola only on its way north to Prince Rupert; to return, I had the luxury of a five-day cruise — two to Prince Rupert and three to Vancouver, avoiding the long fjord into Bella Coola, which would have taken almost a day traversing it both ways.

My parents must have suffered some anguish in deciding whether to send me — an overactive 10-year-old, with little or no appreciation of risk — to Bella Coola on my own. And it was not only a safety issue that created concern but also a financial one. Even though they were running a business, my parents were required to divide the small profits 50/50 with Frank and Rena, leaving very little for extras, including food. So I would have to go alone.

I was delighted. I knew, of course, like every other 10-year-old, that I was capable of taking care of myself. I knew everything I needed to know.

We borrowed a car, a dark green DeSoto, and we were off to the Union Steamship dock, where the SS *Cardena* was lying at berth. Although huge by my standards, these ships were small but sturdy, as they needed to manoeuvre into the tiny bays and inlets where the gyppo loggers (who worked for small-scale logging companies rather than the sawmills or lumber companies) had their camps and be tied up to small docks or log booms.

I was ready for this adventure, but my mother was nervous. A shy person by nature, she summoned up her courage and sidled up to a young priest she saw going aboard. She asked him if he "would keep an eye on Fay." He agreed. I was not sure that I wanted this sinister-looking man in black interfering with my plans during my two days of freedom, but it turns out I needn't have worried, as he was an alcoholic and didn't surface for the whole trip. We then proceeded to my cabin, where we met a young woman of about 25 who was to share the stateroom with me. The same question was asked, "Would you keep an eye on Fay?" That done, my parents left, and I was on my own!

Ship exploration was first on my list, and I intended to do a thorough job. The first thing I learned was that the doors to the deck were heavy and it took all my 70 pounds to pry them open. The second thing I learned was to be mindful of the very high steps so as not to cut my shins on the metal threshold when prying open the deck doors. Out on the deck, there were a few canvas chairs and a diagram of some sort, with numbers on it. Later, I learned it was where one played shuffleboard. No one could say that we, on the West Coast, in the 1940s, were not sophisticated.

On the bow, there was a lot of activity as huge winches loaded supplies in order of the various destinations as we sailed north. Enormous quantities of food, large oil drums, cables, logging equipment and machinery were systematically placed inside the hold of the ship. It was mesmerizing.

That completed, the hold was closed and a small runabout, complete with outboard motor and a small bulldozer, was lashed to the deck. The whistle blew, the moorings slipped, and we were at sea!

The dining room was my next destination. It was an awesome sight. I was used to an oilcloth tablecloth, a knife, a fork and a spoon, but this dining room was the ultimate in elegance. There were starched white linen tablecloths with linen serviettes to match and so much silverware I wondered if the table could hold it all. What should I use first … and second? Wide-eyed, I sat down and looked around to see what the others (the ship's officers and the other guests) were doing with all the utensils. Then, the food began to arrive: first the soup, then salad, then the main course and finally the dessert. More silverware and food than I had ever seen. It was a dazzling experience and one that would be repeated three times a day!

After dinner and a little more wandering, I returned to my stateroom, as it was, after all, time for a bathroom break. Like all children, I had left it to the last minute. But I could not get into the room; the door was locked and bolted. Hearing some scuffling inside, I waited, hopping from one foot to the other, until the door finally opened and my roommate appeared at the door, tucking her blouse into her skirt. She opened the door just wide enough for me to sidle to the washroom, but enough for me to catch a glimpse of a young soldier on the lower bunk. I completed my activity and left. The door closed behind me and I heard the distinct click of the bolt. Perhaps another 10-year-old would be aware of what was going on, but I was oblivious and too busy to be concerned. Besides, she wasn't bothering me, and for that, I was happy.

Whales rolled alongside the boat in large numbers, and porpoises entertained us by the hour with their jumps and laser-like charges through the water. There seemed hardly a time when you could not see these magnificent mammals swimming and diving, as if dancing to the rhythm of the ploughing ship.

Throughout the day, when the boat docked at a cannery (and there were many up the West Coast at that time), I bounded up the gang-plank and went through the cannery, watching with fascination as the fish were brought in, scaled, gutted, de-finned and sent down the assembly line for the women to cut and stuff into cans for processing. Most of this prime quality fish was sent to England as part of the war effort.

The canneries had various accommodations for the workers. In the past, there had been separate quarters for Japanese and Chinese workers. The Indians[1] usually set up their tent villages nearby. But in 1942, there were no Japanese allowed on the coast, so the work went to the Indian and Chinese workers, along with a few Caucasian people. I usually got back to the boat in time to see most of the cargo unloaded and pallets of canned fish loaded and packed into the hold. It is a sight that I find intriguing to this day.

As the ship continued north, the ocean became quite rough and I noticed fewer people about. When I arrived at the dining room for lunch, there were no passengers, just the captain, first mate and purser. I was invited to join them at their table and did so for the rest of the trip. We were moving through the Queen Charlotte Strait and Queen Charlotte Sound and, apparently, the other passengers weren't feeling well during this section of the journey.

The following morning, we arrived in Namu, a large cannery with a

---

1   I mean no disrespect to Indigenous Peoples when I use the term "Indian" or any other word commonly used to describe their life. These were terms that were widely used in those days and, therefore, preserved in these stories from so many years ago.

reduction plant sitting almost on the wharf. The stench of the herring being reduced into fertilizer was overwhelming. Huge boatloads were brought in to be processed, which eventually resulted in loss of food for salmon. The salmon consequently went into a steep decline. We did not realize it at the time, but surely someone in the vaulted halls of the fisheries department should have known. My uncle, married to my aunt Dona (of measles fame), supervised the reduction plant. Had he known the devastating effect it would have on the fisheries, neither he nor anyone else up the North Coast would have condoned it. But 1942 was early in the white man's history of the North Coast and none of us could have predicted the consequences.

Dona and her six-month-old son boarded the ship there, and we continued on to Bella Coola.

I never did see the priest again.

• • •

Bella Coola, a beautiful, mystical valley, lies 450 kilometres north of Vancouver, at the end of a long fjord that runs inland 100 kilometres from the ocean. The mountains rise up 3,500 metres on either side of the narrow valley and stand as sentinels, protecting it from the inclement weather of the North Coast. It has an interior climate rather than a coastal one.

The first known settlers were the Indigenous Peoples but even their history is a mystery. The present Bella Coola First Nations are Salish, as are the Okanagan and those of the Fraser River Delta. No one is sure how they became isolated 400 kilometres away from the others of their tribe, and it is thought that this present group has only been in the valley for the past 600 years.

Norwegian adventurer Thor Heyerdahl spent several months in Bella Coola. He was intrigued by the rock carvings in the Marquesas Islands of French Polynesia and their similarities to the ones in Bella Coola. There were other similarities as well, such as their methods of cooking and their dialect. Heyerdahl surmised that the original Bella Coola First Nations, due to their easy lifestyle, abundant food and the security of their protected valley became indolent and were not prepared for the enemies that came overland through the mountains.

He believed that the rock carvers were driven from the valley, escaping their invaders and settling on the outer islands of the coast. Heyerdahl proposed some even accidentally travelled far enough offshore for the strong southerly current to carry them to the Islands of the South Pacific and a new paradise. This, of course, is speculation, but carvings as far away as New Zealand bear a definite resemblance to the ones in the Valley.[2]

They also carved great totem poles, grinding colourful rocks and mixing the powder with fish oil to make various paint colours. To my sorrow, on a trip to San Diego a number of years ago, I found dozens of Bella Coola totems residing in one of the buildings in Balboa Park — many more, I think, than there are in the Smithsonian. At some time during the 1920s or 1930s, people from U.S. museums arrived in the Valley. Chainsaws in hand, they cut down and removed these totems. Perhaps, they felt, they were preserving them, but was it right? Where were the B.C. and Canadian governments when this was happening?

The big question of my family's story is, how did my grandfather, a Macdonald from Glengarry County, Ontario, my step-grandfather from Boston and my beautiful grandmother from Bohemia, the Austrian part of Czechoslovakia, all find themselves in this remote mystic valley at the turn of the century? I will try to put this together, all the while knowing there will be many missing pieces in this puzzle.

Family Background

Why didn't I ask more relevant questions when I had the opportunity? Normally, I never shy away from asking questions; yet, when it came to asking the important questions on family history, I came up short on gathering the information I would like to have now.

In my defence, I did ask about my first step-grandfather and was told it was something I did not need to know. But there were other things I — or my mother, aunt or uncle — could have and should have asked. This leaves me with somewhat sketchy images of the life

---

2 I have included more fascinating details of the history of the Bella Coola area in Appendix I.

my grandparents had in Bella Coola, but I will shade it in as well as I'm able.

Before I continue with my adventures in Bella Coola and beyond, I think it's important to give some family background.

My Grandmother — Emma Mueller/Quaas/Riesterer/Macdonald/ Gledhill

I'll start with my maternal grandmother, Emma, who was the only one of my grandparents who was not born in Canada. Her Austrian family had moved to the Bohemian section of Czechoslovakia (now the Czech Republic), the most affluent part of the country. I don't know why they moved there, but obviously, the financial situation was less than perfect, as five of the sisters in a family of 13 came to North America in the late 1800s. My grandmother was the youngest in the family and, at age 13, followed the eldest sister to Vancouver, before it was even declared a town. My grandmother was pretty and petite, had a sweet nature and loved to paint. She also played the zither.

After some time in Vancouver, she went to stay with another sister in Maple Valley in the Skagit Valley region of Washington State.

I would like to know more about my grandmother's life and especially her first marriage. But people at that time were generally not forthcoming with their stories. When I was young I did ask her about her life, but I was quickly brushed aside and told, "It was not important."

All I know about her first husband is that his last name was Quaas. They had two sons, the first of which died and the second was my beloved Uncle George, who lived to be 94, in spite of his many logging injuries. She and her first husband may have divorced, or he may have committed suicide, or he just left. These things were never discussed, and George knew nothing about his father.

My grandmother was a young woman when she was left alone, probably 19 or 20, with a baby and no means of supporting herself. What was she to do? Help came by way of a well-to-do family in Nelson, B.C. Robert Riesterer owned breweries in Nelson, Port Moody, Vancouver and Victoria. He and his wife had two sons, Charles and Robert, and they were awaiting the birth of their third child. Emma was recommended to be their housekeeper and governess, and she and George moved to Nelson to live with the family.

Unfortunately, Robert's wife died in childbirth, as sometimes happened in the days before advanced medical care, leaving a widower and three children. My grandmother stayed on to care for the children of whom she was very fond, especially baby Clara. She must also have become very fond of Mr. Riesterer — and he of her — as four years later, they were married. At age 51, he was 27 years her senior.

Grandma Emma

We'll never know if it was a marriage of love or convenience, as a year or two later, in 1902, fate dealt another cruel blow and Mr. Riesterer died suddenly, probably of a heart attack.

As I understand it, Emma was left with a comfortable home and income to look after herself and the children, including George, and see them into adulthood. The story might have ended there, but it didn't.

Enter my grandfather, John Daniel Macdonald, a prospector from Ontario, who had seen the last spike of the Canadian railroad driven in B.C. at Craigellachie, and who had a few gold claims, some of them producing. I have gone to Nelson to try to find information on the mines, but "Jock" Macdonald was a common name for prospectors and miners at that time and we had insufficient time and information to find out very much. Supposedly, he was a relative of Sir John A. Macdonald, although unproven, and a bit of a gambler. Rumour has it that he lost his mines with a few rolls of the dice.

In any case, he somehow met and convinced a pretty young woman to marry him and go homesteading in Bella Coola, where he owned around 100 acres of prime timber.

It was fortunate for me that she made this decision, but I have questioned her reasoning more than once. Many people have told me that this delicate, artistic lady should not have been a pioneer in this remote part of B.C., but a pioneer she was, and she lived and endured there for most of the rest of her days.

She gave up a comfortable life, and the Riesterer children were sent to live with guardians. Strangely enough, even though I feel that she essentially abandoned the children, the families remained close. I lived with "Auntie Clara" (Robert Riesterer's third child — the baby when my grandmother was with Robert Riesterer) when I was going to high school in Vancouver, and she remains, in my memory, one of the most wonderful women I have ever known: kind, competent and ahead of her time, and she loved my grandmother. I consider her daughter, who is 10 years older than me, a cousin and a true friend.

My grandparents and George went to Bella Coola, where my grandfather built a two-storey log house. They even had a piano. My mother, Flora, was born, and even though life was not easy, they were comfortable enough. Then, in 1912, when my mother was three years old, another disaster occurred. My grandfather and some men had gone out to clear some land. They had set the powder and fuse to blow out an old stump and he got behind a tree, the usual protocol. A large piece of the stump flew up and hit the tree he was standing behind, causing a large limb (a conch burr) to fall directly upon him, killing him instantly.

A wooden coffin was constructed, and he was placed inside. My mother remembers climbing into the coffin with him, sure he was not dead because his eyes were still open. Someone carried her out, closed his eyes and pulled down the lid. He was buried in the yard beside the house. There is no marker and no longer a house, leaving no memory of where he is buried.

Sam Gledhill, who was to be my grandmother's fourth and last husband, adored my grandmother and, in probably 1916, she married him. They had two daughters, Clara and Dona, and thus became a family of six. At age 15, George went away to the logging camps in order to relieve the family's financial burden. My mother always said, "Sam was a very kind man and he treated me, his stepdaughter, as well or better than his own two girls."

And in 1941, it was Sam who met 10-year-old me, in Bella Coola, after my eventful trip on the SS *Cardena*.

Sam and my grandmother lived happily, if not comfortably, in the old rustic house that Sam had cobbled together, until his death. (The original house, a nice one that my grandfather Macdonald had built, had burned to the ground a couple of years after Sam married my grandmother). After Sam's passing, my grandmother stayed with us in Vancouver for a short time and then spent the rest of her life with her youngest daughter in Victoria. She died in 1955, at the age of 78, of pneumonia, and is buried in the Royal Oak Cemetery. I regret that she never met my son Ken, her first great-grandchild, who was born that year.

She was a kind, sweet lady, and I understand why Auntie Clara loved her so much.

My Third Step-Grandfather — Sam Gledhill

Sam — my grandmother's fourth husband — arrived in the Valley before both my grandmother and my grandfather, and even before the Norwegian settlers. Born in Lowell, Massachusetts, near Boston, in 1869, he sailed around Cape Horn and landed in Bella Coola sometime in the 1880s.

He may have still been in his teens, but he was the third white man in Bella Coola, after Alexander MacKenzie made his famous overland trip across the continent to the Valley. Mr. Clayton bought the existing Hudson's Bay store (originally a fort or trading post) and turned it into a general store, where Sam would eventually work.

A sketchy diary tells stories of Sam at the turn of the century, carrying the mail by horse-drawn wagon in the spring, summer and fall, and by sleigh in the winter, from Bella Coola to Anaheim Lake, a distance of 65 kilometres, over some of the roughest terrain in the province. The Norwegians eventually built a road to help with part of the journey, but when the road ended, it was a steep climb of over 2,000 metres through an inhospitable mountain pass. As difficult as it was in the summer, it was gruelling in the winter. In his 20 years of mail delivery, he travelled 32,000 kilometres and never missed a trip.

In spite of it all, he was always cheerful and ready to help anyone who needed or wanted a helping hand — and many did. He was messenger and troubadour to the whole valley, travelling the entire length, bringing news of neighbours and friends, their trials, successes, births and deaths. And deaths were not infrequent in the Valley in those days. People up and down the route had nothing but good things to say about him.

When asked if he ever got lonely on these excursions, he explained, "You can never really be lonely going up and down the Bella Coola Valley. You kind of get attached to the mountains and streams and all those things, and in time, they become just like the furnishings of your home."

Sam married my grandmother, taking on not only a wife, but also her 14-year-old son, George, from her first husband, and her four-year-old daughter, Flora (my mother), from my grandfather, Jack Macdonald, who had been her third husband. She and Sam, in turn, had two children, Dona and Clara, my half-aunts. After this, Sam no longer carried the mail to Anaheim Lake but did continue On Her Majesty's Service for the next 20 years, travelling 3,000 kilometres between Bella Coola and Atnarko with his old wagon and his faithful horse, Ned.

It was very much a pioneer life, fraught with danger and hardship, but everyone in the Valley was living under the same circumstances so no one felt deprived or oppressed. They just got on with the tasks at hand.

During their life there, Sam and my grandmother suffered many catastrophes. The first one was the fire. Most of the homes were made of bare wood or logs, and all heating was with wood. It does not take much imagination to realize that a rogue spark flicked out of an unattended fire or a hot ash that was carelessly ignored could cause a smouldering fire that grows quickly into a raging inferno. I don't know what caused the fire that razed my grandparents' house (the one my grandfather had built), but I do know that all was lost except the cow, a few pigs, some chickens and Ned, the horse. Neighbours rallied to help rebuild, but Sam, for a reason known only to him, rejected their help and chose instead to make a wagon shed into a house. It was unsatisfactory housing, but they lived in it for several years until the next catastrophe occurred.

As my aunt Dona tells it, she was left at home, at about age 16, to look after the animals, milk the cow and do general chores while Sam and my grandmother went to Bella Coola. It was an overnight trip in those days, even though it was only 30 kilometres away. A sudden windstorm came up and several large trees blew down on the property. Knowing she had to get the animals into the barn, she tried to herd them in, but the animals were frightened and ran away when she tried to direct them. Realizing that she needed help, she ran a mile down the road to her friend's place and asked her to come and help. Between the two of them, they got the animals into the barn, milked the cow and thought about their options for the rest of the evening. Peggy could stay with Dona, or Dona could go to Peggy's for the night. They decided on Peggy's place and had a good home-cooked dinner and a relaxed and pleasant night. In the morning, on returning to the homestead, they realized that their decision had been a good one. A huge tree had fallen through the house, landing in the bedroom where the girls would have been sleeping. Once again, Sam refused help from neighbours and winched the house together. While the repairs were being made, the family slept in the barn. It was December, and the snow was flying, so there was always frost on their hair and on their blankets when they awoke in the morning.

There were other incidents that proved this wonderful valley was not the Eden that some liked to think it was. The Bella Coola River flooded often, due to the snowmelt from the high peaks that surrounded the valley. Some years were worse than others. One year, the entire valley was completely awash, and many people had to camp on the mountainsides until the river's surge subsided. Sam, my grandmother and family made their home in a root cellar on the side of the mountain for several days until they could return to the house and begin the tedious and heartbreaking clean-up necessary after a flood. Many things were lost, but, surprisingly, some of the old pictures were spared. They were yellowed and not of good quality to begin with, but they do serve as a record of early life in the Valley.

Sam lived the rest of his life in Bella Coola and died in 1951. He is buried in the far corner of the cemetery. For some reason, there is no mention of him in the small museum, which is strange, considering he was such a longtime and enduring resident of the Valley.

My Mother — Flora Macdonald

My mother, Flora Christine Dobson, nee Macdonald, is more difficult to write about than my father, who was colourful, mercurial and social. She lived most of her life in his shadow and seemed to have no part in decision-making. I'm sure that if she had had a vote, we would not have lived the nomadic life that we did. When he said "Move," we moved. When a question was asked, he answered. At social gatherings, he did all the talking and she listened quietly, removed from discussions. That is not to say that she was a doormat; she just found it easier to go along with whatever he thought or decided. In many ways, she lived through him.

She did not have his quick, insightful intelligence; instead, she took a measured approach to most things and checked and re-checked everything she did. Common sense was her forte. She was very attractive and, until her death at 96, she always looked at least 10 years younger than her age. Her disposition, much like her mother's, was quiet, sweet and non-judgmental. She was well-liked by those who knew her and was extremely loyal to her friends. However, she was not one who did much to help other people. She never became involved in any organizations, be it school or charitable, and she never volunteered for anything. When my father died when she was in her late sixties, I tried to get her involved in a social or volunteer agency so that she would be less isolated, but it was to no avail.

She was born on June 22, 1909, in Bella Coola Hospital, which was a small hospital at the time and not much larger now. Three years after my grandfather was killed, when my mother was six years old, my grandmother married Sam Gledhill. They moved to Vancouver where Sam had a small house, and she began school in an area now known as the lower east side. At the time, it was certainly not the elite section of Vancouver, nor was it the dreary, drug-infested area that it is now. They remained there until her half-sister Clara was born, and then Bella Coola beckoned, and they all returned to the Valley.

Here, among other adversities, education was a problem. There were not enough students for the government to allow for a school and teacher. Some of the Norwegian residents wanted a school, but a group of Seventh-day Adventists, who had also settled there, did not see the need. After much pressure and pleading, some of the Seventh-day Adventists were finally persuaded to send their children to school, which allowed for sufficient numbers to qualify for a one-room school and a teacher.

Shortly after this hurdle was crossed, another little girl, my aunt Dona, was born, in the old log house. When it was time to register her, the officials demanded the signature of the nurse who delivered her. The only other person in the room was my nine-year-old mother, so she signed her name as the nurse! I had not heard this story until Dona recited it at my mother's graveside.

• • •

Bella Coola was, and still is, grizzly bear country, and when walking on the road or through the woods one is always on the lookout for bear scat, bear sounds or the ominous glimpse of a brown furry head with a long snout. One day, when she was about 10 years old, my mother was sent out to look for Kate, the cow, who had somehow escaped the fenced pasture and lost her bell. Not far from the barn, she thought she could hear her crashing through the bush and began calling her name. She finally chased her out onto the road to find Andy Christianson, one of their neighbours, looking very shaken. She had not been chasing Kate. "You were chasing a grizzly bear," he said. "He came within a foot of me, running as fast as he could." At that point they both hugged each other, unnerved from the experience. He walked her home, although he was probably more frightened than she. The cow, wherever she was, was left to find her own way home.

At the age of 13, my mother was sent to Manitoba to live with her father's sister, a Mrs. MacIntosh, partly because of the poor education in Bella Coola. It appeared that this aunt thought that her brother had some money and that she might be in line for some, especially if she took care of his daughter for a while.

It soon became apparent that there was no money to be had, and the aunt became increasingly cruel. She had been through several miscarriages, had no children of her own and, with little money herself, felt burdened by having to feed and care for another person. No doubt she was a bitter old lady with little understanding of how to care for a 13-year-old girl. My mother described her time there as a horrific experience. She was fed potatoes and little else, the weather was unbearably cold in winter and she had insufficient clothing. She did, however, survive, in spite of the fact that on at least one occasion, when my mother arrived home later than expected, her aunt locked her out, in the middle of winter. That night, and I don't know how many others, she stayed in the barn.

After two years of misery, she went to Vancouver where she boarded with two families. Apparently the husband of the first family tried to rape her. She escaped to another family, who were good to her, and she was able to complete her schooling. She graduated from Britannia High School in 1927.

At this point, she was offered an apprenticeship to become a pharmacist, but with no means of supporting herself, she lost the opportunity. (It's interesting to note that, in 1927, a university degree was not required to become a pharmacist.) Instead, she found work with the C.P.R. Telegraph. It was a good job that paid well, with a paycheque arriving every two weeks without fail. The struggle for money was not over, but it was greatly alleviated. This was a happy time for her; she felt important and valued. These memories stayed with her vividly, and when she was suffering from early dementia in her nineties, she told me repeatedly about the telegraph office, and how careful she had to be, as there could be no errors in the messages. She also said that when they wired Victoria, they would hear about the sunny weather and blooming flowers in February. "I didn't believe them then," she said.

She met my father who was logging at the time and had become friends with her half-brother George. George not only liked my dad but also thought he seemed more of a gentleman than other loggers, so he introduced him to my mother. At age 20, she married my father and was forced to quit her much-loved job. At that time, married women were not allowed to work in most jobs. This could not have occurred at a worse time. It was 1930, the start of the Great Depression, and my father did not have a secure job. To complicate life further, a year later, I appeared on the scene.

Dad, never one to take charity or go on "relief," did odd jobs, such as filing saws in Stanley Park, selling silk stockings door-to-door and selling subscriptions for *Liberty* magazine. The magazine sold for five cents a copy, so the profit for him must have been minimal. Their accommodation was a windowless two-room basement apartment, and they often had to choose between buying milk for me and putting 25 cents in the meter for heat.

They were lean and tough times in those Depression years on the West Coast. There were work camps, soup lines, men going from door to door looking to work for a meal and people dying of starvation in the streets.

Although my mother overcame many adversities in her life, she never became mentally strong and was unable to handle even the smallest amount of stress. She succumbed to a nervous breakdown at about age 18, and was headed for another one at age 34, when we were in Pitt Meadows, before we escaped to the Portage, where Dad luckily found another position. At the same time, while most people who were scarred by the Depression became penurious and miserly, she did not succumb to those traits. Although our family was never wealthy, when we did have some money, she was as generous as she could possibly be.

When she was in her fifties, my father had a bridge-building business up and running, and they built a beautiful home in West Vancouver overlooking the water, with a view stretching from Lions Gate Bridge to Vancouver Island. She was proud of the house and decorated it comfortably and elegantly. She loved to be invited out, but reciprocity was difficult for her. Usually, my father was the one to phone and invite people for dinner. She prepared a good meal and was happy with the outcome, but she would not take the initiative. Perhaps she lacked confidence and felt that no one really wanted to see her, or perhaps she was just a little bit lazy.

My mother, at age 80, known to her grandchildren as "Grammy"
(which I am also called by my grandchildren) — 1998

She was healthy and active her entire life and travelled until she was in her eighties. By the time she was 90 and living on her own in an apartment, it was clear that she needed help. Her memory was slipping badly, and she began to accuse others of incompetency (not her usual demeanour). She moved to an excellent retirement home for two years and then had to be transferred to its intermediate care section. She was extremely angry at this move, as she felt she was being moved into the dismal basement apartment of Depression years, even though this one was on the main floor and she had two large rooms with huge windows overlooking a garden. There had been some scarring after all.

To some degree, she transferred her dependency on my father to me. She would not attend the entertainment that was offered in the home unless I went with her. I had to persuade her to come to the lounge for afternoon tea and do most of the socializing as other residents joined us at the table.

She lived the rest of her life being well taken care of by both staff and family and, at 96, she slipped out of life as quietly and peacefully as she had lived it.

My Father — Harry Dobson

My father was born in the last hours of the 19th century in Buckingham, Quebec. He saw and remembered events and inventions that occurred in the 20th century, such as Halley's Comet (which can only be seen from earth with the naked eye about every 75 years), the first motorcars, the crystal radio sets, the cylindrical records played on one of Thomas Edison's first gramophones and the first telephones.

He left home at 17 and never saw his parents or most of his siblings again. There are two stories given for his abrupt departure: one, which he tells, and another, told by his brother, Bun, who was just three months old when my father left.

My father's version:

He finished school at age 16 at the top of his class — but it was 1916, the First World War was on and he wanted to enlist. He went off to the recruiting office, lied about his age and was accepted into the army.

His mother learned about this little escapade and promptly went down to the recruiting office and had him delisted! She was a devout Catholic and her fond hope was that he, the oldest in the family, would become a priest. He was furious with his mother for blowing the whistle on him, as well as for other real or imagined wrongs, and he had no intention of becoming a priest, so he left, in anger.

His brother's version:

My uncle Bun said that my father and his brother Bill were constantly fighting. At this point, there were eight children, six boys and two girls, and the war between the two older brothers was causing chaos in the family. It was suggested that one of them leave. Since Harry, my father, was the eldest, he would be the one to go.

My father's version seems to be the more likely, as, early on, there were problems between him and his mother. Because of her strong Catholic faith, she did not want the family to associate with anyone who was not Catholic. He could not understand why he couldn't be friends with someone who was Protestant. I'm quite sure that he broke that rule, as well as others, which would have resulted in a sharp blow across the face or ear. This enraged him. He did not like the ceremonial and ritualistic services he was forced to attend as an altar boy, and he did not like the constant praying at home and sprinkling of holy water whenever there was a thunderstorm (and there were many) or any minor crisis. And he did not want to be a priest.

Uncle Bun says that their mother was sweet-natured and kind (her picture seemed to reflect that) but here, again, the stories differ. Maybe she was always of a gentle nature or maybe she mellowed as time went on, and Bun, the eighth child, benefitted from that transformation. I think that, as most mothers, she was trying to do the best for her children.

Their father was either the head of the chemical plant in Buckingham or the head of a section of the plant. They had a comfortable home that he had built in the town, and he obviously had a fairly good income. The boys all went to the Christian Brothers' school and the girls must have gone to the convent to be taught by nuns.

According to my father, the Christian Brothers were excellent teachers, but they were very strict and a bit harsh with their discipline. The cane came out when errors were made, especially in arithmetic. As I understand it, he did not feel the cane too often, as mathematics was his strong suit, but knowing his volatile personality, if he had been struck, his rebellious personality would have surfaced. He spoke English and French fluently and although he never had occasion to speak French after leaving Quebec, he was still fluent to the end of his life.

Regardless of the reason, my father left his family without telling anyone where he was going, and he never contacted them again. He found his way to Winnipeg and got a job delivering mail from LaPas to Churchill by dog team. He was 17 years old, with no experience with dog teams, reading a map or compass or surviving in the sub-Arctic. Alone, and without guidance or experience, he made the trip (possibly with the help of an "Indian trapper," as they were referred to at the time) but arrived in Churchill with his toes badly frozen. He was admitted to hospital where he overheard the doctor saying that he would amputate his toes in the morning. This, of course, was upsetting to a 17-year-old boy. He was able to make contact with Joe, the trapper he had met along the way, and Joe said, "Do not worry. Be sure your window is left unlocked tonight. I will come for you at two a.m. and take you to my mother. She will care for you."

At the appointed hour, Joe slipped through the window, carried my father to his sled and took him to his mother's log cabin. Every day, she made a concoction of spruce pitch and other unknown ingredients gathered from the woods and massaged his toes with the mixture. He was there all winter, being cared for and receiving daily treatments from this good woman.

One spring day, with all of his toes still attached to his feet, he was sitting on the porch when the Northwest Mounted Police rode up. "We have been scouring the district for your bones," they said. "We could not trace you the night you fled the hospital, so we figured you had perished."

Who knows if it was the potion or the massage that saved his toes but one thing is certain: this kind lady saved him from being crippled and allowed him to live a normal and productive life.

He left the North and "rode the rails" all over the United States and Canada. He worked in mines, and the bedtime stories he told me were often about the mines' "pit ponies" that rarely saw the light of day. They all had names and personalities, and he made the stories exciting and not as dreary and sad as one might expect.

He worked on farms and finally in the logging camps of B.C., where he met Uncle George, my mother's half-brother. George liked my dad and introduced him to my mother. They were married in 1930 and I was born in 1931, at the height of the Great Depression.

My father worked many different jobs so we could survive those desperate years, but at least he always worked. He found a job at the *Vancouver Sun* newspaper and stayed for about three and a half years, but it didn't last, and he went off on a fishing venture. He never stayed long at a job, as he did not like working for someone else. We moved often. He was resourceful, brave, adventurous, intelligent and funny. He was also volatile, impatient, sometimes harsh, opinionated and judgmental. His restless nature made life — my mother's and mine — unsettled, unpredictable and fascinating.

Bella Coola, then Back to Reality

After my eventful trip on the SS *Cardena*, I hopped onto my step-grandfather Sam's old flat wagon, pulled by Ned, a very old horse, and we began our 30-kilometre journey up the valley to Firvale. We had never met before. He was, by my standards, an old man. He must have made the trip the day before and spent the night on the old wagon, waiting to take me up the valley in the daytime.

He said very little and let me chirp and chatter on about the wonders of the mountains, the farms, the waterfalls, the sunshine and what-ever else came into my young and empty head. He listened patiently, much the way Matthew did when he picked up Anne in *Anne of Green Gables*. He was a kind man who adored my grandmother, and my mother always said that although she was his stepchild, he always treated her as one of his own. The trip took the entire day, but what an experience it was, moving slowly through the soaring mountains, deeper and deeper into the valley.

Bella Coola, with Sam and Grandma Emma
holding Dona's baby Malcolm — 1942

My grandmother, whom I adored, was eagerly awaiting my arrival, and I was instantly introduced to an entire new world. The house was made of bare wood planks in their natural state. Not a drop of stain or varnish had ever been applied. The stairs led to a loft area where I was to sleep, and the kitchen was rudimentary beyond belief. The living room was large and boasted a sofa, one chair, a table, four dining chairs and several of my grandmother's paintings on the wall. To say it was rustic would certainly be an understatement — and I loved it! Across the road was even more excitement: a barn with a cow, several chickens and a pig. Ned the horse lived there too. I could tell that this was going to be a marvellous summer. And it was.

I was allowed to ride Ned, who, at 30 years old, was not about to gallop or buck. I went fishing in the Nusatsum River and caught several trout that were cooked in a pan over an open fire by the side of the river. I was also attacked by a very large and belligerent rooster, who ripped my scalp and pulled open the skin on my temple. We had him for dinner the next day.

Too soon, August had come to an end, and it was time to return to Pitt Meadows and reality. The trip home, which took five days on the ship, was again spent visiting canneries and villages and enjoying the elegance of the dining room with its white linen tablecloths and copious amounts of silverware. While this experience didn't include a hooker for a roommate or an alcoholic priest, there were other memorable times, like sitting on the back deck with a full moon shining and one of the passengers playing his guitar. It had been a magical time for me, and I wasn't quite ready to re-enter the real world.

• • •

When I arrived home, my two little bantam hens rushed to meet me. Banty, maybe due to her tenuous beginning, was still slim for a chicken, but she was healthy, and I was still her mom. Bunty, more robust and prettier, was tentative, but with a little coaxing jumped on my finger and got her neck rubbed.

At that time, we were plagued by flies. Pitt Meadows, being mostly a bog, was a good breading ground, and even though we tried to keep the screen doors closed, the constant coming and going of many people allowed the flies sufficient time for entry into the store and restaurant area, where they accumulated around the windows. The next day, armed with Banty on one finger and Bunty on the other, I entered the store, held the chickens up to the windows and pointed to the flies. Either due to their natural instinct or their good training, it took them two minutes to clear those two large windows of the entire population of flies. It became a daily ritual, practiced only when no customers were around.

The Crossroads, as our place was called, was at the intersection of two busy roads. One was the main road up the Valley from Vancouver, and the other began the circular route around the peat bog. We were only a few hundred metres from the Pitt River Bridge, a narrow plank structure that was very slippery when it rained — which was most of the time. Cars mostly slithered across the bridge with drivers' shoulders hunched, desperately trying to avoid sliding into another car. On the other side of the bridge was the Wild Duck Inn, a notorious watering hole for local farmers, loggers and mill workers. Many nights, especially Friday and Saturday nights, cars would screech through the crossroads, careening and swerving, often resulting in a serious accident and sometimes death.

We were usually closed by 10 p.m. — before the inn closed — but one day, in the late afternoon, two men came in for gas. They had been drinking but did not seem too impaired. They paid for their gas, asked directions to Mission and got back into their car. Instead of following my father's instructions to continue on the paved highway, they turned an abrupt right and raced down the unpaved bog road. They missed one of the many bad curves on the road and ended upside down in a ditch — dead. As my father was the last person to see them alive, he was called in to testify at the trial. We did not have a car at the time, which made this a long and costly trip. The trial went on for several days, the station had to be closed, there was little money coming in and things were not going well with Rena. She and my mother were not getting along. Rena came and went as she pleased (in the Duesenberg), leaving my mother with unrelieved 12-hour days. Never able to tolerate stress, my mother was coming close to a breakdown. It was imperative that we leave.

I'm not sure my father had even been to Vancouver Island other than the summer he quit his good job and decided to go commercial fishing, but his descriptions of this wonderful Shangri-La were compelling. He had found a 100-acre piece of waterfront property with two houses on it, and he would be paid $10 a month to work as a caretaker. He bought a green Ford Model A truck from a friend, and in April 1942, at Easter, we headed out, with no thought to the school year. My parents were in the front seat and I was in the back, sitting on the cold metal floor of the open truck, surrounded by many of our possessions, including a crate for Banty and Bunty and several others full of healthy large clucking New Hampshire chickens. A separate crate held a large rooster named Flatfoot, who crowed most of the way. We were a curiosity driving down the highway to Vancouver and an even greater curiosity on the ferry to Nanaimo, with our Tobacco Road truck and our rooster in full voice. I think he was a tenor.

LIFE IMPROVES

The Most Wonderful Place in the World … Almost

It wasn't very far from the C.P.R. Dock in Nanaimo to our new home, but the trip seemed much longer, and for good reason. The first nine kilometres were by paved road, until we crossed over the Nanaimo River Bridge, after which we turned a sharp left towards the Indian reserve and then a sharp right onto a dusty, rough gravel road. Sitting on the hard metal floor of the old truck and bumping over potholes and underlying corduroy was less than comfortable, but at 11 years old, I was excited about the prospect of a new adventure and the discomfort only added to the anticipation.

We passed only two houses over two miles; all the rest was bush and trees. We laboured up a steep and precipitous hill, at the top of which was a farm belonging to Jane Gordon, a woman in her sixties, the daughter of an Indian Chief and a Scot of no particular lineage. Since her older, infirm brother had left, she worked the farm completely on her own.

We continued our journey another mile and came to a large iron gate. From here on in was our new caretaker property — 100 acres of it! From the gate to the house was one mile, and we noted that once inside the gate the road was a bright orange red. We later learned that it was refuse from the boilers in the mine used in the coking process. There were many working mines in the area at that time; ash, no doubt, was readily available and probably free to anyone who would haul it away. In spite of the ash fill, the road was even rougher than the gravel road, as large sharp rocks and potholes had to be navigated around. Still, it was beautiful with the many huge fir trees on either side interspersed with gnarled arbutus and flat rocky outcroppings covered with rock plants and lichen. The chickens and I lurched along, hanging on as best we could — even the rooster had stopped crowing — and we finally arrived at the top of a very steep and winding hill. We carefully wound our way down the hill to the bottom — and the ocean. We were awestruck.

The Portage, and the small white house — a former Hudson's Bay trading post — at low tide at the Portage

A large bay spread out in front of us, enclosed by sandstone rocks carved by the wind and the ocean into marvellous designs. On the left side of the bay, the rocks rose to a high point, on top of which stood a small white house. We later learned that it was a log house covered with siding and painted white. It was over 100 years old, which was old, by West Coast standards, and had been a Hudson's Bay fort or store. It was marked on the navigational charts as the White House. Later, when they cut through the logs to enlarge the windows (they were always small in the early days, one reason, it was said, being to guard against Indian attacks), they found that the chainsaws could barely cut through, as the logs had become so hard they were almost petrified.

Behind us were a small barn, a chicken coop, a shed for storing grain and machinery and a mature orchard with many varieties of fruit, such as plums, apples and pears. In the orchard, and looking quite bemused by all the commotion, was a beautiful Jersey cow. We immediately named her Beauty.

There was also a small building, which, on investigation, housed an imposing pump with a handle, and we soon learned that no one should ever pass the pump house without pumping at least a dozen times to fill the water tank on the back porch. There was no running water, no electricity and no telephone, but we were so delighted with our wonderful place that the lack of amenities did not bother us — at least for the moment. Besides, after Pitt Meadows, almost anything would be paradise.

Our house at the Portage

We deposited the chickens in the coop and headed up a small hill to the big house, which was to be our new home. It was a brown-shingled house with a front porch and a long field in front of it. As we climbed the path, we could see a beautiful lagoon on one side, and beyond, Northumberland Channel and the cliffs of Gabriola Island. We stood there amazed, not believing our good fortune. My father had not been dreaming, we were indeed in the most wonderful place in the world.

A stately cedar tree stood about 50 feet from the house with seating carefully surrounding the trunk. A stone path led from the tree to the house, and in front of the house, two huge rocks, painted white, served as a gate. To the right of the house and down a path was the all-important outhouse (by this time, I was an expert on outhouses) and, farther along, a small chicken coop, complete with a bantam rooster … a husband for Banty and Bunty! This probably came as a shock to them, as neither one of them had ever seen a rooster their size before, and in his own way, he was quite handsome. His lower layer of feathers was white, but he looked as though someone had emptied their basement of leftover paint and thrown the dregs at this poor chicken. He was bright blue, bright red, bright green, in no particular design, with a splash of yellow and brown. My father immediately named him Joseph. As he was the only one with any religious training, he explained to my mother and me that this man in the bible, Joseph, had a coat of many colours; so Joseph he became.

The house was large, with four bedrooms upstairs and one on the main floor. Entry was through the kitchen, which had a sink (but no water) and a McClary wood stove. The dining room, in the corner between the kitchen and living room, had two huge windows overlooking the lagoon and the strait. The living room also had four huge windows, two overlooking the lagoon and the strait and two with a view of the bay and the white house on the point. There was a fireplace, which, we would find later, was the most essential feature of this room. There was also a bathroom containing a large bathtub with no taps. The upstairs bedrooms were all finished in tongue and groove and painted in calcimine colours of pink, green, blue and pale orange, all with large windows.

I make frequent mention of the windows because it was wartime and blackout time. We were directly across from Nanaimo, which had an army camp on the hill above it. The camp was, in fact, just two miles across the water and easily visible. A vulnerable location. Our first task was to find 10 very large blankets to use as window coverings, then to sew on hangers to hook onto the nails above the first-floor windows. Although it was a nuisance to hang the blankets every evening, it turned out to be a happy necessity, as the blankets blocked out the cold as well as the light. As we later discovered, the furnace was non-functional, and our only heat was from the kitchen stove and the living room fireplace. This made winters a cold affair in this spacious and uninsulated house.

Our next discovery was the portage and grounds. At the end of the long field in front of the house, we saw a large depression in the ground. On close inspection, it revealed a massive amount of clam and oyster shells and a few crab skeletons. This was the remains of a potlatch ceremony site and probably a midden (an old dump for domestic waste), all abandoned when the government banned the potlatch and confiscated most of the Indigenous artifacts. Potlatches were common on the B.C. coast and were important to the natives for social gatherings, paying back debts, showing the power of the tribe and distributing wealth and property. The ceremonies often lasted 10 days, the tribe having taken several years to amass enough wealth in order to hold a potlatch and, in the end, often impoverishing themselves. The B.C. government, in what they felt were the best interests of the Indigenous people, banned the potlatch and in doing so changed their way of life. It must have been a wonderful sight to see their canoes converging on this spot — having come north from Yellowpoint, south from Nanaimo, and west from Gabriola — hearing the drums and watching the dancing, singing and other festivities.

Further on from the midden was the portage itself. In the early days of the Nanaimo area, this piece of property was a long peninsula with a narrow and low-lying piece of land at this point. The Indigenous people, on returning from their fishing grounds at Dodd Narrows, would portage their canoes across this piece of land and carry on to their reserve at the mouth of the Nanaimo River. During the turbulent mining and logging days of the late 1800s, many men were imprisoned for disorderly behaviour. Nanaimo was famous for having more beer parlours per capita than any city in the Northwest. There were many fights and other misdemeanours, which led to stints in the jail and therefore an abundance of manpower to work on the portage project. The job was to make a cut, through solid rock, 100 feet long, 10 feet wide and eight feet deep, at this low and narrow spot in the peninsula, rendering the far side of the cut an island. It was an amazing feat when one realizes that the work was all done with pick and shovel and perhaps some blasting. The lower part of the cut had to be done only on low tide, as it filled on anything above a half tide. The purpose of the cut was to allow the Indigenous people to take their boats (they now all had 30- to 35-foot power boats) through the channel and not have to go around the point, which was a long and often dangerous journey. It was a good thing for us too: on the nights we wanted fresh salmon for supper, we would run down to the portage when we saw a fish boat returning and buy a lovely six-pound coho, for just 50 cents.

Property owner, Mrs. Bonney, overlooking the cut that the imprisoned miners made at the Portage

There were many other interesting parts of the property as well. In addition to the one bay we saw on our arrival, there were two smaller ones with sandy beaches and surrounded by the same wind-carved sandstone.

The reef, which formed part of the lagoon, was a work of art in itself, rising out of the water and topped with sandstone caves. It was wonderful to explore when the tide was low, and it revealed hundreds of pools teeming with sea life. At the end of the reef and almost adjoining Duke Point was a lovely reversing falls, evident when the tide rose and fell, allowing the lagoon to be refreshed with new water twice a day. From this point to the end, about half a mile, the lagoon was enclosed by land: Duke Point on the one side and "our" property (we thought of it as ours) on the other.

The property was actually owned by a man who, at that time, was the manager of one of the large pulp mills up the coast. This was to be his and his wife's retirement home, and we were to be the caretakers until they were ready to retire. The man they had bought it from was reputed to be a poet; although, I have never seen any evidence of his work. He seemed to have had a better time building quaint little fairy tale houses and charming little bridges about the property than writing any poetry of note. I, of course, loved these enchanting little places, and as an only child with no other children around for many miles, I was a regular visitor with my imagination as my only companion.

The Trip to School

We settled into our new accommodation quickly. There wasn't, in fact, much to settle, as our possessions were few and utilitarian: a sofa and chair for the living room, a table and a few chairs for the dining room, a kitchen table and chairs, a bedroom suite for my parents and a single bed for me. Not much furniture for a five-bedroom house, but it was all that was needed.

With the Easter holiday over, it was time for me to face going to a new school again, in the middle of, or in this case, the last part of the school year. It was going to be a four-mile hike, mostly through heavy bush, but apparently there were trails if you knew where they were. The lagoon ran a half-mile south of the house and was enclosed by our property on the one side and Duke Point on the other. On the Duke Point side, there was a small house that had once been inhabited by English mystic Brother XII's secretary Madame Zee (an intriguing story; see Appendix II) but now housed a small family with a daughter, Margaret, who was 13 years old. Contact was made with her so that she could show me the way to school. She was a blond girl, a little heavy and with a sullen disposition. Still, she was someone to walk with and teach me the way.

During World War II, daylight savings time was in effect the entire year. The walk was four miles, and we needed an hour and 15 minutes to make it to class on time, which meant leaving the house at 7:30 a.m. (6:30 standard time). It was dark. I headed out with a flashlight and my lunch box, down the twisting trail along the lagoon to meet Margaret. She was not yet there when I arrived, and I was nervous standing there alone and hoped she would hurry. Suddenly, I heard a voice saying, "Who are you?" It was a man's voice, so I responded, "Who are you?" No answer. Then it came again: "Who are you?" By the time Margaret arrived, I was shaking, but happy to see her, although I sensed that she was not going to be an easy person to like.

"Margaret," I said, "there is someone out there who keeps saying, 'Who are you?'" Margaret listened, and it came again. She gave me a disgusted look and said, "You are so stupid. It's only an owl."

I felt chastened and embarrassed, but also relieved that there was no immediate danger. I followed her silently to school along the road, past Jane Gordon's farm (the only sign of habitation on our route), down the hill and onto a trail. The trail was soft and quiet and lined with tall trees, salal bushes and huckleberry bushes. The swamp we crossed over via a moss-covered log was beautiful and, at this time of year, full of exotic skunk cabbage. Most people do not regard skunk cabbage as exotic or beautiful, but in Europe, it is called swamp lantern and much appreciated. It does have a strong odour, but if one can ignore this simple form of protection, it is truly beautiful, with its yellow centre and graceful protective spring green leaves. I loved them then, and even more in the years to follow, as they were my first harbinger of spring after a gloomy and lonely winter.

Our journey continued until we reached the school field at exactly 8:45 a.m., with just enough time to get inside, take off our coats and be at our desks by nine o'clock. Margaret, for all her disagreeable nature, was quite a good teacher. She knew most of the plants along the way and taught me their names. I was an eager student, but she considered me more of a nuisance than a companion. Perhaps this was her way of asserting her superiority. Whatever her motives, she taught me well, and the following year I was able to lead half the class on a plant identification field trip while the teacher led the other half.

Margaret also warned me of wood ticks, rampant in the spring in that area. Each night, after I arrived home after running a mile around the beaches, I took off my clothes, shook them out and inspected my body for the tiny dark red insects with black feet, similar to a very small ladybug. These ticks were considered quite dangerous, as they could inflict a person with Rocky Mountain fever if they became embedded under the skin. I had found a few that had not yet broken the skin, until one day, I found one burrowing into my skin on top of my collarbone. My father sprang into action. Local knowledge said that if you doused the tick with kerosene and held a match behind it, the tick would back out. This particular tick had not read the script very carefully and proceeded to burrow deeper. After an hour and much painful digging, all parts were finally removed. I still carry a small scar as testimony to my battle with the tick.

June arrived along with summer holidays, and Margaret announced that she was moving to downtown Cedar, which, at that time, consisted of a store, a post office and gas station, all on the same premises. This meant, of course, that I would be travelling this route to school by myself, which I did for the next three years. Strangely, it did not worry me too much to lose the unhappy Margaret. In the winter, it would be just breaking light as I arrived at school, and I rarely arrived home before dark. There were cougars around at certain times of the year, which I tried to watch for, but with my poor eyesight, I could not have seen them. I did feel their presence. My salvation was probably that there were sheep in the vicinity and the cougars preferred lamb to me.

One thing that did worry me was the wild cattle that roamed loose in the area. The cows did not frighten me, but there were bulls mixed with the herds and they were concerning. The trails were narrow and the salal on either side was too dense and high to go through — I just had to carry on through and hope that none of the animals decided to become belligerent as I was making my way between them.

One experience haunts me to this day. Part of my journey to and from school took me past the Indian reserve, usually a quiet part of my route; however, one day, late in January, two of the boys died. They had gathered camas root, roasted it on an open fire and eaten it. Camas was one of the staple foods of their diet, but only the blue camas is nutritious and edible. White camas is deadly — hence called the death camas — and this is what they had eaten.

The drums began to beat and the mourning and calling ensued. *Boom-boom-boom-boom*, interspersed with agonizing cries. It went on for about a week. It was eerie and frightening to hear as I passed by each morning and again at dusk. They had no interest in me, of course, and would not have harmed me, but it was one time in my life when I felt the hair physically lift from the back of my head.

Obviously, I survived all of these encounters, and at the end of three years, when it was necessary to go away to school, I emerged a much tougher young girl, both mentally and physically, with a deep appreciation of both the beauty and danger of nature.

Beauty

We hadn't expected to find her there when we first arrived at the Portage, but there was the Jersey cow, watching our every move with great interest. She was beautiful too, with her large brown eyes framed with a darker shade, looming out of a cream-coloured face, which is why we called her Beauty. At that time, we did not realize that not only was she going to be a pleasure to watch as she grazed throughout the property, but she would also become a very important and essential part of our lives. Beauty was lovely and docile and willingly gave us her milk and manure, expecting no more than a warm barn and a little hay in the winter.

Neither my father nor I had much success milking her, but she and my mother had a little love affair from the start. As soon as my mother began milking, the milk would flow and, with seemingly little effort, Mom would have a bucket of milk in no time. We settled into an evening routine: after supper, my parents headed for the barn, Mom to milk and Dad to feed Beauty and clean up the barn. I cleaned up the kitchen and did the dishes. When they returned, we poured the milk through clean white gauze into a metal creamer, complete with a spigot on the bottom, and then carefully washed everything so it was ready for the next morning. The butter we made from the heavy cream was either sold to people in Cedar or traded for the food stamps necessary to buy rationed items like butter, sugar, meat, gas and liquor. We mostly traded for sugar, which we needed for preserving all the fruit from the orchard. A Jersey cow does not give a huge volume of milk, and between the three of us, we were able to consume all the milk, mostly skim.

My mother with Beauty at the Portage

Beauty also gave us two calves in three years and was pregnant with a third when disaster struck. Usually, she grazed in the long field in front of the house or in the orchard, but on this December day, she had wandered up the steep hill beside the white house. The hill was rocky and covered with moss and it sloped to the ocean after the crest. It was a foggy morning and my mother noted that she could not see or hear Beauty, so she went out to look. Eventually, she could hear the bell but couldn't see her — and then she saw the skid marks on the moss. She immediately realized that Beauty had fallen into the ocean at least 10 metres below.

My father was summoned. He ran to the lagoon, rowed the boat through the portage across the bays and around the point. By the time he got there, Beauty was afloat, but exhausted. They could not swim her around the point as they had planned, so they did the next best thing. In December, the tides were high, and the west side of the point had several large sandstone erosions that were flat on the bottom, covered on the top and about 10 metres long and five metres deep. The tide was high enough to pull her into one of those caves so that she was at least out of the water and safe for the moment. They rowed back to the bay, loaded some hay and blankets into the boat and returned to the cave. The tide was on the ebb by this time, which made this route now inaccessible. Nor would they be able to row over to milk her. They thought that perhaps the next day they could get her into the water from the cave and swim her around the point to the bay, but on consulting the tide tables, it was obvious that this was the highest tide of the month and that they would have to think of another way of getting a cow out of a cave three metres above the beach and around the point to safety. In the meantime, she had to be fed and milked.

They made a trail down to the cave: it was steep and slippery, but they managed to get enough food and water down to sustain her and milk her twice a day for two entire days. During this time, my father was engaged in sourcing enough lumber to build a ramp in the hope that we could get her to co-operate and go down a steep ramp to the beach. It had to be steep because even on a low tide there was very little beach at the bottom. My dad wasn't much of a carpenter, but what he built was strong and heavy. On the morning of the third day, they rowed the ramp around and tied it near the cave. In the winter, the tides are low but only at night. The ramp in place, we started the move about 4:30 p.m. It was getting dark, and we knew we didn't have time to spare. Beauty trusted my mother, and I'm sure she knew that we were trying to save her; so, with my mother coaxing and Dad and

I steering and holding, we got her down the ramp and onto the beach. Phase one completed.

Our problems, however, were not over. It goes without saying that a cow is not an agile animal.

The cave that we were able to pull Beauty into for temporary safety

It is also a heavy animal with sharp pointed hooves not suitable for walking on a wet, sandy, silty and slippery surface, interspersed with large and small rocks. On her first step she sank to her knees, and we realized that we would have to "plank" her around the point. Dad and I put a plank down and she gingerly walked along, being coaxed, pulled and prodded. Then we moved the plank forward and repeated the exercise. It was hard work; the planks were heavy and wet, Beauty was heavy and slow and we were wet and exhausted. It was almost midnight when we finally got her off the beach, onto dry land and into the barn. As we closed the barn door, we looked up and saw that it had started to snow. One day more and she would have died in the cave, as we would not have been able to get her out. Her calf was still-born a month later, and she never bore another, but she continued to give milk (a smaller amount) — and she was still our Beauty.

The Portage: Pros and Cons

Except for some obvious drawbacks, life at the Portage was idyllic.

One of the negatives was money, which was always in short supply. Dad tried to fulfill his dream of making money while enjoying life on the fishing grounds, but the only boat he could afford was small, 32 feet, with an old one-lung Easthope motor. The engine was the most reliable on the coast, but maximum speed was about four knots. This meant he could fish the area around Dodd Narrows, Nanaimo and perhaps as far as Lasquteti Island, but it would not allow him to travel to the farther, more productive fishing areas. We could hear the chug of the old engine when he was only a mile away and it would still take him half an hour to arrive home.

The boat that sank in the lagoon

He kept the boat in the lagoon where it was safe from the winds that prevailed up and down the channel, or at least we thought it was safe, until we looked out one morning to see that it had sunk in the lagoon! As I left for school that morning my parents headed down to try to salvage it, and when I arrived home that afternoon the boat was floating again. I'll never know how those two small people managed it with a rowboat and a line but, somehow, they did. I do know that a great deal of work ensued, cleaning caulking and painting. I had to do a great deal of the caulking and hated every minute of it. To my mother's delight, and mine, Dad gave up fishing after that first year. I guess he sold the boat; I don't even remember the name of it.

After that, he did some odd jobs, like clearing land for the Nanaimo airport, which made me happy for the three or four months it lasted because I got a ride partway to school.

My long and somewhat dangerous walk to school every day was a distinct downside, and the lack of a proper heating system gave rise to some very cold winter nights in the large draughty house, especially after the fire had gone out.

Our only entertainment was a battery radio, which we listened to for only two hours a night. We lit the fireplace and sat in the dim glow of the Aladdin Lamp hissing its way through the evening. At intervals, we would stand and back up to the fire — where we would get our jeans almost to the smoke point — and then sit back down. The first few seconds were very warm and exciting as we wondered if our skin would survive, but we quickly cooled down and would have to repeat the exercise a few minutes later.

One New Year's Eve, we treated ourselves and turned the radio on to hear the celebrations going on elsewhere, but when the network shut down immediately after the broadcast, we forgot to turn it off. In the morning, we were awakened by church bells peeling and realized our mistake. It was the last gasp of energy from the precious battery. This was a small disaster as it was a few months before we could afford a new one. Large batteries in those days cost $12, an impossible sum for us to raise in a short time.

The positives, however, far outweighed the negatives. The mouth of the Nanaimo River came in to the left of the little white house, and when the tide was low we donned our boots and walked in the eelgrass-covered rivulets. When we stepped on something hard, we knew it was a crab and slid a pitchfork underneath and carefully lifted him into a bucket. We did not take females. Jack Point yielded all the oysters we ever needed, and we gathered them by tapping them off the rocks with a screwdriver and a hammer. All the shells were returned to the beach as they contained the spawn. Clams were abundant in the lagoon, and it must have been a sight to see two adults, one child, one horse, a cow, two dogs and five cats all heading for the clam-digging grounds. The horse and cow looked on, and the dogs jumped around, but the cats got right down to business. They were there with us, legs in sand and water, scavenging any clams that were damaged by the shovel and thus available to them.

In the fall and winter, there were ducks. With the shotgun in hand, my mother would wait until there were three sitting close together and get all three with one shot. Shells were precious and never wasted. Tip, a spitz-retriever cross, would spring into action and pick them up one at a time and bring them to shore. Very occasionally, we shot a deer. This was rare, though, as we had no refrigeration and we wasted nothing. Beauty gave plenty of milk, which we kept cold in a metal container with a spigot on the bottom. I drank gallons of skim milk because the cream stayed on top, and we made butter from the cream. My job was to wind the churn, for hours it seemed, until the butter came. Then I washed, salted and shaped it. I whined a lot about all this work, as well as other jobs like blackberry picking, but no one seemed to pay much attention to my complaints. The chickens gave a good supply of eggs, and we had chicken in our pots fairly frequently.

The orchard yielded a wide variety of apples — Transparent, Northern Spy, Russets and others — with various keeping qualities. In winter, they were kept in hay on bunks in a small cabin on the hill behind the house. Our dessert was usually apple crisp, apple pie or apple sauce, all with whipped cream. There were plums, pears and blackberries too, but they were difficult to store. As there was severe sugar rationing, we traded all our meat, liquor, butter, eggs and some gas coupons for enough sugar to can most of the fruit. Mom used a thin syrup to eke out the supply. She grew a large garden, some of which had been planted with asparagus several yeas before, so from April on, we had an abundance of vegetables. Like the pioneers, we bought very little — just flour, salt and yeast to make bread. All was well in paradise.

Well, almost well. Joseph, the bantam rooster, was creating a problem, and my father was more than a little angry with him. It seems that Joseph was happy for just a short while with his two beautiful new brides, Banty and Bunty, before he decided that he was destined for bigger things. The bigger things came in the form of the large New Hampshire hens who lived by the barn with Flatfoot the rooster. It didn't take long for Joseph to back Flatfoot into a corner and intimidate him to a point where he could no longer crow. The chickens, who roamed free in the daytime, began disappearing. Three weeks later, they reappeared, each with eight or ten little chicks in tow. It soon became apparent that every single chick was a progeny of Joseph. Dad was furious. Half-breed chickens are small, so it takes two to make a meal, their eggs are small, so, again, two for the size of one, and these chickens were wilier than their docile mothers, were hard to catch and almost impossible to keep in a coop.

One morning, about the time he was angriest with Joseph, I was finishing breakfast before heading out for school, and I asked my father, "Dad, can chickens swim?" As with many fathers who don't always pay full attention to their offspring and who don't wish to say, "I don't know," he said, "Well, all animals can swim." I left for school with an idea in my head, and when I got home I went straight to the upper chicken coop. I took Joseph off the perch and went down to the lagoon. Here was a small wharf with water that wasn't so deep that I couldn't jump in and save him if I had to, but it was out of his depth. I carefully put him in the water and was delighted when he swam slowly but manfully to shore, shook himself off and ran up the hill and back to his coop. I did notice, however, that there was a little list to his walk, but attributed it to hill climbing and cold water.

At supper that night, I said, "You were right, Dad."

"Huh? Right about what?"

"Chickens can swim," I replied.

"How did you find that out?" he asked.

"I threw Joseph into the chuck and he swam to shore."

I had his attention now. He gave me a strange look and said, "Where did you find him?"

"On his perch in the chicken coop."

"You couldn't have!" he said angrily. "I killed Joseph this afternoon."

"Well," I said, "he's alive now, and I guess he's had a very bad day."

What had occurred was this: Dad had been outside working and had a crowbar in his hand when Joseph, unwisely, had chosen that moment to saunter down the path. Dad reached over, gave him a mighty blow on the head, threw him in a pile of leaves and stumps and left him for dead. Sometime later, Joseph woke up and stumbled back to the coop to recover. It couldn't have been long after that when I came along, removed him from his perch and put him into the cold ocean water. A very bad day in the life of a rooster.

Joseph lived to a ripe old age. He never did get over his passion for the big chickens and, ever after, he walked with a decided list to the right.

Long Harry

Long Harry was a tall, solid Indian of about 80 years. He was from the Nanaimo reserve three and a half miles away. He liked to visit my father occasionally and would walk the seven miles there and back as if he was just visiting next door. But Long Harry upset me one day when Dad asked him to stay for lunch, and Long Harry came to me and said, "Old man say, tell old woman I stay for lunch." I was shocked that he would call my parents old man and old woman; after all, my mother was in her early thirties. I considered it quite disrespectful. My parents, of course, understood it for what it was — a man making himself understood as best he could.

Long Harry stayed for lunch and showed Dad how the Indians made their fishing lures. Then he held one thumb up — it seemed at least six inches long — and aimed his finger at it to demonstrate how to put the line through the lure. I was quite intrigued.

Then talk turned to Long Harry's father. Around 1867, when Long Harry was six years old, two white men were murdered in the Nanaimo area. The government, at that time, appeared to have a penchant for rounding up Indians as they were always considered the usual suspects, and his father was rounded up and accused.

Long Harry's description was as follows:

"They accuse my father. He not guilty of murder, but they say so. They build a gallows on Protection Island and they take my father there. They put rope around his neck and open trap, rope slip — he land on feet. Everybody say, 'No hang him, no hang him, he innocent!'

But they put rope around his neck again, and I see them hang my father. Little while later, they catch white guys who do the murder — but they hang my father on Gallows Point. That why it called Gallows Point."

I have searched the archives in Victoria to find evidence of this incident. I found other similar stories, but I could not verify Long Harry's account as I did not know his Indian name nor his father's, but I do believe that what he told us was true.

The Beginning of the End at the Portage

Change to our idyllic life was inevitable. The owners of the property, Mr. and Mrs. Bonney, were due to retire and wanted to move into the big house and be lords of the manor on their estate. Before they could do this, a great deal of work was required as they could not move into the house in its present condition, with no running water, no electricity and no furnace. In addition, they had decided to raise mink as a lucrative pastime. Mrs. Bonney's father in New Westminster was raising mink and, as he was becoming quite elderly, would pass the breeding stock on to them.

A great deal of construction was going to be required as it would be necessary to bring in electricity, find a constant source of water and build a refrigerator house, as well as the many pens that the mink would require. It would also mean refurbishing the 100-year-old log house on the point for us to occupy. It was at this point that Mr. Bonney decided that he needed help to build and oversee the work and enlisted my father as working supervisor and as a partner in the mink business.

The first part of the job entailed building a small lake at the top of the hill so that the water could flow with a gravity feed line. My father did all the clearing on his own, felling the trees and blasting the stumps. I was surprised that my mother was not more concerned about my father doing this as she had lost her own father when she was only three, in a land clearing incident in Bella Coola; but she never questioned whatever was put before her, whether it was my father blasting stumps or me walking eight miles through the bush.

After the land was cleared, a huge bulldozer was brought in to scoop out the soil. Shortly thereafter, the crater began to fill with water, and we had our lake of about 300 metres long and 100 metres wide. Pipes were salvaged from the Nanaimo River and laid down the hill to give a good source of water for the two houses and the refrigerator house. This water was not to be used for drinking but for all other purposes, as we were not sure about the purity or bacterial count of this new supply.

The next project was to get the power lines up to the property from the highway three miles down the road, through inhospitable terrain, and to convince B.C. Electric to do it. This was not an easy sell, but somehow, either by the persuasive ability of my father or some clout from Mr. Bonney or the stars being aligned just right, the power lines were brought down and we could flick a switch for light for the first time in three years.

By this time, I was in Grade 7 and had finally convinced my parents that I needed a bike. I had pleaded and cajoled for two years and finally, at Christmas, I received my shiny new bike. Proud of my new vehicle, I cleaned, polished and oiled it every week. The rock and gravel road was not ideal ground for a bike. The trip to school was longer as I could not use the cut-off trail, and I had to push the bike up a few long hills, but I was happy to have it and could usually make it to or from school in an hour.

One day, however, on my way to school, I hit a rock at the top of a short steep hill, one mile from the house. Over the handlebars I went, heading face first into a huge rock on the side of the road. At the last second, I threw up my head and landed chin-first into the rock. I lay there, unconscious, for about an hour, and when I did come to, I tried to collect my thoughts as to my next move. I could not stay there, as no one would even begin to look for me until at least five o'clock. My chin was very sore, but there wasn't too much blood and my legs and arms seemed to be in working order. Nothing else was bothering me, so I thought I might as well carry on the remaining three miles to school. When I picked up my bike I saw that the front wheel was parallel to the handlebars. This caused me to amend my decision and I headed for home, dragging the bike along.

My mother was upset when she saw me, and my father was called in for a consultation. It was decided that we go to Nanaimo to see the doctor, which was a heavy decision, as it would cost money for gas and for the doctor.

We left the house with me in the front seat of the truck and my mother relegated to the back, sitting on the spare tire — the only time this had ever happened. I was delighted.

We arrived without an appointment, as we still did not have a phone, but were taken right into the office. The nurse was given the task of cleaning out the gravel from the wound but when the doctor came to look at it, before doing the stitches, he said, "That won't do. Give me the gauze. If we don't get this dirt out now, she'll have a black line there for the rest of her life." He did get it out, but it was painful, and I wanted him to stop. I am grateful to him now as the scar is almost imperceptible and fits neatly into a little area for a double chin.

• • •

I had always been a reader and loved books whenever I could find them. We had no books at home except *The Complete Works of Shakespeare*. I read that over the summer. My father sometimes bought the early sci-fi paperbacks and I read them, much to my mother's horror. At school, there were a few books available, and I read them during the lunch hour. There were no other girls in my grade, and of the six boys who were my classmates, five were very rough, and the one who was decent went home for lunch. The classroom had deteriorated to a level where there was little discipline. The teacher (who was also the principal) was unable to cope with the three grades (5, 6 and 7) in one classroom, either academically or as a disciplinarian. The classroom was chaos and very little teaching or learning took place. I withdrew from the melee and just read books.

About this time, I developed a carbuncle (a painful pus-bearing inflammation under the skin) on my knee. As it worsened, I was no longer able to walk and had to stay home from school. There were no antibiotics in those days (it probably could have been lanced by a doctor but, as explained above, we didn't — or couldn't — go to a doctor very often), so it was treated by applying poultices and hoping for the best. One night, it finally broke, pulling out seven cores of tissue. What a relief it was! It was still weeping and sore and heavily bandaged when I returned to school a few days later, biking with mostly one leg the entire way.

While I was away, a plot of some kind had developed among the Grade 6 girls. Was it because I had all the Grade 7 boys to myself at one table? Was it that they felt I was being elitist by reading books at noon, or was it that they had discovered girl power? I don't know. After school that first day back, I limped out to get my bike and start the ride home when four or five Grade 6 girls began to grab the bike. Then a few boys appeared, one, the brother of one of the girls. I stood there surrounded, wondering what it was about, when the first blow fell and then a kick to my knee by one of the boys. Blood erupted from my knee but not as fast or as hard as my very quick and violent temper. They had not reckoned on the fact that I was unusually strong due to my three years of walking and running eight to 10 miles a day, plus being the pitcher on the school mixed softball team. When it was all over, there were two black eyes, three knocked-out teeth and a large pile of hair on the ground. None was mine.

I rode my bike to the store to pick up the mail, and Mrs. Rayer, the owner, was shocked. She took me into her kitchen, washed and bandaged my leg, and I headed home, again riding one-legged all the way.

When I got home, I related what had happened and announced that I was not going to school the next day. My father thought for a minute and said, "You can do that, but if you do, they will think they have beaten you. If you go and face them, they will know you are strong and will respect you."

I wasn't sure whether I wanted to be respected or not, but the next day I headed off, unhappily, to school. When I arrived, the entire school was waiting. They fell back to create a lane to allow me through and I went up the steps without a word being uttered.

I was called into the principal's office to relate the incident. I don't know who reported it, maybe Mrs. Rayer. He asked me what I would do if it happened again. "I would do exactly the same thing," I responded. He said nothing more and there were no reprimands for anyone. I feel he was a weak man in the wrong profession, and he certainly was not skilled in conflict resolution.

At this point, it was obvious that I could not continue at this school and hope to gain any kind of education. Work on the buildings was about to begin, and Dad had hired a master carpenter who he knew. He also hired Jim, the husband of the family we had come to know in Pitt Meadows. Margaret and Jim had sold their property in Pitt Meadows and moved to Vernon, but Jim had no job. It was decided that I would go to Vernon with Margaret and Sharon, their daughter, who was five years my junior, live on their new property with them and go to a school that was academically acceptable. Jim would stay at the Portage and help with the construction.

It sounded like a wonderful adventure to me, so on February 1, I was off to Vernon and a new school, true to our habit of never starting a new school at the beginning of the term.

It was exciting taking the train through the Fraser Valley and the high country, and arriving at the Vernon train station in the snow at -23 degrees Celsius. New experiences awaited.

Vernon

Margaret and Sharon met me at the train station in Margaret's old truck. It was newer than our old Ford Model A, and three of us could sit in the front seat, a luxurious concept as far as I was concerned, having been relegated to the hard metal surface of the truck deck for the past three years. Margaret was a big lady, almost six feet tall, and the truck suited her well.

We drove 10 miles east to Lavington, a small rural community situated among rolling hills. Margaret and Jim, with the profits on the sale of their farm in Pitt Meadows, had bought the old house and part of the land that had been owned by James Buchanan, a wealthy Scottish distiller, who may have used it as a hunting lodge. British Columbia abounds with hunting lodges built by the gentry, such as the Astors, in the early 1900s. The house was large and all on one floor, which was unusual for that climate or that era. It had five huge bedrooms, a large living room, a dining room, two kitchens and one bathroom. It had been a lovely estate with beautiful grounds but, although it had not been "let go," the house and the grounds were in less than perfect condition. Jim was not much of a worker, which my father was to find after hiring him to work at the Portage. In fact, he was bone lazy. Neither was he a fix-it type of man. Consequently, there was much that required fixing in their house, including the furnace, which worked little or not at all. It was uncomfortable enough to live on the coast in a house with a non-functioning furnace, but in the interior climate it resulted in pipes breaking and leaking, causing the halls and bathroom to be covered in a thin layer of ice. We skated or slid to the bathroom for the months of February and March.

Margaret was not a practical person, but she was kind and artistic. It was not long before she had Sharon's room painted and wallpapered in pink tulips and mine done in large yellow daffodils. It may not be the décor one would choose now, but for an eight-year-old and a 13-year-old, it was lovely, and it created the feeling of warmth even on those cold winter days and nights.

My bedroom was the nicest of all at the back of the house, with a view onto the open woods. Usually, in the morning, I could look out onto the snow-covered acreage and see at least 30 mule deer foraging for food and, along with them, the same number of ring-necked pheasants, the males parading in full colourful uniform. With the backdrop of the white snow and green trees, it created a sight that could not properly have been captured in a painting or a photograph.

I caught the school bus, which stopped not far from the house, and made instant friends. It's not hard when you are jammed on a bus with up to 50 other children. One of the stops was the Coldstream Ranch at the western end of Kalamalka Lake. The land had been acquired by an Irish military officer who developed it into a cattle ranch. In 1891, it was sold to Lord Aberdeen, who planted orchards, sub-divided some of the land and sold it to the British gentry. Since then, it has become a residential community for Vernon, although some agricultural land still remains.

The high school in Vernon was brand new and I loved it. It was situated within the city park, which had beautiful trees, flower gardens and streams running through it. An idyllic stetting.

I made friends with Patsy Laidlaw, a very attractive girl who was having trouble with English. I was able to help her, and she, in turn, was friendly and often invited me to her home for lunch. Later in her life, she became Pat Jordon, one of our first female MLAs (Member of the Legislative Assembly) in the Social Credit Government. English, of course, was almost the only subject I could help her with, as, due to my long period of poor schooling, I was not up to speed in other subjects, especially math. With the help of a determined and dedicated math teacher, Mr. Seaton, from a pioneer family in B.C. (Seaton Lake is named after one of his ancestors), I caught up and passed the rest of the class and, at the end of the term, was promoted to Grade 9A for the coming year. It had been a stigma being in the B group, but all the Lavington students had been placed there for the first year of high school to get them sorted out academically. It was not going to make much difference to me because I was not going to continue school in Vernon in the fall. I did not know where I was going to be but, sadly, I knew it was not going to be Vernon.

• • •

One of the many things I loved about living in Vernon in the winter was the ice skating. On the coast, there was very little ice, and in rural communities, there were no arenas available. After school in February and March, we took the bus home, did our homework and had supper. Then we walked a mile and a half through the snow to the elementary school and the outdoor rink constructed by some of the men in the district. In the day, the elementary school children used it at lunch time, and after school and in the evening, we older students could skate, after which we had to clean the ice and re-flood the rink so it would freeze into a smooth surface again for the younger ones' use the next day. No maintenance people to pay, no supervision required, and there never were any major problems or injuries. This was a wonderful experience for me, who had never really skated before and had never experienced prolonged cold weather, or walking with the snow crunching underfoot. I loved it all.

All too soon, spring arrived and the snow disappeared, replaced by hills covered with a variety of tiny colourful wild flowers, and then, later on, acres of apple trees adorned with pink and white blossoms — again a sight impossible to capture with paintbrush or camera.

One day at school was particularly memorable: I was sent to the office on an errand and found the principal and staff huddled together looking worried. Getting as close as I dared and straining to hear the conversation, I learned that Franklin Roosevelt had died. Who was going to take his place? He wasn't going to see the end of the war, which we were told was imminent. It did not have the impact on me of John Kennedy's assassination years later, but it was a very important incident at that time. I had gone through the war without knowing a lot about what was happening as, at the Portage, we had limited contact with the outside world. Now I was now old enough to appreciate the enormity of the war and the concern over Mr. Roosevelt. I marched back to the classroom with the important news — and no one believed me! Fifteen minutes later, the news came over the PA system.

I experienced yet another incident that could have had serious consequences and taught me a very important lesson. The school picnic at Kalamalka Lake was to take place at the end of the week and the usual excitement and planning was underway. I was looking forward to swimming and diving, and it did not occur to me that many of the children did not know how to swim. Being a coastal, I automatically assumed that everyone could swim. At the end of the wharf, I jumped in and encouraged my best friend, Joyce, to do the same. "I can't swim," she said. "Oh, come on," I said, "it's easy, and besides, I'll help you." Although she was a little younger, she was much bigger than I, and when she jumped in, she went down like a rock right to the bottom, about three metres below the wharf. When she came up and was about to go down again, I grabbed her wrist and the wharf but she was very heavy. I knew that I couldn't hang on to her for long and I certainly couldn't get her back onto the wharf. I was screaming for help and desperately trying to hang on. When I knew I couldn't hold on for much longer, her brother appeared and the two of us got her back onto the wharf and safety. The incident haunted me for months and never again did I put pressure on someone to do something they could not or should not do.

The end of the school year was approaching, and I was going to have to leave all my new friends and return home. It wasn't that I didn't like the Portage, but after the misery and isolation of Pitt Meadows and the somewhat solitary life of the Portage, I was enjoying having friends and finally learning something at school.

My mother was going to come to Vernon for a short holiday, as most of the construction had been completed and the crew of men she had cooked for had gone home. On my way to school, I walked over to the train station to meet her — and she didn't recognize me! Instead of the pencil-thin child she was expecting, there was a somewhat porky creature rolling towards her — certainly not her daughter. What had happened? Well, it turned out that although Margaret was a wonderful, warm, artistic woman, she could not cook. Her husband thought that a cake had to be soggy in the middle to be edible. I cannot remember what I got in my lunch bag, but I know that Sharon got brown sugar sandwiches every day. Furthermore, at lunchtime, our group went over to our favourite restaurant to have banana splits, sodas or whatever fattening foods took our fancy. And I was no longer walking or biking eight miles a day. After school, I would come home to find nothing much to eat, so I'd gobble up several crackers, each one covered with a quarter of an inch of butter. This plus the sudden onset of puberty allowed me to balloon— everywhere — and to gain 30 pounds in the bargain.

This, in turn, did cause an incident that could have been very serious. Leaving my mother to go to Margaret's, I was walking to school, looking older and more voluptuous than I felt. A car approached and the lone male occupant asked directions to Kelowna. I said, "Keep going, turn right after the train tracks, go past the school and follow the road out of town."

He did not appear to understand and said, "Well, please get in and show me the way, and I can drop you off at the school."

"No," I replied. "It's not far."

"Please show me the way," he insisted. "I'm not good with directions and may make a mistake."

Foolishly, I got into the car, and he locked the doors. When we got to the school, I said, "Thank you. I'll get out here."

"No," he said nastily. "You're coming with me."

"No. I have to get out here. I have to go to school."

"You're not going to school; you're coming with me."

For some reason, I didn't panic. I reached over, turned the key in the ignition, pulled it out and threw it in the back seat. In the confusion to get the key, he slammed on the brake, and I opened the door and ran. Even then, I was not sure what he was up to; in those days, 13 was still naïve.

A Surprise Summer at the Portage

My return to the Portage, in June 1945, was far more exciting than I had expected it to be. As well as my father being there to meet me, there was a tall young man who looked a lot like my father, but he was much younger and taller and maybe a little better looking. It was my uncle Bun (his name was Bernard), who was three months old when my father left home at the age of 17. He had just been discharged from the air force. He was free, had a little money and decided to have a look at the West Coast and maybe try to find his elusive brother.

Somehow, he had obtained our former Vancouver address and began knocking on doors. The upstairs renters in the Franklin Street house had heard that we had moved to "The Island," somewhere south of Nanaimo. Bun took the ferry to Nanaimo. On the boat, Bun met a man to whom he explained that he was looking for a brother who had left home 27 years prior and no one had heard from him since. The man had a car and a little time to spare, so they got off the ferry and drove south along the highway, stopping at stores and houses along the way. Finally, someone sent them along the cut-off road to Cedar, and at Rayers store, they were given directions to the Portage.

It was a dreadful road and the man must have wondered why he had let his curiosity get the better of him, but they eventually arrived. My mother opened the door and said, "You're Harry's brother, aren't you?" The man, realizing that Bun had found his family, turned the car around and drove off. Bun did not even get a chance to say thank you.

There ensued a happy summer for me. We swam every late afternoon when he had finished work and the tide had come rolling in over the warm sand. We played checkers, cards, snakes and ladders … and the gramophone! The whole house echoed with "The Bluebird of Happiness," sung by John Charles Thomas, and songs from *The Student Prince* and *The Merry Widow*, music I had never heard before.

Then the mink arrived. They were vicious little creatures that were always ready to bite as they ran up and over the insides of their cages so fast you could hardly follow them with your eyes. And did they smell! An acrid, pungent smell that dictated that their cages must be situated a long way from the house and cleaned regularly.

My father, with our dog Ranger, holding JoJo, our pet mink

They had their young, but only my father was allowed near the pens for fear of causing them distress. They will eat their young when they perceive danger. One day, a mother mink died, leaving two orphan kits. What to do with two motherless babies? My father decided to put the male kit in with another mother in the hope that she would adopt him. He put the kit in the cage, and she carried it into the nest. All seemed well until the next morning when there was no sign of the kit. The mother had eaten it.

That left us with the baby female to try to raise by bottle feeding. This needed to be done several times a day and, since I had some time between minor housework and helping my mother with the canning of tomatoes, fruit and some seafood, I became the surrogate mother. Mink are one of the most ferocious mammals on earth and no one that we had ever heard of had ever tamed a mink. We called her JoJo and kept her in a cage on the porch. For her lunchtime and afternoon feeds, we all gathered on the porch and she ran from one to another as a bit of a game. One day, she ran to Bun and up his pant leg — on the inside! He wasn't worried as he thought she would come out at the large hole at the knee of his jeans, however, she made a turn, passed the knee hole and continued on up. Bun, of course, panicked and grabbed his pant leg just soon enough. JoJo panicked too and let the entire contents of her bowels go, noxious smell and all. It ended happily, with no apparent damage to either Bun or JoJo. In fact, the only casualty was Bun's jeans, which were not salvageable and were duly buried without ceremony.

Most of the construction had been completed. It was the end of August and time for both Bun and me to move on. Me, to Victoria to live with my aunt Dona and her husband, Bill, and their two children. Bun decided to stay on the West Coast for a while longer, and he too headed to Victoria to find a job and assess the West Coast winters.

Since it was time for the Bonneys to move into the house, my parents also had to move to the small log house on the point, which had been slightly remodelled and decorated.

Sadly, in the 1980s, this beautiful property was desecrated in favour of a huge industrial park and a ferry terminal. I was told that the house would be moved and preserved at a heritage site, but on my one trip back, to witness the devastation, I found the little white log house pushed over the bank on its side, not far from where Beauty had slipped into the ocean, for nature to deal with. A careless waste of history.

2
Reaching Maturity

DIFFERENT FORMS OF EDUCATION

Victoria

I moved to Victoria in September, to go to school, and lived with Aunt Dona and Uncle Bill and their two children, Malcolm, who was five years old, and his three-month-old sister, Pat. At last, I changed schools at the beginning of the school term. The house they lived in was of a decidedly peculiar design with the bedrooms and bathroom branching off the kitchen, and the never-used living room somewhere down the hall. There was a solitary bedroom upstairs, which was to be my domain for the next 10 months. There was also a basement of sorts, a dank, dark excavation under the house with a dirt floor, a place I never wanted to go.

The house was situated in what is now the industrial part of Esquimalt and at a crossing between the road and the railroad track. In fact, the train ran no more than 10 metres from the side of the house. The first few days were exciting as I levitated from the bed at midnight when the train came churning down the track, blowing its whistle and ringing the bell. But a 14-year-old adapts well to noise, confusion and change, and after the third night I never heard it again.

I was looking forward to going to school in Victoria and eagerly bounced off to Esquimalt High on Head Street. I was in Grade 9. Settling into my desk, I tried to look happy and made some gestures of friendliness to some of the girls. My advances were met with scowls and stony silence. This had never happened before, and I was bewildered. Each day, I tried to make contact with someone — anyone — but I received the same rebuffs every time. I was hurt, lonely and homesick for the first time in my life. What I had not been prepared for was that Victoria, at that time, was very "British," and the people, even the younger ones, retained their cool, reserved attitude until they either got tired of ignoring you or had observed you for long enough to decide that you were of no particular threat.

Finally, after about two weeks, a girl named Dodie walked up to me and said, "You go home the same way I do. Why don't we walk together?" From that day on, we were fast friends.

After the breakthrough, things went well. In fact, I enjoyed my year there more than any of the eight schools I attended from Grades 1 to 12.

I joined the journalism club and wrote the high school news from Esquimalt, which appeared weekly in the *Vancouver Sun*. My readership was undoubtedly small, but I felt literary and important. I also joined the radio club. The local radio station, CJVI, allowed high school students to take over the station for three hours every Saturday morning. Again, we probably didn't have a devoted following of listeners, but it was fun, a little scary and very good experience. Two announcers were chosen from each school, along with two scriptwriters and two technicians. I was chosen as the female announcer from Esquimalt, and Bill Stevenson (in Grade 11) was the male announcer. My most memorable experience was doing an hour-long program on American musical-composer Jerome Kern the day after he died. Needless to say, since then, he has been one of my favourite songwriters. I don't know how many others went on to have media careers, but Bill Stevenson became a well-known sportscaster in Canada for many years.

Although I didn't pursue a communications career, both the experience with the newspaper and the radio prepared me for the work I did in later life with radio and television.

Esquimalt High was a small school at that time, with about 300 students. I might not have had the same opportunities at a larger one.

My aunt and uncle seldom went out in the evening, but one night, in early November, they decided to go to a movie. They put the children to bed and left me in charge. All was quiet and I was doing my homework on the kitchen table when there was a mighty crash from somewhere very close. It sounded as if it had come from the room where the baby was sleeping. I ran into the room, but she was sound asleep, and nothing seemed amiss. I ran into the little boy's room and he was asleep as well. I searched all over the house and could not find anything that could have caused such a terrifying noise.

Well, I had to do it. I had to go down into that horrible basement and find out what had happened. I was shaking, but I made myself go down and look around. Still nothing. Back upstairs, I returned to the baby's room, and then I noticed it: the huge mirror that had been part of the dresser set had broken away from the small pieces of plastic that contained it and crashed to the floor, missing the baby's head by inches. Now I really was shaking. What if it had landed on her? What were my aunt and uncle going to say? Would they think I had something to do with this? Was it my fault? I sat in the kitchen for two hours worrying about their reaction and my fate. When they came home and I showed them what had occurred, they were shocked and grateful that nothing had happened to the baby. And when I told my uncle how frightened I was to go down into the basement, he just laughed and said, "I don't blame you, I'm scared to go down there too!"

One night, in late February, with a nasty cold and insufficiently dressed for the cold Victoria wind, I stood in line for an hour waiting to go to a movie. The lineups were long as there were few theatres and the entire naval base came to town Friday and Saturday nights. There was no other entertainment — no discos, no nightclubs, no live music of any kind — so everyone ended up at the movies.

Two days later, I had pneumonia, and as the days went by it grew progressively worse until was decided that I should go to the hospital. This presented a dilemma for my uncle. He was a Scottish-born Presbyterian, and I had always argued with him about his vendetta against Catholics and Catholicism. He felt the religion was bad and, therefore, so were the people.

With the chutzpah and idealism of youth (no one knows more than a 14-year-old), I debated this position. Although my father was born Catholic but didn't practice, and neither did I (in fact, I didn't practice any religion at all), my uncle decided that I must be a Catholic, as no one else would put up such a defence on their behalf. He did not want to take me to St. Joseph's Hospital, as he would not come to visit me there — it was Catholic at the time, and he wouldn't set foot in a Catholic hospital. The only solution was for me to go to the Royal Jubilee Hospital, but register as a Catholic.

So there I was, very ill, lying in a 15-bed ward (all other patients being non-Catholics). My temperature went up and up, and my bed was constantly soaking wet. The nurses changed the sheets and pads two or three times a day, but as soon as they were changed, they were wet again. A Catholic priest — a thin, cadaverous-looking young man without a trace of happiness on his face — came to see me twice a day. He would say, with a grimace, "And how-w-w are you-u-u?" It was eerie and frightening. One day, when my temperature was over 105 degrees Fahrenheit (it was measured in Fahrenheit at the time) and rising, he asked me if I would like extreme unction. On the verge of delirium and not knowing what it was, I said no. He left, maybe intending to try again another day … if I was still here. Finally, my mother, who had come when she heard how sick I was, spoke to the nurses, and he did not come again.

But he was not the only one with a serious demeanour. The doctor was looking very worried, as I was not getting better. It was 1946, the war was over, but the new wonder drug, penicillin, had not yet been released for civilian use. Unfortunately, that drug appeared to be my only hope, so the doctor made a trip to the naval base and pleaded with the military doctors until he was able to obtain a sufficient supply.

The injections were administered every three hours. The penicillin was thick and viscous and, because of this, required a very large gauge needle. Each injection was painful, partly because of the needle size and dose frequency, and partly because the layer of fat I had laid down the year before in Vernon had been absorbed by my bed through perspiration. I weighed 85 pounds. Finally, when my temperature reached 106 degrees, the penicillin began to do its job: the fever broke, and I slept for two days.

On the third day, I woke up and was allowed to go to the bathroom. I was weak and wobbly, but alive. In the bathroom, I met a woman who calmly said, "My husband died last night." I replied, "Oh, I'm so very sorry," to which she answered, "It's all right, you know; he's with God and happy, and sometime soon I'll be with him too. I'm Catholic, you know, and we believe that."

This conversation shocked me, and I grabbed the vanity to keep from collapsing, but back in bed I thought about it. If Catholics believe this so completely, what a wonderful, helpful religion it is. I told myself I must remember to discuss this with my uncle.

Two days later, I was discharged from hospital and my mother took me shopping. I felt reasonably well that day, but the next was most unpleasant. After a month in a hospital bed, my muscles had become lazy and soft, and they completely seized up. I could not straighten my legs or walk. I could only crawl a few feet. I soon got better but it was a lesson on what not to do when you have been in bed for a month.

After gaining about 10 pounds, I went back to school having lost seven weeks, with just May and part of June left in the school year. The principal called me into his office and very kindly said, "You will write your final exams, but if you do not pass them all, I will not hold you back." I did pass them all but have always thought how kind and thoughtful he was to assure me that I would not fail.

I still love Victoria, but every March, I get a chest infection or pneumonia. Antibiotics are easier to come by and easier to administer now, and my confinement is never as long. It is, however, the one month of the year that I would like to be elsewhere.

Magee

Grade 10, Vancouver, and school number seven: Magee High School. Again, I was actually starting at the beginning of the term. Uncle Bill had bought property on the water in Victoria and they were building a house, so it was not the ideal place for me to live or be underfoot.

My step-aunt Clara and her husband, Frank, lived in the Kerrisdale section of Vancouver, and I was excited about spending the next year with them and going to a prestigious Vancouver school. Huge chestnut trees lined the street in front of the house, providing shade yet allowing dappled sunshine through. The house, of 1930s vintage, was neat. It had a spacious living room containing some lovely antiques, a large dining room with a carved oak dining suite, two bedrooms, a bathroom, a kitchen and a small yard with a tiny garden. This was in sharp contrast to many of my former residences, which were usually large and draughty, with basic furniture and sprawling, untrimmed grounds. I wasn't sure how I was going to behave as perfectly as the house demanded. My aunt and uncle were older than my parents, but they were kind, cultured and caring. Uncle Frank had a gentle sense of humour, and Auntie Clara was lovely in every sense of the word.

It all looked and felt wonderful; however, I had not anticipated some of the obstacles that lay ahead.

The first shock came on the first day of school when I went to register. None of us was aware that because I was an out-of-town student, I would be required to pay a monthly fee of $25. This came as a huge blow, as my parents were paying for my room and board, and I knew they could not pay more. I went to my aunt in a state of despair and explained the problem. Her answer was, "Don't worry, dear, I'm sure we'll think of something." I was upset that she seemed to take it so lightly. I was doomed never to finish high school, doomed as only a 15-year-old could be. I was beaten and consumed with my bad luck and the injustice of it all. I suffered all afternoon and into the evening until my aunt came back to me and suggested, "Why don't you babysit? You could put an ad in the *Kerrisdale News*. There are people around here with children who would probably like to have an evening out."

My ad read: "Babysitter available after school and evenings, vicinity 43rd and Maple. 25 cents an hour to midnight, 35 cents an hour after midnight." The calls rolled in, and I was in business. I babysat six nights a week, usually making $1 to $1.35 a night, which was just enough to pay the wretched school board their $25, with a dollar or so extra to go roller-skating with my friends on Friday night.

The second blow came when I started classes and the jumble of the previous years of moving, being in country schools and losing time to illness caught up with me. This school, in an upper-class neighbour-hood, was, academically, the best public high school in Vancouver. I knew no French (they had all studied it since Grade 7), and math, never my best subject, was beyond me. Social studies was okay, as long as they kept to geography, as I had studied four courses of geog-raphy, but had missed all the history in the moves. Mercifully, English was the one subject in which I could hold my own.

On the first day of French class, the teacher said, "*Mademoiselle Dobson, ouvre la porte, s'il vous plaît.*" I sat at my desk. He said it louder, but still I sat; the third time, he yelled, and someone in the class said, "Open the door, stupid." Outside the door, I only guessed that he was yelling at me to come back in. I slithered into my seat, shamed and humiliated.

After a day or two of this, I went to him and said, "I'm sorry, Mr. Sutherland, I have never taken French before."

"What are you doing in my class then?" he asked angrily.

"Well, if I don't pass Grade 10 French, I won't have time to make up enough in Grades 11 and 12 to be accepted at university."

Known to be a tough teacher, he looked at me warily, and finally said, "All right, I'll give you exercises to do every day. Bring them to me at eight thirty in the morning and I'll correct them and give you more."

Much to his surprise, I think, I was there every morning at 8:30, my homework done. After a month, he cut me down to three days a week, and by Christmas, I was well ahead of the rest of the class. He turned out to be a wonderful person as well as a wonderful teacher, but there were some repercussions from all this. Whenever someone was not doing his or her work to his satisfaction, he would thunder at them, "Look at Mademoiselle Dobson. She came here not knowing a word of French and now she is ahead of you all." It probably did not endear me to the rest of the class, but I didn't care. I was not there to be the most popular girl in the school (not much chance of that anyway) and I had French under control.

One of the many regrets I have is that I never told Mr. Sutherland how much I admired him for his teaching ability, for his trust in me to succeed and for his dedication. He was indeed one of the truly committed teachers, so much so that he died young, of a heart attack. I attribute his untimely demise, in part, to his sincere efforts on behalf of his students and his frustration at their often indifference to school and to the course.

Having French somewhat under control, I attacked the other subjects. Math was the biggest problem; the teacher had written the math text for the province and was not very interested in helping the slow students, no matter what the reason.

This is where the babysitting helped. While not a financial bonanza, it paid my fees and gave me a great deal of time to study. Usually, I could get the children to bed by eight o'clock, clean up the dishes, if there were any, and study for the next three hours. And did I study: not only did I complete my homework, I also caught up on much of the education I had missed prior to coming to Magee.

A third and minor problem was the clique system that had evolved in the school. Most of the students in the area had lived there all their lives. They had gone to elementary school together, on to junior high, and were now in senior high together. They had no need to include a newcomer into their midst. The elite of the lot wore cashmere sweaters and went out with the boys on the basketball team (also considered the elite). Then there was the sub-elite group who wanted to be in the elite group but were kept mostly on the fringe. To be honest, with my schedule, there was not a lot of time for socialization, but those of us who were new to Magee formed a loose alliance, walked to school together and roller-skated on Friday nights. We weren't really misfits, but we weren't the elite either, or even sub-elite. Not one of us owned a cashmere sweater or went out with a basketball player … or anyone else for that matter.

By the end of the year, a few things changed. I had gained weight, as my lovely aunt had an "iron fist in a velvet glove" when it came to my poor eating habits. If I said, "No, thank you, Auntie Clara," to squash, cottage cheese or any of the long list of foods I did not like, she said, "Yes, dear, just try a little." I was not going to argue with Auntie Clara, nor leave anything on my plate. She did a great deal of wonderful baking, which I grew to like, so the combination of hormones and food blew me up 30 pounds — not a pretty sight on a five-foot-two frame, and certainly of no interest to the basketball team.

All the studying did pay off, and I managed to pass my exams reasonably well, including math, although I just scraped through with a C. The other good news was that I was coming back to the same school next year, to familiar ground, a few friends and my wonderful aunt and uncle.

Last Years of High School

It was comforting to return to the same school for the second year, but less exciting than I was used to. In fact, it was relatively uneventful. I continued babysitting and studying, but it was by now a routine and much less stressful.

The year progressed fairly quickly and graduation for the Grade 12 students began to loom on the horizon. I was only in Grade 11, so while I was not involved in the frantic activities, I still found it quite absorbing. The rule of the school was that no one should be left without a date for the dance on this important occasion. To ensure that everyone was properly engaged, a draw was set up with boys' names in one box and girls' in the other.

The auditorium was tense with angst and excitement as the names were pulled from each box, paired and called out. This person would be your date for the night, until midnight. The usual histrionics of the involved students ensued: snickering, groaning, writhing and sighing. This matchmaking practice was done at most schools at the time, but Magee students included a little addendum to the procedure. It was a well-to-do area and students had access to more disposable income than in other areas of the city. The boys set up their own insurance policy: among themselves, they chose the two girls they considered the least attractive in the Grade 12 class, known as Dog #1 and Dog #2. They all contributed to a fund and when the draw was made, the boy who got Dog #1 received most of the insurance money. The rest went to the escort of Dog #2. And all abided by the rule of going to the dance and staying with their date until midnight.

While the dogs' identities were supposed to remain a secret, pretty much the whole school found out who they were well before graduation.

The top male catch (he thought) was a handsome, wealthy, arrogant young man. He was the one to draw the winning ticket (or losing, depending on how you look at it). He took the girl to the dance and, as I understand, behaved in his usual superior and unpleasant manner. At the dot of midnight, he rushed her home at top speed so that he could carry on with the girls of his class — the inner circle elite. There was a small retribution in the speeding ticket he acquired rushing to get her home and out of his life. It took up all the insurance money and more. Those of us on the lower rungs of society were very pleased to hear the news.

• • •

I finished Grade 11 with good marks, except for a C+ in math, and the following year I would be off to school number eight.

Dad and his partner at the mink ranch had parted ways, and we were "on the road again," so to speak. It was decided that my mother and I would live together in Vancouver while my father and uncle would go off to build railroad bridges around the province. They had scraped together enough money to buy out an older man who had a small bridge-building business with contracts to build these bridges. They accomplished this by my dad pooling the $200 from the sale of his old truck and $800 from the sale of 80 acres of prime timber in Bella Coola that my mother had inherited. These days, it would be worth millions. I don't know what my uncle contributed, but it was enough to pay for a down payment on the business. They paid the rest as they earned money.

As it was three years after the war ended and housing was in short supply, the only place we could find was a dark, dreary, 200-square-foot basement apartment in a house. It really wasn't an apartment, but rather an L-shaped room with the long part of the L becoming a kitchen and bathroom, and the other part, the bedroom. A dresser with a large round mirror, similar to the one that had fallen and almost hit my three-month-old cousin two years before, was my desk. There were no windows. It was just one step up from a cave. We entered this dismal abode through the basement door, walking past a huge octopus of a furnace and brushing by my dresser desk.

The outside and upstairs of the house were nice enough to look at. It was owned by an Orthodox Jewish family and the only time I ever saw the upstairs was when I was called upon, on Friday nights, to go up and turn the lights on or off, as they were not supposed to do any work on the Sabbath, and turning on a light was considered work. I liked Friday nights because it was quiet. Other nights, we were treated to a loud, full-scale war between the daughter, who was about 25 years old, and the son, who was about 22 — far too old to be carrying on in this manner. One night, I almost called the police as she was holding a knife to him; we could hear every word downstairs. She was obviously an unstable person, and when she wasn't fighting with her brother, she was on the phone fighting with her boyfriend who, she said, was a doctor. One doctor off my list, I thought — if he wasn't smart enough to get rid of her, he wasn't smart enough to be a doctor I would go to.

It was difficult to concentrate on my heavily science and math-oriented homework with the nightly noise all through my twelfth year. I was always grateful to hear the door slam, knowing that at least one of them had left the house in a rage.

The itinerant life of roaming the province had its advantages and its very definite disadvantages. It had made me independent and self-sufficient, but it had also left many gaps in my schooling. We never moved at the end of the school term, so sometimes I studied geometry twice but no algebra, or geography but no history.

I was the only girl in the physics class at my new school, King Edward High School, and I was having some difficulty with the subject but could not understand why. The concepts were clear to me, but my equations were not working out.

I did not recognize Billy (my "husband" from our childhood wedding, now called "Bill") until I heard his name. He was in my class and having no trouble at all with the subject. As I was new to the school and he was the only person I even vaguely knew in the class, I asked him if he could help me with my problem. He said he would.

Later that evening, he came over to the apartment, working his way past the furnace and the laundry tubs to reach my area. He took a look at my equations and said, "That's right, that's right and that's right, as far as the equations are concerned, but you'd better learn to add, subtract, multiply and divide." With that, he said, "Goodnight," and left. From then on, physics was no longer the mystery that it had been.

King Edward was the largest school in the city and drew students from all social and ethnic backgrounds, many of whom were not planning to go to university, which made the environment very different from that of Magee. I soon found two very nice girls to walk to school with, and we, in turn, found three very nice Grade 13 boys to walk home from school with. One of them, Gordie, became my boyfriend.

We were walking home one day, along 12th Avenue, when Gordie was called aside by two young Asian men. I walked ahead for half a block, and when he caught up to me, I asked, "What did they want?"

"Nothing," he replied.

"Well, obviously they wanted something," I pressed. "What was it?"

"They wanted drugs."

"What did you tell them?" I asked.

"I told them that I didn't know, but to go down to the docks on the east side and they might find what they were looking for."

I wasn't sure what he was talking about. Drugs? I had never heard of them but was sufficiently impressed with his worldliness. Little did I realize that, in time, this behaviour would become commonplace in downtown Vancouver. We were so naïve and sheltered.

Not long after this incident, Gordie, who sometimes talked about his old girlfriend, telling me what a hard time she had given him and how volatile and unstable she was, presented me with a beautiful Parker fountain pen. I was overwhelmed as I knew he could not afford such an expensive gift, until I realized that this was a goodbye offering. He was going back to his volatile, unstable girlfriend, and I was being dumped!

It was the first and only time I was the dumpee — and it hurt! I moped, I whined, I sobbed and I suffered, and then I finally realized that I wasn't suffering because of the loss of Gordie but because my pride had been badly bruised. It still hurt, but I soon recovered when a friend introduced me to her brother, who was in his first year at the University of British Columbia.

When graduation came, I was drawn with the boy "dog" of the school — no insurance here — but I wasn't worried because my handsome new boyfriend was going to pick me up after the dance at 12 o'clock sharp.

UBC

At the end of the term, my mother and I were able to find a better place to live, in a large, older home converted into suites. We had a bedroom, bathroom, living room and spacious kitchen. We even had windows — big ones — and my desk, a real desk, was in the living room, as was my hide-a-bed.

My father, still with his familiar refrain, "Girls are too dumb to go to university," finally realized that arguing with me was in vain. "What do you think you are going to take?" he asked me. Quickly, I replied, "English, philosophy, history."

I didn't get any further before he said, "Like hell. If I have to feed you for four more years, you'd better have a job when you get out. You won't get a job with a philosophy degree."

I hadn't planned on this reaction, but I did like to eat, so I signed up to take an aptitude test at the University of British Columbia. The results came back: Forestry, Engineering. So, off to the forestry department I went, all smiles and brimming with enthusiasm, only to be met with a very angry man who said, "We don't take females in this department. We don't even have female bathrooms in the building!" I suggested going to another building, but he would not accept that — or me.

What other options were there? I knew my personality was not suited to being a nurse or a social worker, and teaching did not appeal to me. There was, however, a new faculty on campus in the home economics department offering a bachelor of science in nutrition. And that is how I backed into my profession.

The "Home Ec" courses should never have been taught at university. But the nutrition courses were good, and after the first year, we were able to concentrate on nutrition, organic chemistry, biology, bacteriology and biochemistry.

It was a good four years. I became vice-president of the Varsity Outdoor Club (as the president's position was reserved for males only).

In a cooperative effort, we built a ski cabin on Mount Seymour, which slept over 100 people and was designed by one of our own student architects. The boys' dorm was on one side and the girls' dorm on the other, and no one ever crossed the line. No drinking was allowed, and no one broke that rule either.

A particularly amusing incident occurred when I was in first year. An organization called Phrateres, which most first-year students joined only to drop out of in second year, was putting on a pyjama party. It was to be held at Brock Hall, a large and elegant building on campus. It was one of the few such buildings, as after the Second World War, most buildings were hastily constructed or Quonset huts brought in to accommodate the influx of discharged military people who were receiving an education courtesy of the Canadian government. At this time, most of the military had graduated, but the ugly buildings were still in use and new ones were still on the drawing board. It was a wonderful time to attend UBC. There were only 5,000 students, products of the Depression and Post-Depression, when people had kept their families small due to the severe lack of money.

But back to the pyjama party. Anne, a new driver, and the sister of Bill, my new boyfriend, picked seven of us up in her mother's large 1949 Ford, and we all piled in, wearing pyjamas and curlers and some carrying teddy bears. We noticed that, as we drove into Brock Hall, we scraped the back bumper due to a combination of the the load of girls we had in the back seat and a large dip in the pavement. No harm was done, and we carried on to the party.

The party was over at about 11:30, so we decided to go home via Spanish Banks, a lovely beach, but also, at night, a well-known "necking place." We thought we would drive along the beach and get our kicks from spying into all the various cars with the aid of our high-beam lights. We were having a hilarious and silly time as only 17-year-olds could appreciate, when Anne slammed on the brakes hard. There we were, looking into the car of Anne's boyfriend, Anton, and he and his lady friend were not discussing physics. Anne quickly put the car into reverse, hit a log very hard and tore off the gas tank! Now we were in trouble. We had to sheepishly knock on Anton's door and ask if he could help us. He was not pleased to see us. Reluctantly, and looking quite disheveled, he struggled over to our car, assessed the damage and decided he could do nothing. He returned to his car and resumed his activities.

So there we all were, on Spanish Banks at midnight, in our pyjamas, with no phone and no way to get home. Somehow, another girl and I were elected to hitchhike to the 4th Avenue village gas station to get some help. And we did, to the puzzlement and amusement of the people who finally picked us up.

There was only one person on duty that night, a young man, also a university student, who was not too sympathetic to the plight of eight silly females. We used all the feminine wiles we had and finally convinced him that it was almost a matter of life and death. Our friend was going to be killed by her parents!

He must have grown up on a farm, as he grabbed a coil of wire and some pliers and we all headed to the beach. In very short order, he had the tank wired on and we were set to go with the admonition to drive slowly and carefully as the tank would not hold for long.

We were all sworn to a secret pact as to how it had all happened. The story: the extra weight and low-slung design of the car had caused the big dip in front of Brock Hall to tear off the tank. Shame on the university to have such a steep gully that could damage cars!

A few days later, when the car had been repaired, Bill, who usually did most of the driving, said, "Come with me. I'm going to drive over that dip and see how the car drags and take it up with the university." I tried to dissuade him, but it became apparent to him that there was absolutely no way that the incident could have occurred as we had described it. Nevertheless, I clung to the story in all sincerity. I think he must have approached Anne with his suspicions, but he never told their parents, nor did he go to the university for repayment of the mechanic's bill. To this day, I do not know whether Anne blames me for telling him, which I did not, or whether she accepts the fact that he figured it out on his own. As for Anton, it was the end of the relationship, for which we were all happy. We all knew that he was a low-lifer who was not suitable for Anne, and the last time I ever saw him, many years later, was when he was working on a fishing boat up in Ocean Falls.

University life continued, much as it does for everyone, with its successes and failures along the way. I joined an upscale sorority and some of the Magee girls were now my "sisters." So there I was, now one of the elite, going to parties in elegant homes in Shaughnessy or Point Grey and never inviting anyone to my home, a downscale apartment in a marginal area of Vancouver.

My UBC graduation photo — 1953

A Blooming Good Summer

It was April 1953, in Vancouver, and I was awaiting entry into my painfully earned dietetic internship at the Montreal General Hospital in the coming September. I had spent two exciting and exhausting summers working as a waitress at the Banff Springs Hotel, the first year in the elegant Alhambra dining room and the second year in the equally elegant and more fun golf course clubhouse. Graham, my future husband, and whom I had met at the Banff Springs two years previously, was studying dentistry at McGill University in Montreal. The medical and dental students had an abbreviated summer, in that they finished late and returned to classes early, so he would not be returning to Banff for the summer. Because of this, I decided to remain in Vancouver and spend my last summer at home with my mother.

My name went up on the university employment board and, within a day, I got a job working at the *Vancouver Sun*, the same tall red roofed building my father had worked in many years before. Unfortunately, the job (a mindless one typing addresses or something) did not suit my skills or my personality, and I realized, very quickly, that I had better pursue another endeavour. Back went my name on the student board, and very shortly thereafter, an interesting call came in.

"Hello, is this Fay Dobson?" a cultured male voice said.

I replied it was.

"Well, I have a flower farm in Hatzic, and I'm looking for a new hired hand. Would you be interested?"

His name was Bill Jack, and he explained that the job would involve driving a truck, delivering flowers to the train station or airport, maybe picking up some gladioluses, helping at flower shows and other odd jobs. "By the way," he added, "can you drive a truck?"

"Of course," I answered, telling a large white lie, as I had just received my driver's licence three weeks earlier.

"And can you double clutch?" he continued.

"Certainly," I said, enlarging enormously on my repertoire of white lies.

"Well," he said, "may I come over in about an hour to see you, bring the truck and see how you do?"

I agreed. Hanging up the phone, I went straight to my father, who, by some twist of fate, was in town that day to buy a new truck. Normally he was off building bridges in Northern Alberta or somewhere else in B.C.

"Dad," I asked, "can you double clutch?"

"Yes."

"Well, can you teach me?"

"When?" he asked.

"Right now. I have half an hour to learn before this man comes to test me."

Dad and I jolted around a few blocks in his brand new truck. I learned fairly quickly and got home minutes before Bill arrived.

He was a pleasant man, about six feet tall and 40-ish. He was well spoken and polite, but the truck was almost a wreck. It was a large old two-tonne green panel with back doors that closed occasionally, if you applied enough brute force, and a clutch that always stuck.

It was an interesting ride. I learned that you had to flick your toe under the clutch to get it to move, which resulted in a lurch. At this point, the back doors would fly open, so it was necessary to jam on the brakes so the back doors would slam shut, and you were on your way ... until the next stop. He either liked me, felt I needed the work or was just having some fun because as we came to a stop in front of the apartment, he offered me the job.

As it turned out, Bill had several university degrees, had been the reeve of Mission, the head of the Liberal Party and head of the local library board, all while running the farm. His father had been a medical missionary in Taiwan and had returned to the Fraser Valley to begin growing and hybridizing gladioluses, peonies and iris. At this point, his parents were elderly, and Bill was running the farm. He was an avant-garde thinker, as I was to learn, and had reasoned that girls needed jobs, were as capable as boys in accomplishing work and were often more organized. He was an early, strong women's advocate. He liked women, he liked me and he adored his only daughter. He also took great delight in proving to the "guys" on the farm that a girl was as capable as they were. One fell off the roof when I sauntered out in my new designer jeans to be introduced as the new hired hand.

My moment in the spotlight was only that — a moment — as Bill pointed to some very large boxes and said, "These need to be loaded onto the truck now for delivery tomorrow morning on the first train."

The boxes were two metres long, a metre wide by a metre tall and full of peonies. They were heavy. I leaned down to pick one up and could only raise one end. I said, "I don't think I can lift these onto the truck." Bill replied, "Oh, in a day or two, you'll be throwing them in and not even thinking about it." With that, he walked off leaving me to figure out what I was going to do.

In my two years waitressing at the Banff Springs, I had learned to use my body to carry the heavy trays of dishes, silver and food. You learned to run with the tray above your head, shifting the weight in such a way that you did not really carry the whole load. Being the smallest in the dining room, with the station farthest away, I had become quite good at this manoeuvre. Could this principle be applied here? I got hold of the box and swung my body back and then forward. The first box wobbled onto the bed of the truck. The second went a little farther, and by the fifth box, they were hitting the back of the cab with some authority. The guys watched in silence. My next challenge would be wrestling the old truck to the train the next morning.

I went back to the house where I would be living with Bill's family for the next few months and Bill asked, "How did you make out?"

"Fine," I replied. "All loaded up and ready to go." I saw a vestige of a smile and a slight crinkle around his eyes.

"Good." he said.

I had been given the option of living in a small cottage on the property or with the family, which consisted of Bill, his wife, Dolly, and four children, in the big, beautiful but dilapidated Tudor house. Although I was never timid, the thought of being alone far out on the edge of a very large field did not appeal to me. Besides, I did not think I wanted an evening visit from any of the other hired hands.

It proved to be an interesting summer. Dolly needed to learn to drive, so I taught her using my vast driving experience. The children, a nine-year-old boy genius, a seven-year-old girl and twin boys of five (who only spoke twin talk) did not know how to swim, so I taught them.

Bill was building a library in one of the many rooms in the house, and he asked me if I knew how to stain and varnish. This time I said no.

"Well, I guess you're going to learn," he stated.

So I stained and varnished all the shelves and woodwork in the library, built to accommodate his extensive classical book collection.

In the evenings, we often listened to classical music, which I had never really heard before. I have always said my degree gave me a profession, but not an education. I learned about symphony and opera, not all of which my untrained ear could assimilate, but I listened and learned, and Bill loved teaching this unsophisticated young woman.

One day, he said, "I need you to go to Vancouver to pick up some roofing material." Again, I asked, "How will I lift that heavy stuff onto the truck by myself?"

"You won't have to. Just get out and stand on the platform and all the young guys will load the truck for you in no time." And that is exactly what happened!

"Now," he said, "when you go through Port Moody, do not speed." (In that truck, he must have been dreaming.) "The police want to make money and will pick you up at the slightest provocation."

I promised not to go over the speed limit, and as I got into the truck, the twins were standing in front with big smiles on their faces. I shooed them away, backed out and headed for Vancouver. I found the industrial park, got the truck loaded by all those nice young men and headed back to Hatzic. The load was heavy and steering was difficult, but I held the road, creeping along at 25 miles an hour. Going through Port Moody, I heard the eerie sound of a siren. It can't be for me, I thought, I'm only going 25 miles an hour. But it was for me, I realized, as the police car pulled in front of me, spewing gravel in my path.

"Show me your driver's licence," said this little toad of a man. Without a doubt, he was the ugliest policeman I had ever seen. I produced my driver's licence, which I had picked up from home only an hour before. I had lost it two weeks earlier and some kind person had mailed it to my home just that day.

"Where's your chauffeur's licence?" he demanded. I wasn't driving VIPs; I had a load of tarpaper and roofing material in the truck. "You should have a chauffeur's licence, and besides, you are overloaded. You should be carrying two tonnes, not three." How did he know that?

"Why did you pull me over in the first place?" I asked him. "I wasn't speeding or doing anything else wrong."

"Your front licence plate was bent in two," he said "and that got my attention." Then I remembered those two little twins in front of the truck before I left the farm — that's what they had been up to. Also, it was unusual for a young woman, in those days, to be a truck driver. In fact, I think, he was told to go out and make some money for the municipality. They were simpler times then, and this was one way to increase the coffers, as not much else happened in those small and sleepy communities. He gave me a $25 ticket — a lot of money back then — and I had to face Bill with the ticket.

It was the only time Bill showed any impatience with me. He seemed to feel that I should have been able to talk my way out of the fine. I shook my head and remarked, "If you could have seen how ugly and mean this man was, you would understand."

It was, however, a portent of things to come. Never in my life have I ever been able to talk my way out of a ticket of any kind, whether I was guilty or not.

The last major, and without a doubt, the most enjoyable job I had was to set up the flower display at the Pacific National Exhibition at the end of August. The truck was filled with flowers and vases and all the equipment necessary to make a spectacular showing. Even the old truck looked semi elegant. The exhibit took up one end of a large building and took a full day to set up, but it did look spectacular. Without prejudice, I think it was the best floral exhibit at the Exhibition, and I took many orders for the many corms, bulbs and rhizomes that we sold.

And then the summer was over, and I was off to Montreal. It had been no easier than working at Banff, but the wonderful and challenging experiences stay with me to this day. Bill became a lifelong friend, extending to his third wife (25 years his junior). As I said, he did like women. He gave me many of the plants that still grow in my garden. He was generous with his time and his knowledge, and he showed me another dimension to life.

Montreal Experience

The winter of 1953–54 was like any other in Montreal: cold, slushy, sometimes snowy and always dismal. At that time, there was no subway system and the bus and streetcar routes were inadequate. When transportation did arrive, it was usually so overcrowded that the side doors were open and people were clinging to other passengers and hanging out over the traffic lanes. Long line-ups appeared at the stops and eventually snaked down the street. When there was no more room, buses simply didn't stop, leaving people waiting on the street for an hour or more.

Usually, the temperature was -15 degrees Celsius. While this was normal in Montreal at that time, something else was going on that was not. Women were terrified. They would not allow a man to stand behind them in line, or when they were boarding a bus or streetcar, or walking up stairs. It was the winter of "The Slasher." This person would get behind a woman, scalpel in hand, and slash her legs. In those days, women wore only skirts or dresses — no pants. Because the cold made her legs somewhat numb, she would not feel it until the hot blood began trickling down the back of her legs. By the time she realized what had happened, the culprit had disappeared. Each day, the papers reported more women who had been slashed, and each day, women became more nervous and wary.

I arrived in Montreal in September 1953 and began my dietetic internship at the Western Division of the Montreal General Hospital. Located on upper St. Catherine Street, separate from the main hospital, it was the new private section of the hospital and the patients were treated more like hotel guests than patients. They had their own liquor supply, boasting Courvoisier, single malt scotch and fine wines. Their meals were elegantly prepared and presented. The nurses were always ready when the call button summoned them. Whatever private patients wanted, they got.

My second month was something of a shock when, for the remainder of my internship, I moved down to the main section of the hospital at lower Dorchester Street and St. Lawrence ("The Main") — author Mordecai Richler's old haunts. One had to negotiate down The Main through drug addicts, prostitutes and street fights to reach the hospital. It was intimidating at first, but we soon realized we were safer here than in most other places in Montreal. "*Garde-malade*" was sounded and everything stopped. The fights abruptly ended as we walked the gauntlet between the two or more antagonists. As soon as we passed, the fight resumed with equal vigor. Everyone on the The Main knew that if anyone from the hospital was attacked or harassed, the hospital would refuse treatment to the perpetrator. These were the saddest, poorest people of society, but their syphilis, diabetes and overdoses were treated at the hospital without question and without charge. For the medical and dietetic interns, the young nursing students and the people in allied fields, it provided a valuable learning experience, medically and socially.

Some of the dietetic interns lived in quarters provided by the hospital. Four of us were assigned rooms in the student nurses' residence connected to the hospital by a tunnel under Dorchester Street. The staff dietitians worked 9 a.m. to 5 p.m., but the interns worked 7 a.m. to 7 p.m., for which they received room and board and $10 a month. Each month, we were sent to a different section of the hospital to learn the procedures and workings of the area.

One of my early rotations was on two women's medical wards. Three times a day, the food carriers came down from the main kitchen to the small kitchens on each ward, and the maids put the food on the plates, water, juice and condiments on the trays, and delivered them to patients. After the meal, they collected the trays, washed the dishes in the sink (there were no dishwashers then) and cleaned up to be ready for the next meal.

It did not take long to notice that, on most days, either one or both maids on the women's wards didn't turn up for work. The dietetic interns then had to cover the staff shortage, and we certainly learned the procedures and workings of the wards firsthand. It did not take long to understand their constant absenteeism. The maids were poorly paid and usually living in near poverty. The one way they could supplement their income was by working on the men's wards, where they were busy soliciting business — a far more lucrative endeavour.

The head dietitian, a spinster, finally realized that the maids were missing a great deal of work and called me into her office one day. She asked me if I had any idea why we were having so many staff problems on these particular wards. So I told her. She sat in shocked silence, and I realized that I should not have told her the cold, hard truth. I left the office wishing I could retract my words and that I had just smiled and pleaded ignorance.

February found me on the 7th floor in the main kitchen, supervising food preparation, scheduling staff and ordering the food required for the week. It was a large, old kitchen, with dark oiled floors. I suspect some of the equipment had been there since the hospital opened in 1821, over 130 years before. It was, at the time, the oldest hospital in Canada. The equipment was battered and bent but had to be used for another year and half, when the new hospital would open in a better part of town.

In my supervisory capacity, I was going through the kitchen one afternoon and ventured into the pot washer's domain. It was in a dark corner of the kitchen (there weren't many bright areas). He was sloshing the battered pots around in some of the dirtiest water I had ever seen. It was a grey-brown colour, with chunks of old food floating about. The pots themselves were greasy and dirty and still contained the remains of that night's supper, or maybe even supper from several nights prior.

I said, "George, you must redo all those pots with soap and clean water and rinse them properly. This is a hospital, and we cannot have patients who are already unwell getting sick from the food." George was a sullen, stocky, unkempt man of about 45, with a mouth that drooped in both corners. He wore a permanent scowl. He looked at me with hate in his eyes and did not say a word.

By 6 p.m., everyone had left the kitchen but George and me. He was clattering around in the pot area, and I was in my small office in the far corner of the kitchen, confirming the next day's orders. By chance, I glanced up to see George coming towards me with a knife in each hand, and I knew this was serious. But I also knew that Graham, my future husband, was still working in the dental clinic in the basement of the hospital. This was where all the McGill dental students did their practical work. I quickly picked up the phone, hoping he would answer. Three rings and he thankfully picked up the phone. I quietly said, "Graham, I'm in the kitchen and I'm in trouble," and hung up. By this time, George had reached the door of the office and began to threaten me. Obviously, the incident in the afternoon had been brewing in his head and he decided to take action. I was trapped. There was no escape route, and I certainly could not overpower him. I needed to buy time. My only recourse was to sit quietly and talk to him as calmly as I could. Soon, George saw the look of recognition and relief come across my face and turned to see a six-foot-tall young man coming towards us very fast. He backed away from the door and sidled off. Graham had made it out of the clinic, up seven flights of stairs and into the kitchen in three minutes.

The next day, I reported the incident and George was picked up and taken to the police station for questioning. I had not realized he had been picked up the month prior and questioned on suspicion of being the Slasher, and released. This time, he was not released. I'm not sure whether or not he was the Slasher. As far as I can remember, the name was never published, nor was the Slasher was ever positively identified. But I do know that from then on, the slashings ceased and the women of Montreal were able to relax.

When I finished my internship later that year, Graham and I were married in the McGill Inter-denominational Chapel. The location was chosen because I had been refused by some other churches since I had not been baptized and I refused to declare any specific religion (and I still don't). It was a small but meaningful occasion, and the chapel was lovely.

Our wedding — 1954

3

New Chapters

A NEW FAMILY LIFE

Vancouver

The old Montreal General Hospital was closing down, and Graham had passed all his exams and boards and had received acceptances from two prestigious American universities for further studies in oral surgery. I was to work for the three years to support us as universities at that time only paid for tuition but no living expenses. I jokingly said, "I'll support you for three years, if you'll support me for the rest of my life."

Then we got the news back from the lab. I was pregnant. That news changed the course of our lives, as we did not think we could rely on our parents to pay for three years of room and board. Graham, with a very heavy heart, had to refuse his much-desired acceptances.

So we were off to Vancouver for a year. He had secured a position with the Vancouver School Board to work on a pilot project to assess the dental health of elementary school children and, at the same time, do the necessary dental work. This would give us time to decide where in the province we wanted to settle.

In September, our first son, Ken, was born under somewhat stressful circumstances. I was three weeks late and finally took the castor oil and orange juice treatment (the inducement treatment at the time, which was almost as painful as the birth itself). He was a forceps baby, and other than a large hematoma on his head, which, we were assured, would resolve itself and cause no harm to his brain, he was healthy. I was put into a semi-private room with a diabetic lady who was about to give birth, and she was very worried. Often, children of diabetic mothers did not survive, and in the delivery room, the last thing she heard the doctor say was, "We'll try to save one of them." When she woke up, she thought that the baby had died. But it hadn't, and she was euphoric. Then, it did die, and she began to cry and scream non-stop for two days. I felt sorry for her, but I could not help. She was inconsolable. I was weak and badly shaken and had a breast infection due, I think, to the unsanitary conditions at the hospital, especially the washrooms. It was a difficult two weeks trying to look after a newborn when you can't even look after yourself, but we both survived, and life carried on.

We found a place with five acres on the ocean in Qualicum Beach on Vancouver Island. Graham had found a suitable place to set up his dental practice in Parksville, six miles away. And so began our rural life on our "estate."

Yellow Leaves

Our white house in Qualicum sat high on a bank, surrounded by an acre of green grass, and looked out to sea. It was flanked on either side by large fir trees and many old maples. The cleared property was connected to the highway by a quarter-mile gravel road that was in constant need of gravel for the potholes and a strong arm with a machete to keep the vigorous growth of spirea at bay.

It was a lovely, clear day in early September when we moved in, with a blue sky hovering over this idyllic and tranquil scene. There wasn't much to move — a small wooden table, four chairs, a crib, a bed, two trunks and a brand new washer and dryer. This was our total wealth, as well as a golden haired one-year-old boy.

Our house in Qualicum

The progression into autumn brought another colour into the picture. The maple leaves turned a brilliant yellow, to add to the white, green and blue, and the scene was even more beautiful. I carried on in a state of euphoria until mid-October when the yellow leaves began to fall, turn brown and cover the acre of green grass in a thick soggy layer. It was no longer beautiful and I pondered how I was going to get rid of all these heavy, ugly leaves.

CKWX was playing on the radio when I heard the voice of Cecil Solly, the omnipresent B.C. gardener, droning on about pansies and primroses and the Yellow Leaf Contest. I began to pay attention. "Yes," he was saying, "send us the largest yellow leaf from your yard and the CKWX crew will come and rake it for you. I sprinted outside and picked up the largest yellow leaf I could see close to the house, although it was by no means the largest on the property. I wrapped it around a large piece of cardboard, packaged it up, sent it off to the radio station and forgot about it. One week later, the telephone rang and it was "Ceaseless Solly" (as we used to call him), saying that I had won the yellow leaf contest and that the CKWX staff would arrive on the Saturday after next, rakes in hand, along with the Rhythm Pals for entertainment. I protested a little, warning him of the size of the yard, but he "tut-tutted" me and assured me it was no problem — the more yard the better. Maybe he was having his own private joke at the staff's expense, as he was not going to be participating.

When I told Graham, he gave me a somewhat exasperated look and said, "How come everyone else wins money and you win a bunch of guys who won't do any work and the Rhythm Pals?" These five men played the foot-stomping, shit-kicking music of the Wild West on a variety of conventional and unconventional instruments. This was not quite our kind of music.

From then on, every time I turned on the radio, I would be shocked to hear the DJ invite everyone on Vancouver Island to join them at the Pettapieces to watch them rake leaves and dance to the music of the Rhythm Pals! What to do now? This was worse than the leaves. What would the locals think about their new dentist? Worse yet, we learned that the contest was sponsored by a toothpaste company with the famous tagline: "You'll wonder where the yellow went when you brush your teeth with Pepsodent." And worst of all, what would the College of Dental Surgeons have to say about a dentist advertising a particular brand of toothpaste? Graham was disconsolate. He was sure that the College would strike him from the register. I phoned CKWX and pleaded with them not to come. "No, it will be all right," they said. "We will come and we won't mention that he is a dentist." Graham was not to be consoled. He had been in practice for only two months! I thought he was overreacting a little. He did not agree. At that time the rules were strict and very clear.

The day before the great event, I lifted Ken into the flimsy wire and canvas car seat and drove our old car over the mountain to Port Alberni, where I bought several dozen donuts and numerous pack-ages of coffee and plastic cups, none of which we could afford. The Rhythm Pals were costing us money. It would have been cheaper to hire someone to rake the leaves.

The day dawned and an unusual weather phenomenon occurred: thick fog, making visibility close to zero. Maybe this would deter them. In any case, I pulled out the enamel canning pot and what-ever else was at hand and began boiling water for coffee. In a short time, a parade of station wagons came inching down the narrow road with CKWX in large letters attached to the roofs. When they arrived at the house, they jumped out, wearing brand new red blazers that shone like neon through the fog and holding brand new gleaming bamboo rakes, except for the announcers, who were holding shiny black microphones.

"How far away is the water?" one asked.

"One step back and you're in it," I warned them.

"Do you get fog here all the time?" was the next question.

"It's the only time I've seen fog here," I said. And, in fact, in the 13 years we lived in Qualicum, it was the only time we ever saw fog.

Meanwhile, the Rhythm Pals, in red plaid shirts and jeans, were setting up shop in the corner of the living room. They had commandeered the four chairs and the two steamer trunks we owned for seating arrangements for everyone else.

People began trickling down the road and coming into the house as I offered coffee and donuts and ushered them into the living room. The Rhythm Pals fired up their instruments and the party was on. Graham, always gracious, was doing his best to be a good host, all the while living in terror that they were going to mention his profession. The party rolled on with much foot stomping, hand clapping and dancing. In the end, only about 50 people turned up, but I had a few anxious moments wondering whether the old wooden floors would stand up against 50 not-so-small foot-stomping adults assaulting it. It did, thanks, I guess, to the solidly built edge-grained fir floor.

Then we received our prizes. The grand prize was that the announcers assiduously avoided naming and broadcasting Graham's profession. In addition to that we received six boxes of laundry soap, six packages of Pepsodent toothpaste and still-new bamboo rakes. Hardly a leaf had been turned. Then they and the Rhythm Pals packed up. Everyone left and we breathed a sigh of relief. If anyone from the College of Dental Surgeons heard about it, they never commented, and Graham continued practicing for the next 40 years. And never again, to my knowledge, did CKWX ever run another Yellow Leaf Contest. But they could have; from then on, I only listened to CBC.

A Night of Terror

The word "*qualicum*" in the Pentlatch language (northern coast Salish) means "a place to dry chum salmon." There is also a strong wind that occasionally blows between the areas of Deep Bay and French Creek that is called a qualicum. Indian lore states that one of the ancestors had control of the wind and would call upon it to blow when she felt that circumstances were not to her liking. She has been gone now for over 1,000 years, but she still invokes her wrath from time to time.

We had been told about these strong winds. They did not occur often, and they did not last long, so when I took my Christmas cakes out of the oven on December 5, 1957, and the power went off, I was not concerned. A branch or a small tree had probably fallen across the power line, I thought, and it would not be long before the hydro company would have us up and running again. Without electricity, the motor in the pump house could not function and we would be without water. As was our usual drill, one of us ran to the bathroom to get as much water into the tub as the pressure would allow, and the other milked the pipes in the kitchen to carry us through the hour or so we were expecting the blackout to last.

I stepped out onto the back porch to retrieve my cakes and felt the velocity of the wind, which was picking up speed by the minute. But wait, this was not a qualicum! We had been told qualicums come from the north — this was coming from the east. Back inside, I lit the garbage burner (wood fired), which adjoined the electric stove, and Graham started the fireplace in the living room. This would provide enough heat to maintain us for a while and I could boil water for vegetables and cook some meat on top of the garbage burner. The Coleman lamp was activated and some candles were lit, and we were quite cozy in our little nest.

The wind continued to blow — hard. By nine o'clock, it was too strong to even step outside and we could hear the large fir trees beside the house creaking and groaning with the force of the wind. Then, with the cry of a trunk giving up, one of the large trees crashed to the ground with a thud. A thud that was unique and final. One has to have heard a large tree fall to truly understand the dead finality of it. We did not know how close it had fallen to the house and were grateful that it had missed us. But ... when and where would the next one fall?

I began to think of the people in London, during the Blitz. They would hear the scream of the bomb and only knew they were safe when it exploded, possibly on a neighbour's house. We felt like that, the three of us huddled around the fireplace, waiting, the wind relentless and unabating. Then, another scream followed by a thud, which made the house vibrate but did not hit it. It was too close. The wind increased and a third tree came down, this time with one large limb hitting and collapsing the front porch. It's an odd feeling, to be trapped in a situation such as that: in danger but with no place to run and no place safer than where you are.

By 2 a.m., the house was still standing and intact, except for the porch. We could detect a slight reduction in the force of the wind, and an hour later, it was just a stout breeze. We finally slept, the three of us on a mattress, in front of the fireplace, grateful that by some miracle, we had been spared.

When daylight came, we surveyed the damage as well as how much of the forest had landed in our space. Only about half of the porch had been taken out, a piece eight feet by ten feet. On the ground were six fir trees, each about three feet in diameter, lying parallel on the grass from five to 20 feet from the house. If the wind had been slightly more to the east, every one of those trees would have landed on the house and we would have all been killed.

Trees blocked the entire driveway, and there was no way out. We were too early in our residency to own a chainsaw to enable us to cut our way through. The phone was dead, cut off at the same time as the power, as both telephone and power lines were on the same poles.

That day, we were in survival mode, collecting wood (but not able to use the trees that had arrived on the grass the previous night), keeping the fires going in order to keep the uninsulated house above 12 degrees Celsius and eating food that did not require much water for preparation or cooking. That night passed peacefully, but the next day we were looking for some kind of help. Where were the hydro people? Had they forgotten that someone lived down this little road? In the afternoon, we made our decision. Graham, machete in hand

and Ken on his back, and I, with a backpack full of baby things and a few toiletries, began our trek to the highway. From there, we would have to walk two miles to get to a hotel. We weren't sure how we were going to pay for it, but we couldn't stay as we were, with no water and the house becoming ever colder as the temperature dropped.

Suddenly, we saw lights. It was a hydro truck with two men wielding chainsaws and working their way through. When they got to us, they said, "Don't worry, you're okay. We'll have your power on in a few minutes." We asked what had happened.

"We had a full-scale hurricane," they told us. "There were 126 large trees across the highway between Parksville and Qualicum." It was a distance of 13 kilometres. "They are cleared now, and power is on, but it has taken a while to get to all the smaller properties." When we heard that, we were amazed they had come so soon.

Back to the house we went and stood outside, waiting. Shortly after, *all* the lights came on. Not only the lights, but the radio was blaring and the stove burners were glowing red. Unbeknownst to us, Ken, though only 15 months old, had done his bit to help and had switched on everything he knew to get light and heat into the house. It was fortunate that we had not made our escape.

It was obvious that something had to be done about the still-standing trees that now posed a threat to our home, but they were on our neighbour's property. It was owned by Mr. Milner and Lady Milner. It was an estate that was the same depth as ours, with about a kilometre of waterfront and about one third of a kilometre from the highway. Lady Milner was an Irish countess, known to be a haughty, domineering and austere woman. Graham phoned, made an appointment to see Mr. Milner and headed out. The door of the Milner home was opened by one of the Irish maids dressed in a black uniform with a white bonnet and apron. Lady Milner was called. She was a handsome woman about six feet tall and solidly built. She told Graham to sit on a stool in the hallway until he was called. At this point, Graham's red hair was sending out sparks for being treated like a schoolboy, or one of Lady Milner's serfs. At length, he was called in to see Mr. Milner, a five-foot-two gnome of a man, who was perfectly charming. "Of course," he said, when told the story of the trees. "Take out any of the trees that endanger your house and send me the bill." They shook hands and Graham left. I don't think he saw "the Madam" on the way out.

We vacated the premises for the day, and the trees were felled by a competent woodsman. All but one large tree in which the eagles had built an aerie and which, according to the faller, could not reach the house if it did come down. For the ensuing 12 years that we lived there, we were awakened each morning to eagle cries. Still, I was never completely comfortable with that tree, and I never again lived in a house with a large tree near enough to do any harm if it did decide to topple.

ANIMALS – DOMESTIC ... AND NOT

Pheasants, et al.

In 1958, Qualicum and Parksville were two very small towns, six miles apart, nestled beside the water on the east coast of Vancouver Island. They were resource based, mostly with logging, fishing, a little farming, and a small but growing tourist industry. For a young dentist and his family, it was a struggle eking out a living, as work was seasonal and also because everyone perceived the dentist to be wealthy. Consequently, he was paid last, if at all. Often, payment was in the form of manure, fish or the odd chicken, making it difficult to pay for the many dental supplies that were required to keep the practice going.

One incident that illustrates this attitude occurred when I went to the local ladies' shop to buy some white stockings to go with the white uniform I wore when I assisted Graham in the office. A lady whose family had a large dental bill with us was in the store buying some quite expensive clothing. Her bill alone would have paid for a month's dental supplies.

She saw me, and said, "Oh, we haven't been able to pay our bill these past few months; we have had some rather large oil bills this winter, you know." I simply said to her, "So have we." When I reported this to my husband, it was not the patient he was angry with, but me.

In order to supplement our income and do something different, Graham decided to become a gentleman farmer and raise a few exotic pheasants. There was a man in Parksville who raised golden, Manchurian and ring-necked pheasants, and Graham thought that this would add a little class to our tiny estate — aside from the fact that he knew nothing about raising pheasants or any other kind of bird or animal. Each pheasant egg cost three to five dollars! This at a time when I was buying medium eggs from the store instead of large, because they were three cents a dozen cheaper. He bought a clutch of eggs. Now what? "Well," I suggested, "you need a hen, preferably a bantam, to sit on the eggs and look after the chicks when they hatch." I neglected to say "broody bantam"— one who is in the mood to sit on eggs for the next three weeks.

Graham went off to the office and announced to the children who were patients in his practice that he would pay 25 cents for a bantam hen. The following day saw us with six bantam hens at 25 cents each, and not one of them broody. After explaining that they had to be in the right frame of mind to want to sit on eggs for three weeks, he finally came home with a broody bantam hen. We settled her in a little nest in the corner of a shed and slipped the eggs under her. She fluffed her feathers and settled nicely into her new home.

A week passed with all going well until one morning, on going out to feed her, I found devastation. The hen was dead, the eggs eaten and the nest destroyed. Graham was furious and ready to shoot the dog who he was sure was the culprit. "No," I said. "This is not the work of a dog, but a mink. You can see how the neck is ripped open, the blood drained and the eggs sucked dry." Shaken but not defeated, Graham bought another clutch of eggs, this time only ring-necked, which were less expensive than the others. He also borrowed a vintage solid oak incubator from two aristocratic English brothers who had a farm at French Creek.

The incubator had been idle for many years but roared into action the minute it was plugged in. The pheasant eggs were neatly tucked in and safe from marauding wildlife. Incubators, however, are not as free from work as one may imagine. In the nest, the hen turns the eggs regularly. In the incubator, they must be turned by hand. The hen also supplies heat and moisture to the eggs; the incubator supplies heat, but moisture must be added. When the chicks hatch, the incubator does not look after the chicks, keep them warm, scratch for them or tuck them in at night.

In spite of this, Graham, with his new toy, offered to hatch eggs for other people. We received chicken eggs, guinea fowl eggs and goose eggs. We filled the incubator but, as he was at work all day, it fell to me to turn the eggs several times a day and keep the humidity at the appropriate level. At this point, I had a two-year-old and was eight and a half months pregnant.

The pheasants hatched first, and we borrowed a brooder from the same two English brothers. I phoned the pheasant man to find out what to feed these fluffy yellow chicks with brown stripes. The first three days, chopped hard boiled eggs; the second three days, chopped hard boiled eggs and dandelion greens; the third three days, the same plus chicken mash. After that, just chicken mash. Four days after the pheasants hatched, the chicken chicks arrived. They were put in with the pheasant chicks, which turned out to be a big mistake. The pheasant chicks picked the beaks off the chicken chicks, rendering them unable to eat. I tried keeping them in my oven but could not find a way to feed them and, eventually, most of them died. We managed to get the brooder sectioned off for new arrivals, which were delivered every few days, and meet their dietary needs, depending on their age.

Well past my due date, the geese hatched, looking more like small serpents than birds, with their wet coats and long snake-like necks. They received the usual offerings for the newly hatched: hard-boiled eggs, but they would not eat. At this point, I was tired, cranky and exasperated, and when Graham came home, I said somewhat unpleasantly, "You look after your damn geese. I can't get them to eat!" Off he went to the shed where he remained for quite some time. When he came back to the house, he wore a look of amusement and some satisfaction. "Did you get them to eat?" I asked.

"Yes."

"How?"

"Well," he said, "I looked at them for a long time and then I thought, geese usually eat under water, so I got a pan, put the food in it, covered it with water and they gobbled it up!"

I thought, for a city boy, this was quite smart.

At nine and a half months, I finally produced our second son, Ron. Long and thin — a little like the geese.

All the birds grew and thrived, in spite of our ineptitude, and when they were large enough to fend for themselves, they were returned to their respective homes — the chickens, the guinea fowl and the geese. But the pheasants were ours. We built a very pretty pen for them, incorporating the trunk of a large cedar tree, and placed the pheasants inside. At this point, they were easy to care for by just giving them wheat, water and a few greens to pick on. They were attractive birds. The first week went well but then, one morning, when I went out to feed them, one pheasant was dead, still in the pen, but with a leg and a wing pulled off. The raccoons had discovered fine dining. Pheasants do not roost but rather sleep on the ground, and if one was too near the edge of the cage, the raccoons would reach through with their agile little hands and grab whatever they could. Usually, a wing or a leg.

We bought a cock pheasant that we named George, for no particular reason. George would alarm the other pheasants and us that a raccoon was looking for a gourmet meal. I would grab the flashlight, Graham the gun, and the raccoon would be disposed of.

One night, when George gave the call, we looked out the corner of the bedroom window and watched a raccoon patrolling the circumference of the pen and standing on his back legs to try to find an entry. The moon was full that night and the light shimmering on his silver coat as he moved around the pen was a magnificent sight. We looked at each other and said, "We can't continue to do this. They are natural predators, and we have put their favourite food within easy reach. They cannot be expected to know they are our pets."

That particular raccoon was spared that night, and all others, from then on. Shortly thereafter, we had a few good pheasant meals, and it was no longer necessary to bury any more raccoons.

Obedience

Graham was a people person. He didn't dislike animals, in fact, he always made a fuss over the various friends' and neighbours' dogs and cats, scratching them behind the ears, rubbing them under the chin and around the neck, remarking on their attractive markings, good dispositions or other appropriate attributes; he just wasn't keen on including an animal in the family. He didn't relate to them and got a little impatient when they didn't respond as humans do.

I had grown up with a variety of animals, was quite comfortable with them and felt that the children should have a pet so they could learn to appreciate animals' idiosyncrasies, strengths and limitations — and with whom they could share their woes when their parents were being mean, brutal and non-understanding. He proposed a "rent-an-animal service," which didn't exist then and still doesn't. When we lived in Vancouver, he bought me a lovely Siamese cat, but a few months later as we were preparing to move to Qualicum, gave it to my mother who, he said, "needed a cat so she wouldn't be lonesome without us."

Our property in Qualicum was beautiful but a bit remote. One day, a man came into Graham's office and said, "I have a dog for you. Your wife is alone with your children all day and should have some protection. I have a good, strong one-year-old Alsatian that would be a good pet and a good guard dog. You can have him." When explained that way, how could he refuse?

This animal, named Chief, turned out to be a beautiful, strong 110-pound dog. So strong, in fact, that when we tied him to his heavy, solidly built doghouse the first night, he simply moved it up the steps onto the back porch. When we tried to get out the back door the next morning, we discovered it blocked by the doghouse and noticed Chief looking quite pleased with his accomplishment.

Graham was six feet tall and weighed 175 pounds. I was five-foot-two and weighed 105 pounds, five pounds less than the dog, who, of course, had four legs to my two. With all this going for me, it was decided that I should be the one to take him to obedience training. Miss Dunlop had a kennel nearby and was well known for her prowess in dog training and obedience. She was a doggie type of lady — solidly built, sporting an English tweed skirt, tweedy sweater, brown cotton stockings and green shoes with flaps. Chief and I signed up for Miss Dunlop's classes.

It was a lovely June evening and 15 of us turned up with our freshly washed and brushed dogs. Chief was by far the best-looking dog there. He towed me around a little but was generally well behaved, until a yappy little dog, a bit smaller than your average cat, began nipping at Chief's back leg. Chief turned with speed and grace and picked up the little creature in his mouth … and stood there. Attached to the little dog's leash was a large, triangular-shaped lady making a rather large fuss. I pried the dog from Chief's mouth but not before Miss Dunlop came charging onto the scene, green flaps flapping, hair askew and anger in her eyes. If I could not keep my dog under control, she said, we would be asked to leave the class! Embarrassed and chagrined, we made it through the class and got into the car. Chief was not at all perturbed by the incident and seemed to feel it was rather a fun evening.

Chief, our untrainable German shepherd

Upon arriving home, I related it all to Graham. He knew the woman with the mouse-like dog, and I could see he was more amused than sympathetic, until I announced that he would have to take the dog from now on, as Chief was just too strong for me to handle. At that point, the amusement left his face and he grew quite serious. "I'll tell you what," he said. "About half an hour before your next class, I'll give him a little shot — just a half dose to calm him down — and you won't have any more trouble with him."

The next week, a very calm Chief and I set out for obedience class. Miss Dunlop was duly impressed with how well behaved he was and complimented me on all the hard work I had done with him the past week. I smiled and thanked her.

For the next few weeks, we continued in this way. Although Chief didn't learn much about "sit," "stay," "come" or any of the other doggie commands, at least he didn't gobble up any of the other dogs.

Dog trials were coming up and it was touch-and-go whether Chief would be allowed to compete. Finally, since he had made such progress in his social skills, Miss Dunlop decided he should have a try at passing the course. In fairness to the dog, I had not practiced much at home with him, as, when he was not tranquilized, he was not that easy to work with, even on familiar territory and without other distractions.

The night of the trials arrived, and Graham gave Chief his shot, and just a little extra, to be sure that he would be suitably sluggish. Unfortunately, the "little extra" seemed to energize him and he bounded around in the car like a pup. A 110-pound pup.

The community hall was set up with the proper equipment for the trials, with seats around the perimeter for spectators. The judges were there, in their tweeds and shoes with flaps, and we were all there with our dogs. One by one, we were called, and one by one, they all passed, some better than others. And then it was our turn. Chief did not perform as well as some others, but I thought we might just squeak through, until I had to take him off leash for the sit-stay-come routine. As soon as the leash was off, so was he — over the fencing, out the door and down the main street, with me in hot pursuit. I finally caught him, dragged him back to the hall and tied him with a short lead to a very strong post. I sat in ignominy for the rest of the trials.

A young man with a German pointer went through the drill perfectly and obviously won first prize for his efforts. As he came off the floor, a judge motioned him over to compliment him on his skill and diligence. Across the room, watching all the accolades and smiles, I saw the German pointer lift his leg and proceed to use the judge's leg as a fire hydrant. The young man was not aware of what his dog was up to, and the judge did not feel it until her shoe was full of doggie urine. The ensuing moments were filled with embarrassment, apologies, exclamations and rushing for towels, while I was laughing harder than I had in the whole eight weeks of obedience classes.

The Chicken Caper

What are friends for if not to laugh with, be sad with, holiday and hike with, or to involve you in some project you might not otherwise have considered. Such was the case with our friends, the Walkeys, from Duncan. Because we had a little land — five acres, with one useable acre — they decided that we should raise some chickens.

They had a few fat, healthy hens on their small property and thought we should enjoy the same rewards they were reaping in the form of fresh eggs and the occasional chicken dinner. We demurred, but they insisted. This sent Graham into building mode. He built a chicken coop that looked better than our house, and we were set for the new arrivals.

He had barely hammered the last shingle on when they arrived: 30 little black balls of fluff. For the first week, they lived under the brooder we had used for the pheasants, then we moved them to their new residence. Every night, they were carefully locked in their abode to keep the mink and raccoons from devouring them, and every morning they came bustling out to greet the day. They were the best-kept chickens in the country. They were the elite of chickendom.

After a few months, I thought it was time to start feeding them chicken mash. I knew this was the way to get them going on this egg-laying business and went smartly to Buckerfield's, the local country store, to get a good supply of laying mash. I fed them, and they began to sing, a sure sign that they were getting ready to produce. We checked every day, but there was no sign of any eggs, even though we had made them very pretty nests. Maybe they were still a bit young.

A short time later, my aunt Clara from Vancouver came to visit. I did not have a car and could not pick her up, so she came to the house by taxi. After greeting her, I spoke to the taxi driver. "I see you are raising a few chickens," he said.

"Yes," I replied. "They should be laying soon. I've been feeding them lots of laying mash."

"Well," he noted, "it's going to be a long time before them guys lay any eggs." And with that, he drove off.

I took a closer look at these large black birds and observed that they were very tall and very large, with combs that were getting quite big and very red. Every one of them was a rooster!

When we received unsexed chicks, we knew there would be a few roosters — but all 30? Had our good friends played a trick on us? They said not.

Every Monday and Friday morning for the next several weeks, Graham decapitated one bird, pulled out the guts and handed it over to me. I proceeded to pluck it, but it did not end there. This particular breed also grew hair, so there was a full body of hair to remove before it hit the oven. After 15 weeks of chicken dinners, sausages and beef were a welcome repast.

Cats to the Rescue

On a dark December evening, an early Christmas gift arrived. We were happy with our two boys, but we thought a girl would be nice. I was two weeks overdue, and at that point, I would have welcomed either sex. Graham especially wanted a girl and when she was born, and they said "It's a girl," I asked them to double check! Ron, aged four and a half, thought we should call her Shelley, so we did.

We were just getting by financially. In addition, it seemed that everyone we knew decided that since we lived on the water in Qualicum, a much desired tourist location, we must be lonely and need a visit from them.

Graham would phone from work and say the Browns, or the Smiths, or the Waleskis are coming for supper — or staying for three days. Depending on who was coming and what would suit them, I had created 10 different menus to choose from. However, I didn't have a car enabling me to buy groceries and our small refrigerator, with its small freezer section, did not hold enough to feed five or six extra appetites. Graham would sail off in the morning with our only car and leave it parked at the office all day. Unless I got three children up, dressed and fed by 7:30 a.m., in order to get him to work, and then picked him up at 5 p.m., I was trapped. I needed my own car.

What could I do to earn enough money to buy one? I finally settled on raising pedigreed Siamese cats. I bought my first Siamese female, a beautiful kitten that we named Kim, part of her pedigreed name. She was a lovely house pet and soon learned how to keep the dog in his place. We got another young female we named Sunshine and had them both bred.

Graham began building pens in the adjoining shed next to the garage, and eight lovely kittens were born. When they were old enough, I brought them outside where they could play with us and each other. Siamese have long and strong back legs that allow them to jump higher than other cats, and we enjoyed watching them fly through the air as though they were on springs. Then, tired, they would fall into a heap, one on top of the other. A third female, Velvet, and a handsome male, Beau, both with good dispositions, were added to the group. I had my own Cat House.

Although I am no artist, I made a sign with a Siamese cat on it saying, "Siamese Kittens for Sale." It wasn't long before cars came, making their way down the rough gravel driveway. I have blue eyes, our three children have blue eyes and so do the cats. People would look at the cats and then at my children, and remark, "Everyone here has blue eyes!" I hoped that they knew that their only purchase was to be one of the kittens. I felt sure that they would have good homes as the people were nice and they would be paying a fair amount for the kittens, and even more if I had to write away to get the certified pedigree papers.

In the winter, when there were no kittens, the four cats lived with us in the house. I finally had built a small nest egg. Graham called it my one-way bank account, as he paid for the food, cages and heat in the shed.

We found a car that was in my price range. It was an old Vauxhall that a young man had refurbished and which, I later found, was in about the same shape as the old Hatzic truck. At least I had had some good training. The three kids and I rattled up and down the highway between Parksville and Qualicum and somehow managed to survive and feed the summer guests.

I later learned that all the locals felt the same at the end of the summer. It was called "Qualicumitis," a pseudonym for exhaustion.

Ron and Ken with the Siamese kittens

The Siamese kittens ready for a nap

A DIETITIAN'S WORK

Overworked and Underappreciated

Maybe it was the era, maybe it was location, maybe it was luck, or maybe it was because I was born on a Saturday, and Saturday's child works hard for a living — but I never seemed to have to look for work; it usually found me. And that is what happened when, while still living in Qualicum, I was in the hospital in Nanaimo for very minor surgery, the kind that would now be considered day surgery, but in the '60s, you were admitted to hospital for two or three days.

On my second day, the dietitian came to see me. This surprised me, as I did not require a special diet or any adaptations to the menu.

"I hear you are a dietitian," she said.

"Yes," I replied. "But I have not worked in the profession for seven years."

"Oh," she remarked. "I'm sure that your knowledge is current enough, and I wonder if you would be interested in working here for the month of August."

I had three children, the youngest of whom was only 10 months old, I lived in Qualicum Beach, 30 miles away, and I would be the sole dietitian in the hospital. "No," I said. "I don't think I would be capable of the job, and I have family obligations."

She was a pleasant, steady, almost stoic person, but she was desperate. She pleaded with me, "If you don't help me, I don't know what I will do! I have four school-aged children who are out of school for the summer, and my husband has had a severe heart attack. He is being discharged from the hospital and will require a great deal of care. I really need this time off."

And so it was, without any real experience or job preparation, I spent the month of August running a kitchen and staff as the sole dietitian at the Nanaimo Regional General Hospital.

It was a hot summer, and my drive to the hospital began at 6:30 a.m., with an arrival time of 7:15 a.m. At the end of the day, never being able to leave before 5:30, I hit the ferry traffic and after-work rush, arriving home at 6:30 or 7 p.m. Although I had found a capable woman to look after the children all day, I often returned home to three hungry children and a husband who had also worked all day and wasn't sure how to cope with the situation.

The work itself was overwhelming. It involved ordering all the food, accepting the deliveries, supervising the kitchen staff, organizing their work time (including payroll) and checking all the trays going to patients. In addition, there were patients to visit and therapeutic diets to write. This also involved teaching the patients their regimen and explaining why it was important to follow it. As well as all of the above, the hospital administrator often ordered tea to be delivered to his office in the afternoon, where he would entertain other administrators or dignitaries. It was an exhausting job, and at the end of the day I felt like a sucked orange.

I wondered how the poor lady who I was replacing did this job day after day. This job was too much for any one person, much less someone with a personal life. On my drives to and from work I had time to think, not only about the onerous weight of the job, but also about the things that were not being done due to the time constraints. There was no time to monitor the food coming back on the trays and assess what was being wasted and why, in order to adjust the menu accordingly. Food was being stolen from the large refrigerator and the freezer (one day, a side of lamb was taken). There was no time to develop anything new or revise procedures — some of which needed an overhaul — or update educational material. No time, no time!

Towards the end of August, I made an appointment to see the administrator. I explained the workload problem and included in it his constant requests for special teas. I also suggested, not too subtly, that if the regular dietitian did not get some help, he would not have a dietitian at all. She would die of overwork.

To his credit, he listened, and shortly after, instructed human resources to hire another dietitian.

September 1 finally came and, to my relief, I could resume my normal life. About three months later, I received a call from the dietitian, who could not thank me enough. "Thanks to you," she said, "I have a wonderful new colleague. She has been here two months and already she has saved the hospital twice her monthly salary by putting an end to the stealing, cutting the waste and checking that all the food is delivered and accounted for. And, by the way, the administrator's requests for tea have dropped by half."

I don't really know whether or not she had asked for help in the past and was ignored or whether, as many women do, she just kept taking on more work. I do know, however, (and I learned this when I did go back to work) that when a hospital opens a new department or clinic, the administrators make sure there are physicians in place as well as nursing staff and often physiotherapists, but almost never is there provision for even a part-time dietitian. This of course means that if another dietitian is ill, someone else has to pick the workload up, resulting in one dietitian having to work more than two positions. If, on the other hand, nursing is short-staffed, five or six other nurses can shoulder the load of one.

This is not to say that dietitians are the only "little red hens" of the hospital, but I often wonder why we are so invisible. We are almost the only ones practicing illness prevention. Is that not important?

When Mr. Fyke came to Victoria in the late '80s, as administrator to the Victoria General Hospital and later head of the Greater Victoria Hospital Society, he came to speak to us at the hospital. He told us how important our role was and said, "If I could hire another speech therapist, another occupational therapist, another dietitian, I would." The next day, he fired one speech therapist, one occupational therapist and one dietitian.

Later in his career, he said there was wider recognition of the need to place a greater emphasis on primary health care and wellness promotion, rather than the past focus on illness and treatment." But no new positions were initiated.

Cooking with the Guys

A large dark car inched its way slowly down the potholed driveway. Was someone lost? I could usually recognize the vehicle to guess who was coming to pay a visit or deliver groceries, but this one was unfamiliar. I was not nervous about strangers, but having no near neighbours and three children to look after — I always wanted to know who was on the property. A tall man got out of his car. I didn't know who he was, but I had seen him before in the village.

"Hello," he said. "I am Allan Armstrong, the superintendent of schools for the district." Why is he here? I wondered. I was but a lowly member of the PTA. "I'm here," he said, "to ask you to teach home economics at the high school this year. One of the teachers is not able to work, and there is no one else we can recruit on such short notice."

"But I have never taught school before," I said. "And I do not have a teaching certificate."

"Don't worry about that," he replied. "I will look after the certificate, and I know that you have a degree in foods and nutrition. You will do just fine."

"I will have to give the matter some thought and get back to you," I told him. "As you may imagine, I hadn't anticipated this, and I don't think I'll be good at teaching sewing. I do sew for the family, but I doubt I use all the accepted methods required to teach at the high school level."

"If you choose to teach the entire year of foods and nutrition, I will ask the other teacher if she will teach the entire year of sewing," he said. "We really do need you and I do hope to hear a positive response from you."

We chatted for a few more minutes, but my mind was churning. Should I do it? Could I do it? And what about the family? Ken was in Grade 4, Ron in Grade 1 and Shelley was about two years old. How would Graham feel about it? Many questions, and not too many answers yet.

When Graham came home that evening, we discussed the pros and cons: the problem with finding a caregiver (there were no daycares in Qualicum at that time and, in fact, there were few, if any, people who looked after children at all), whether I could do both jobs (no thought, in those days, of the men taking on extra responsibility for the house and children). On the other hand, the extra income would help as it was not a wealthy area and, as mentioned, people were slow to pay their dental bill, if they paid at all.

In the end, I decided to take the job, teaching foods and nutrition only. The other teacher was thrilled to get out of the job as there is much more work in planning and teaching the foods courses. I also negotiated that I would do all morning classes, no breaks, and first period after lunch, so that I could pick up the boys from school and Shelley from her babysitter and be home to do the household chores and make dinner — a nutritious one of course! The other negotiation I made was with the principal. I had learned that a new course was being introduced — Boys' Cooking — and that many of the boys enrolling in the class were well known as the poor and difficult students ranging in age from 14 to 18, and many over six feet tall. The principal and I met, and I asked that if any of the boys were behaving in a disrespectful or disruptive way, I would be able to send them out of class knowing that they would not be allowed re-entry. The principal agreed to this, and I began my new teaching career.

There were five courses to teach, each one requiring preparation, teaching and marking. Four of them had a curriculum to follow, but the boys' course did not. The first day, I gave them the rules: no disrespect or disruptive behaviour, or they were out of the class permanently. Then we went on to the curriculum. What did they want to do in this class? They all took sheets of paper and wrote down their expectations and ideas on what we should do and handed them in at the end of the period. I wasn't surprised to read about pies, cakes, cookies and bread, but there were other good suggestions as well, so we drew up our own plan and began our year of anguish, laughter and learning.

There were 24 boys in the class, which meant that every space was utilized. The lab had been set up for girls, who were smaller and much less physical than the boys, and even for the girls, it was challenging to work efficiently in the small space provided. Most of the boys had never worked in a kitchen before, had no idea about the need for cleanliness, but they all liked to push buttons, twirl timers and engage in some form of disruptive behaviour. The first day, as I was attempting to give a lesson on our first project, I was interrupted several times by one of the boys. I said, "Charlie, that qualifies as disrespect, and I would ask you to raise your hand if you want to say something that would be useful to us all. That is a warning."

The next day, he carried on with interjections, comments and commentary. I repeated my warning and went on with the lesson. The next time he came to class, the same behaviour occurred, and I simply said, "Charlie, you are out of the class. Now." He looked at me somewhat startled, but did not move.

"You heard me," I said. "You are out of the class."

"Well," he said, "when can I come back?"

"You are not coming back into this class, and I made that very clear the first day. Now go."

At that moment, there was a great deal of silence in the classroom as Charlie picked up his books and shuffled out of the room. It also registered with the rest of them that I meant what I said and that any one of them could end up in study period with Charlie if they did not follow the rules.

For the boys' and two of the girls' classes, we started with canning. There was an abundance of fruit in the area that would go to waste, and I was able to buy a large supply at a reasonable price by going directly to the farmers. We were busily canning, labelling and storing the fruit to be used later in the year, as needed, when I was called to the principal's office.

"Why are you doing the canning at this time of year," he asked, "when, in the curriculum, it says it should be done in the spring and that is when all the other teachers have done it?"

"Well," I said, "it doesn't make sense to me to do it in the spring when all the fruit is expensive. Now, I can buy it cheaply and use it throughout the year. The budget for the foods courses is not large and I am trying to stretch it as far as I can."

He grunted a little, noted again that all the others had done it in the spring, but never again did he question me on my modus operandi.

Things were going along well in the boys' class and we were really having a very good time in the process. One day, some of them came to me and asked, "Could we do oysters?"

"We could," I said, "but I don't have the budget to buy enough oysters for the whole class. If, however, you want to collect enough oysters for everyone we can certainly do a lesson or two."

At the time, there were oysters in abundance on the beaches around

Qualicum, but I did not expect an immediate response. In fact, I did not expect any response to my suggestion. How wrong I was! The next day, they appeared with two gallons of fresh, shucked and cleaned oysters. We left the lesson on the nutritional value of oysters and other seafood for a later date and embarked on three days of cooking oysters every way I could think of. They did it all, tried everything and ate every last oyster. I was learning as much as they were in this class. I was finding that boys, given an opportunity, will do more than girls; they will experiment more and be open to new ideas and suggestions. They will try different foods and spices that girls will not try, and if their meals do not turn out as well as they had hoped, they will put on a brave face and eat them anyway. I was really enjoying working with this disparate group.

About halfway through the year, the curriculum for the boys' course arrived. I looked at it and began to laugh. It was the usual bland, uninteresting dogma that came from the home economics experts in Victoria who had not seen the inside of a classroom for 30 years. Blancmange is always high on their list of lessons, as is rice pudding and oatmeal. I took it to class the next day. "Good news," I said. "The curriculum has arrived." They looked at me expectantly, hopefully and a little apprehensively. "Yes," I said. "Our first lesson is how to cut a grapefruit." They couldn't believe it and looked at me blankly. Finally, I couldn't control the smile that evolved into laughter and said, "So, we'll just put that away until next year and continue with our own agenda."

Mr. Armstrong dropped into my classes from time to time, and the boys always behaved like gentlemen. He'd wander about the class with a smile on his face, watching them earnestly make white sauce and grate cheese for their macaroni and cheese.

There was, however, one part of their behaviour that did bother me, and repeatedly telling them was not working. It was a cleanliness problem. They did not see the value of cleaning dishes properly, covering food, washing their hands before working with food or even covering their mouths when they sneezed or coughed. I went to the drug store and asked the pharmacist to order me some agar plates. Then I went home and asked Graham if he could make me an incubator of some sort. He wired an electric light bulb and extension into a large cardboard box, and I had an incubator.

Two days later, the plates arrived, and I took them and the incubator to school. I put the plates on my desk and said, "Neil, come and put your gum on this plate." He looked surprised that I even knew he was chewing gum (which was not allowed) but trundled up to the front and put it on the plate. "Keith, come up and put some of the dirt from your fingernails on a plate, and Matt, come up and cough onto this. The last one, we will leave open for the rest of the period, and then put them all in the incubator."

They were puzzled, and I explained that the agar was a growth medium and whatever bacteria they had donated would grow and we would see the results in a few days. Three days later, we opened the box and placed the plates on my desk. They all came up to the front and watched as I took each cover off the plates. The growth was far better than I had imagined. The fungus from the mouth was beautiful: large grey mounds touching the top of the glass. They almost retched. The other slides were equally impressive. Probably the most telling one was the one that had been left out in the air. It had a variety of interesting growths of different colours and shapes. I didn't have to say much. They understood perfectly what I had been trying to tell them and I never again had to remind them to wash their hands or cover their mouths when they coughed.

School board supervisors from Victoria sometimes came in during class to watch me teach and keep track of what we were doing. One time, one of them gave me poor marks because she noticed the boys hadn't wrapped the garbage the way she thought it should be wrapped. Very petty.

The year was drawing to a close and we had not yet made bread. It was not easy to make bread in a classroom, due to time constraints, but there was a new yeast on the market called "Cool Rise." It enabled you to make the bread dough and then refrigerate it until the next day. Then, of course, it had to be kneaded, shaped and allowed to rise. I said, "Okay, you want to make bread, but you will have to give up your lunch hour to knead, shape and set the bread, and I will have to give up my lunch hour too. We will bake it during the last period of the day. Are you prepared to do that?" Yes, they were.

Day 1, each pair made the dough, wrapped and labelled it and put it in the fridge. Day 2, I arrived in the classroom at noon and there was not a boy in sight. I was annoyed. Then I noticed little mounds covered with clean cloths, sitting on the counters, and I went around to see what had transpired. Under each cloth was an artistic phenomenon. The boys had come in early as the teacher for their previous period was away ill, and they had talked the study teacher into allowing them to come to the cooking lab. They wanted to use their own imaginations to shape the loaves and did not want interference from me. There were cornucopias, braided loaves, loaves in various containers and the odd normal-sized bread loaf in a proper tin.

"Well," I said, when last period arrived and they sat expectantly to see my reaction, "I think this is going to be a very interesting period. Turn your ovens on to four hundred degrees and when it reaches that temperature put the dough in to bake." I didn't have to wait long for the cornucopia to rise to the top of the oven and begin smoking and smouldering along with another one or two of the upright containers. The room became very smoky, so we opened all the windows and headed for the hallway, where I stood laughing and thinking that, in fact, this may be one of their better lessons.

We ended the year with a gourmet barbecue, if there is such a thing. Although the course had been a lot of work and some anguish, it had been a good experience for everyone. My reward for the whole year was that three of the boys went on to chef school and did well for themselves in the industry. The others, at least, knew a few basic cooking skills and probably could have cooked in logging camps or been short-order cooks.

Mr. Armstrong wanted me to come back the following year, but I declined, although I'm sure the next year would have been much easier as I had all the courses organized and just needed to refine some things. In any case, shortly thereafter, we moved to Victoria where my temporary certificate allowed me to do a little substitute teaching. But nothing was ever as much fun as in Qualicum with "my guys."

Transitions

While we still living in Qualicum, an opportunity arose. One of the dentists from Victoria dropped by to say that a new medical building was being erected that Graham could buy into and set up his practice. We had been thinking that it may be time to move to a more urban area — as much as we loved Qualicum and the outdoor life, we were concerned the children would have few opportunities to socialize as they got older. The teenagers in the area usually went to Nanaimo, which was 30 miles away, for whatever events they wanted to attend, be it sports, movies or shopping. This concerned us because some of these trips led to car accidents that resulted in serious injuries or death. We also thought about future education and the availability of other pursuits, such as music, choir and sports.

To add to that, another incident occurred. A very unpleasant lady arrived in our driveway demanding that her unpedigreed, motley-looking female cat be bred to my male Siamese. I said no, knowing that she would sell the kittens at a cut rate and probably not be fussy about the people she sold them to. Of course, that meant she would not get Beau's credentials.

I had to be away for a week and had a man look after the cats. This woman somehow knew I wasn't around and came down, hoping to get her cat into my pens. Fortunately, our cat sitter also shooed her away. But she was not done yet. She came down when he was not there and he had forgotten to lock the pens. She threw her cat in with Beau. After she was bred, she attacked Beau, and when I arrived home, I had to treat his wounds. He was not badly hurt, but my next batch of kittens were not well, due, I think, to some disease her cat had harboured. It was time to wrap up the business.

Velvet and Sunshine were given to friends, who were happy to have the beautiful cats. Unfortunately, Beau had eaten some poison that some unkind person had spread around the area and died, as did the majestic bloodhound belonging to our neighbours, the Milners. We never found out who did this, or how many other victims there were. We took Kim, my original female, with us to Victoria.

Just before our departure, Ken and Ron had one of their frequent disagreements, and Ron, the loser in this case, stomped off to sulk and try to smooth his feathers. Up the driveway, he found a lost orange-coloured kitten and, of course, brought it home. "Can we keep it? Can we keep it?" he pleaded. It was a female, in itself very unusual as most of the orange or red cats are male, while the females are almost always either tortoise shell or calico-coloured. We did keep her and called her "O.K." (for Orange Kat). And so it was that we headed off to Victoria with two adults, three children, two cats, eight sheets of four-by-eight-foot by three-quarter-inch plywood and four large hanging baskets, all packed into our trusty station wagon.

Haile

Not long after our arrival in Victoria, we received a call from a friend associated with the SPCA, telling us that they had just received a quiet one-year-old pedigreed black Labrador who needed a good home. Would we be interested?

Consultation ensued, and Graham, who liked to hunt, agreed that the dog was still young enough to be trained to retrieve the many ducks he planned to bring to our table. Having grown up eating venison and duck and various other wild things, I wasn't interested in the retrieving part, but I did want the dog and so did the children.

He was a lovely dog, although a little timid of men and newspapers, as the previous owner was a man who disciplined him with rolled-up newspapers. Otherwise, he was a friendly and certainly obedient dog.

As we had a red point Siamese cat, son of O.K., who we had named Orange Julius (Julius for short), due to his orange markings on his feet, tail, ears and face, I thought that "Caesar" would be an appropriate name. Graham objected, as he had once known a dog called Caesar who was smelly, sniffly and nasty. We wracked our brains to come up with someone or something that was black and finally decided on "Haile," after Haile Selassie, the Ethiopian ruler.

We lived in Gordon Head, and at the time, there was still a great deal of farmland in the area. The children walked to school through a large daffodil field and tomato fields, and hot houses were abundant in the neighbourhood. Every morning, Haile was allowed to do his morning rounds, which usually consumed about an hour and half of his time, and then he would come home and sleep on the back patio and hope for more activity when everyone got home from school.

After about a year of this kind of freedom, we moved to Beach Drive, a very busy street, and we were forced to keep him in a large, enclosed area and take him for daily walks. We found we could not let him off the leash, as he would run off to do his rounds of the town and come home an hour or so later … if the dog police didn't impound him first, which they did on two or three occasions. This necessitated a trip to the slammer to spring him and a $30 bail charge. This did not please Graham.

Haile

Since we could not let Haile off leash, which prevented him from exploring the neighbourhood, he developed a new trick. The cement wall enclosing him on one side had a steep slope on the other, which housed a very unpleasant and prickly covering of gorse. Haile elected to scale the wall, take a chance on breaking a leg and enduring the punishment of the gorse. Again, we were called to spring him from the slammer. Again, this did not please Graham.

After this happened twice, Graham decided to put up an electric line on top of the cement wall. We watched as Haile readied for the jump; we watched as he made the jump; we watched as his penis hit the electric current as he went over the wall. And we never had to visit the slammer again.

In the meantime, Haile took a holiday to get his retrieval-training badge. He was gone for three weeks for an intense training period. Apparently, he was a reasonable pupil. None of our dogs was ever a stellar performer. He was returned to us with a rubber-knobbed cylinder and a frozen duck for us to continue the training process. We were instructed to take him to the beach each day (no problem, given where we lived, right on the ocean), and throw either the rubber cylinder or the duck out into the ocean and have him retrieve the item. We were diligent. Every day, we took one or the other of the props and threw it into the bay and called "Back!" The first time, Haile would plunge into the water and retrieve whatever we had thrown. The second time he would go, reluctantly, and the third time, he would look at us and say, with his eyes, "You get it yourself. If you keep throwing that thing away, you obviously don't want it." But we persevered. Nevertheless, every day we received the same response, as if to say, "I don't really like swimming, you know." His attitude did not please Graham.

Fall came, and with it, duck hunting season. Graham's brother, Ken, lived in Duncan, and he knew of a good area to hunt. Graham put Haile in the car and left late on a moonless Friday evening. He arrived in Duncan around 10 p.m. and while getting Haile out of the car, the dog escaped. He was off to do his rounds. He was a black dog, on a black night, and he could not be found. Eventually, as always, he returned.

In the early morning, they were out looking for ducks. Graham got the first one, which fell into a shallow lake, and loudly called to Haile, "Back!" Haile plunged into the water, took one look at the duck and swam back empty-mouthed. "Back!" Graham yelled, and again Haile went into the water, swam around the duck and returned. It wasn't frozen. He was trained to pick up a rubber cylinder or a frozen duck, not a soft, warm, feathery bird. The third "Back" did not elicit any response. Once again, this attitude did not please Graham. He himself half-waded, half-swam to retrieve the duck.

That evening, he came storming into the kitchen. "I'm going to shoot that goddamned dog. I almost did today."

"What happened?" I asked.

He related the story. As he was telling it, I began to laugh — inside. The more he told it, the harder it was to contain my hilarity. Finally, I just dissolved laughing and he finally saw the humour of the situation, and soon we were both laughing on the kitchen floor.

The Dory

Graham's enthusiasm for boating paralleled his enthusiasm for animals; thus, our various boats were referred to by Graham as "Never Again the Second," "Never Again the Third," the fourth and the fifth. In general conversation, they were usually referred to as "the goddamn boat." I loved being on the water, and to keep me happy when I wasn't, and avoid hearing my sighing, he begrudgingly learned all the "boaty" lessons required.

We both took our power squadron classes, and I also did the piloting course — the only female in either course. Women were not deemed capable of the mathematics required for coastal navigation. But I would not be the helpless female who could not run a boat or navigate the tricky waters of the coast. Graham should not have to carry the full load of responsibility.

The Dory (or Never Again the Second) was a 14-tonne, 35-foot wooden boat built in 1945. It was solidly constructed of dense fir, with teak decks and mahogany cabin and trim. The square bow accommodated four bunks, then there was the galley and a head. A step up brought you to the lounge and wheelhouse under which the engine churned — some of the time. There was a small back deck, and perched on the stern, a dinghy hung from davits. We bought *The Dory* in partnership with our next-door neighbours, Don and Joan.

The Dory *(or "Never Again the Second")*

It moved at the dizzying speed of seven knots, not a bit faster, and I loved that aspect of it too. Travelling at that speed, one could make tea or cook in the galley without having to hang on with one hand and steady pots with the other. We could enjoy the scenery as it slipped slowly by and we could pass other boats and wildlife without disrupting their peace or serenity. Not that we ever passed any boats, unless they were coming towards us.

To be fair to Graham, the boat did have one little problem: the engine. And this was something I could not help him with. He used to complain that when we were on the goddamn boat, the only place he ever got a suntan was on his rear end, as he always had his head in the engine and his rear end in the air. We had to be towed in to shore a few times by our friends, Jack and Jane, who often boated with us. Graham would say, "Why don't we just open the boathouse door, throw Jack a line and let him take us to wherever we are going?" He was embarrassed. You did not hold your head high while being towed.

There were pros and cons about the co-ownership of the boat. The upside was that whoever used the boat last left it in immaculate condition; the downside was agreement, or lack thereof, on repairs and upkeep. We all agreed that something had to be done with the motor — but what? A new diesel motor would have worked, but it would have meant raising the floor of the wheelhouse to a level that Graham could not stand upright. Don was enough shorter that it would not have affected him and hoped maybe Graham wouldn't mind being bent over most of the time. We pondered and discussed, neither of us having a great deal of disposable income, and finally decided to rebuild the engine on the assurance of Philbrooks Boatyard that "it would be as good as new."

By mid-July, we had new pistons, spark plugs, wiring and whatever it takes to rebuild an engine. The five of us, along with our friends and their children in their boat, were ready to take off for Desolation Sound and beyond.

Graham having a moment of relaxation on The Dory

We were headed north. We came out of Tsehum Harbour, around Curteis Point and through Satellite Channel and Sansum Narrows. The weather was sunny and warm. We were sailing along at near our top speed, enjoying the warmth, the incredible beauty of our convoluted bays and inlets lined with evergreen trees interspersed with the brilliant orange bark of the arbutus trees and the ever-present gulls engaged in their soaring dances across the sky. Just past Yellow Point, and abeam of DeCourcy Island, we paused to wait for slack tide at Dodd Narrows and reminisce about Brother XII, the English mystic and his cult of devoted followers who built a community on this island, and the hardships that they had endured there. Once through the narrow passage, it was a short trip past the Portage, around Jack Point and into Nanaimo Harbour for the night.

The next morning, with the weather still fair, we headed across the Strait of Georgia to a safe harbour in Secret Cove. It was a sunny day, but windy, which made for a much rougher crossing than we had anticipated. The wooden table fell over with a dramatic crash, and a few other items hit the floor and the deck with authority, but the solid old boat ploughed through the water without complaint and the engine, thankfully, chugged steadily along.

The third day saw us round Nelson Island and head up the mouth of Jervis Inlet to Hotham Sound where the Harmony Islands were located. One of the islands was privately owned by an American who did not take kindly to people using any part of his precious land, but his island was the best one to use to tie a stern line from the boat to a tree on shore and drop an anchor off the bow. Fortunately, he was not there at the time, so we escaped eviction and happily had our supper and a good night's sleep without having to listen for the ominous growl of the anchor dragging its cable and the boat shifting position.

But what I did hear in the morning was Graham, not usually an early riser, mournfully calling my name. I looked out the window to see him standing precariously in the dinghy, crab trap raised to about his eye level. Staring him in the face was an enormous wolf eel wound around several times inside the trap. Wolf eels are normally shy creatures and avoid confrontation, when possible, but they are known to have a bite strong enough to snap a broom handle. This was a very large specimen, and it was not at all happy with the present situation. "What should I do?" Graham wailed. "Put him back," I yelled back, not being quite sure, myself, how we were going to get him out of the trap. We had breakfast, discussed the situation and about an hour later, armed with whatever we could find, and wearing thick gloves, we hauled the trap up. To our great surprise there was no sign of the eel. He had bitten a hole in the side of the strong wire trap and escaped.

The day before, Graham had heard a faint sound in the engine he was not happy with. A small rattle, nothing much, and certainly nothing that I would have paid attention to. We had planned to go up Jervis Inlet to Princess Louisa Inlet, considered one of the most beautiful places on earth, but it was a long trip on our slow boats with no help available if something should go wrong. We decided, instead, to go to Egmont, which was not far away, spend the night at the wharf, then the next day go through the Skookumchuck rapids and into the huge inlets behind Sechelt. Here, these large inlets drain their water with every low tide and fill it at high tide. It's a huge amount of water to transfer through a narrow channel with an island in the middle, resulting in very fast water and a slack tide of only six minutes. At this time of year, the tides were very high and very low, so a huge amount of water had to be transferred.

Princess Louisa Inlet

When we got to Egmont, it began to rain, then pour, turning into a downpour. It seemed that there was more water above the boat than there was under it. More boats came to the wharf, including sailboats with everything soaked — sails and decks, sleeping bags and their occupants. We took as many on board as we could, as the old *Dory*, with its furnace, was warm and dry.

It poured the next day too and, although we were comfortable enough, there were now four adults and seven young people between the ages of eight and 15 on board and everyone was getting a little tired of Crazy Eights and Whist.

In the meantime, we calculated our tides and currents and established that we could get through the rapids at 5 p.m. the next day. We waited in high anticipation, cast off at about 4:30 and headed towards the rapids, the other boat in the lead. A tug with a boom of logs was also waiting, and we wondered if we (he had precedence) would all make it through with our very limited time frame. In went the tug, followed by our friend's boat and then us. We did make it through without incident and heaved a hearty sigh of relief. Once we were tied in a sheltered bay, we all (the adults that is) had a good stiff drink and congratulated ourselves on our achievement.

It was a lovely area, and we should have spent more time exploring, but we wanted to go farther up the coast, so it was necessary to make the reverse trip at 6 a.m. two days later. Heads down, we did our calculations again and decided to leave at 6:04 a.m., one minute into slack. We were elected to go first, so we pushed the old boat forward into the narrows, which were as docile looking as when we had first come through. The children were all asleep in their bunks, as we did not want to wake them and have more people around to cause confusion.

Suddenly, this very heavy boat spun 360 degrees in less than three seconds. The old adage of boating, being hours and hours of boredom interspersed with moments of sheer terror, has never been more true. The last of the whirlpools had caught us, and we were completely helpless. The other boat, having seen the incident, turned back, waited another two minutes and, seeing that we were again safely on our way, came through without incident. We all went back to Egmont to tie up at the wharf and try to calm our extremely tattered nerves. In fact, we stayed long enough to walk through the path to the narrows and view the next tide from the land. It was, in the true sense of the word, an awesome experience. At the full flood, it was a seething mass of water with an overfall of at least four feet. It was hard to believe that it could ever be flat and calm. Apparently, people who spend time on the island in the middle of the narrows during the flood often leave terrified and chastened by the experience. I, however, had a never-again of my own: never again will I go through Skookumchuck by boat — any boat.

Desolation Sound

The sunny weather returned, and we continued north to Desolation Sound, stopping at various magical places along the way. From Teakerne Arm we walked to Cassel Lake, which had a small waterfall flowing from it. All the girls (four of them) took the opportunity to go under the waterfall and wash their hair. What a sight it was to see these young, beautiful and innocent young people with the water flowing over them, surrounded by trees, the sun filtering through the branches and they themselves experiencing the pure joy of the moment.

We gathered clams on a pristine white shell beach and after a swim off the boats and when the clams had had time to spit out their sand, everyone came aboard for clams and onions simmered in white wine. It was a true gourmet feast for all, enhanced by the refreshing swim, the fresh air and the fact that when you are on a boat, you are almost always hungry.

Most of the time in Desolation we would find a secluded bay and anchor for the night, but one day we went fishing for red snapper off West Redonda Island. We caught enough for everyone and the children were intrigued watching the fish come to the surface, turn a bright orange and release a large air bubble out of their mouths.

It was about mid-day, and we realized that we were just outside Roscoe Bay. The tide was high, and we could get through the shallow opening at this time. At low tide, it became a small reversing falls. In we went, to find a large log boom and a small logging camp. The loggers were on strike at the time, but George, the camp cook and caretaker, was delighted to see us and invited us to tie to the boom and make ourselves at home. "It won't be going anywhere tonight; loggers are on strike," he said. The reason he was so cordial, we later discovered, was that he expected to visit every boat later in the day and be treated to whatever libation we happened to have on board, complete with hors d'oeuvres!

In the meantime, we gathered up our laundry and plenty of soap and headed to Black Lake, a small crystal-clear lake about a kilometre away. We washed clothes, and ourselves, under our bathing suits, Jack ordering his girls to be sure to wash … "everything." Soap bubbles and foam floated everywhere as we, unknowingly, polluted the lake with our grime and our soap. This is no longer allowed, but in the early '70s, no one knew that we were damaging the environment. The few of us probably did little harm but had it continued with the thousands of boats that later visited the sound, it would have done so.

On our return from the lake, we entertained George, "the mayor of Roscoe Bay," as we called him. We then put our barbecues on the boom, had supper and then roasted marshmallows covered with peanut butter over the fading coals. When darkness came, we retired to our boats. Normally we would have gone to bed, but we weren't ready, and the boys wanted to play cards for a while. We were intent on our game when I glanced out the window and noticed a tug with three lights on the mast. I said, "My God, there's a tug in the bay with a boom under tow — our boom!" The card game ended abruptly as we raced outside to see the tug tying up to the boom and making sure that no boaters were alerted to its presence. We called to our friends as well as three other boats that had come into the bay when we were at the lake (George had had a good night of tippling). Everyone was out on deck, not able to see anything, untying lines and drifting about in the bay. George appeared on the scene, yelling that the strike was over and the boom was on its way to Vancouver. As if we needed this information! The boom and the tug left, leaving us all floating around the bay, trying to anchor and also trying to avoid a collision with each other. After about an hour, we had all found a secure spot, with no danger of swinging on the anchor and hitting another boat. We finally got to bed about 1 a.m.

We slept late that day as there was no need to hurry, since the tide would be high around noon, and we were tired from the loss of sleep and the excitement of the night. George came out in his dinghy to tell us how lucky we were! A few years prior, when a strike came to an end at night, a tug came in and hooked up to a boom and the luckless couple in the only boat tied to the boom that night woke up to find themselves going backwards, past Lund, several kilometres to the south. Apparently tug captains and crew find this manoeuvre highly amusing.

Once out of the bay, we headed south, following the curve of West Redonda Island and into Refuge Cove, where we knew there was a small store. We needed to replenish our food supply and exchange a few stories and information with other boaters. In the store, an American couple were grumbling audibly about the lack of facilities and the cost of the products in the store. There were no washers and dryers and they had had to pay $1.25 for a loaf of bread. The grumbling continued for a while until I could contain myself no longer and finally said, "We are all here for an outdoor and wilderness experience and cannot expect to have modern conveniences in remote places. All the food must be brought in by plane or water taxi at extra expense and if we do not support these people, we may not have a store to come to next year." My comments were not well received and, unfortunately, more prophetic than I would have liked. The store did shut down a year or two later. At the present time, I understand there is a store there again and they do have washers and dryers.

After stocking up, we continued to Squirrel Cove on Cortez Island, where we overnighted and made the decision to circumnavigate the island. We wanted to go into Von Donop Inlet about 18 nautical miles, or three hours, away.

We arrived at the mouth of the inlet about noon and made our way down the narrow channel, watching for a large rock in the middle, covered on a half tide. The inlet opened into a very large pond, and we were surprised to find so many other boats anchored. We soon learned that a man had a market garden at the edge of the bay and the boaters were all taking advantage of being able to buy fresh vegetables and eggs. We, of course, joined in on the buying frenzy.

The next day, we continued down the west side of Cortez Island, stopping in Carrington Bay to dig for some fresh clams. The sun warmed us, the beach was clean and sparkling due to years of accumulation of ground clamshells, and we were anticipating another gourmet feast of clams and white wine later in the day. We resumed our journey at a leisurely pace and then slipped through the narrow channel into Gorge Harbour, our safe and beautiful shelter for the night.

Sadly, it was almost time for us to begin our trek home. Later that evening, we plotted our course for Campbell River. Our friends would come that far with us and continue on their own, as they had a few more days of freedom to enjoy the wonders of the B.C. coast.

The day dawned with a thick fog enveloping us, a boater's nightmare. The only good thing about fog is that usually means there is no wind. With no GPS, just a compass, a chart and a roller ruler, we moved quietly out of our safe haven, hoping there was not too much current to take us off course and put us on to the shallows and rocks off Cape Mudge. With three boats following us, there was no margin for error or we would all be in trouble. With Graham running the boat and me giving him the course and course changes, we made our blind way forward. Four hours later, we found ourselves just south of the shoals on Mudge — exactly where we wanted to be! We gave a sigh of relief as cheers rang out from the other boats and we continued to the government wharf in Campbell River.

The next morning, we gassed up, said goodbye to our friends and began our trip southward. It was a clear, windless morning and we were ready for a relaxed and easy trip to Victoria. We left at about 10 a.m. and decided to cruise past Mitlenatch Island to look at the bird rookeries on this protected island. Thousands of seagulls breed and nest here, and the smell and commotion greeted us a half mile away from this cacophonous community. We were moving along at one or two knots when I heard Graham yell behind me, "Shut it down!" Bewildered, I obeyed immediately, but it was too late. Suddenly, the temperature on the gauges (which I hadn't been watching) went up and the pressure down. "I think we've lost the block," is all he said.

We called in a "PAN-PAN" to the coast guard and gave them our location. They asked if we were in any trouble and we replied, "No, we're just dead in the water."

"We have a seagoing tug in the area with trainees on board, it will be going by at about five p.m. and will pick you up."

It was noon, we made lunch, played cards and read. Graham commented that it was the best day of boating he had had.

Five o'clock arrived and so did the tug, all 100 feet of it, with about 20 eager trainees aboard. "We'll throw you a line," they called. "Stand back!" With that, a 30-pound cannonball arched though the air and landed on our deck. Their aim was good, but to this day I will never know why it didn't go through the deck and onto the bunks below. We tied the line to the Samson post and said, "Ready."

"What's your hull speed?"

"Seven knots," we proudly declared.

"Well, you're going twelve knots tonight," came the reply.

We were not happy with this, as we knew the boat would not be able to follow true and we were afraid that we might lose the propeller.

"Where do you want to go, Campbell River or Lund?" (Both had good boat yards.)

"Campbell River," we said, as we did not want to be on the main land side if we had to get home by bus.

The Dory *under tow by a tug with 20 trainees aboard*

Off we went, and the bow lifted out of the water, creating a wave the old boat had never seen before. We were sluing about and felt very uncomfortable about the whole exercise. Suddenly, a pod of 15 killer whales appeared on either side of us, probably liking the wave, but it seemed more like they were saying, "Don't worry, we're here, we'll look after you." They took us right into Campbell River and then left.

The engine was irreparable, as Graham had suspected. We then wandered around the wharf, looking for someone who might be able to tow us to Victoria. We found a log salvage boat. Inside was a dishevelled-looking man of about 35 and three children between the ages of six and 12. We asked him if he would consider towing us to Victoria. He obviously needed the money and agreed to take us for $100, diesel fuel and all their meals on the trip down. We couldn't believe our good luck. I went immediately to the store to lay in more food for the four extra people.

The following day, we began our trip down island. As much as Graham did not like to be towed, he was relaxing on the rear deck, enjoying the scenery and happy to be rid of responsibility.

Suddenly, I looked up and realized that not only were we on the wrong side of a marker, but we were literally inches from it! Most of the markers are embedded in cement and the cement is close to the surface. It was only our good fortune that we were on a high tide. We quickly realized that this poor man knew nothing about navigation and immediately worked out a series of hand signals. From our boat we navigated all the way down the coast of the island. He followed our instructions faithfully. At meal times, we pulled the two boats together, passed over the food, played the line out and resumed our journey.

The two days it took us went by relatively uneventfully … except for one incident. The children on the towboat were eager to see us pull up as, I'm sure, they had not seen so much good food in some time, if ever. Ron had been pestering to go on the other boat for a change, as the older boy and he were about the same age. We were reluctant to let him go as he was an active and impulsive child, and the other boat was in disarray. As we were almost home, we finally relented, and at lunch break allowed him to go on the towboat. Graham admonished him sternly, saying, "Do not go near the tow rope. Stand well back when the line is playing out. Stay completely away from the stern. Do you understand?"

"Yes, Dad," came the reply.

He got on the other boat, the line was playing out, and Ron's arm was caught in the line! We watched in horror as we heard the snap of the bone and thought for certain that he would be thrown into the water and the propeller. Fortunately, he was not, and we were able to get him back on our boat without further damage.

He did not get as much sympathy as he would have liked, as we were shaken and somewhat angry that he had not done as he was told. We got into our boathouse, fuelled the salvage tug, gave them the leftover food and sent them on their way, hoping they would make it back without incident. Then we were off to the hospital to have a broken bone repaired, after which we would have to face our friends and co-owners of *The Dory* and tell them about the broken motor and that they, probably, would not have a boating holiday this summer.

Graham and me in a dinghy in the Princess Louisa Inlet — circa mid-1990s

Graham and me on Four Winds *(or "Never Again The Last")*

Swap 'n Shop

It was 1970. "Graham," I said, "this house is becoming far too cluttered. We have a number of things we no longer need and I don't want to have around. There is a Swap 'n Shop over in the Tillicum area on Saturdays, and we could load up the station wagon, get of rid of some of it and make a little money as well."

I was always looking for ways to acquire a little cash for the extras that the children needed: music lessons, sports equipment, birthday party gifts and the many other small things that crop up to squeeze the budget.

"Well, you go if you want to — but I'm not going. I don't want people pawing over our belongings, making remarks and bargaining for a lower price on something that is almost a giveaway anyway," came the reply.

"I'll go with you, Mom," said a voice from down the hall. "It will be fun." It was Ron. I knew he liked being with me, and I also knew that he would rather swim into the mouth of a whale than spend any part of the day with his father. Whenever I did leave them alone, when I got home, Ron would be hiding in his bedroom and Graham would be storming around and muttering about that damn kid.

Graham was a perfectionist and wanted his children to be perfect too. The other two managed to conform to his expectations, which, in truth, were not unreasonable. But Ron was different. He was kind and imaginative, but he was hyperactive, sometimes made inappropriate remarks and often pestered his older brother, who would always react, just like his father.

He was not doing well at school, so we had him tested mentally and physically. The report came back: slim and in perfect physical condition, with above-average intelligence and poor attentive skills, which we already knew. He was a good swimmer and won several ribbons for his school, and he could run faster than most, including his brother, which is probably the reason he survived Ken's ire after doing something annoying. I realize it was mainly to get his attention, but Ken wanted nothing to do with Ron and hoped that no one knew they were related — a futile hope with a last name like ours! Ron's best friends were his younger sister and me.

Saturday morning, with the car loaded, Ron and I were about to leave when Graham came out of the house. "Here, take this along," he said, as he handed me a woeful-looking .303-calibre rifle that had taken some serious abuse in its lifetime. "You expect me to sell that?" I asked incredulously.

"Sure, just take it along and see what you can get for it. The barrel has a little bend in it, otherwise it's okay."

"Good for shooting around corners?" I queried. In went the gun and we were off to Swap 'n Shop.

We arrived around 10 a.m., after the initial rush had subsided, and were deluged by people like fresh meat in a swarm of flies. Oh good, I thought, we'll get rid of this load and be out of here in no time. We squirmed our way through the crowd to the back door of the station wagon, got it open and made an attempt to display our treasures. Five minutes later, with no sales to our credit, we were alone in a field of cars and tables.

People who did wander by would cast us a disdainful look and continue on — except for a boy of about 17. He was interested in the gun. As he was examining it, an older man came by, took it from the boy, sighted it and said, "My boy, this is an elephant gun. A good sturdy gun but still won't kill an elephant head on. The only way you can shoot an elephant is up his asshole. Bullet goes straight up and kills him dead as a doornail."

At this point, Ron and I had dodged beside the car — he on one side, I on the other — each not wanting to acknowledge that the other had heard the conversation but both having a laugh inside. I was embarrassed, not wanting my young son to hear that kind of talk, and he was embarrassed, being an 11-year-old and wise in the ways of the world, who did not think his innocent mother could ever have heard that word before. Both gun enthusiasts continued on, and we emerged without comment.

About 20 minutes later, the young man returned, intrigued by the gun. It had a $15 sticker on it. "I'd like to buy the gun," he said. I began to engage him in conversation and he told me that he was hitchhiking across the country. I asked him if he thought anyone would pick him up while carrying a rifle. "I'll just shove the barrel down my boot and cover the top with my jacket; no problem," he said. And off he went with his $15 gun.

It was then that we decided to leave. It was apparent there was not going to be any further activity that day. Our sales amounted to $15 for the gun, three dollars for a lamp and two dollars for odds and ends, not enough to pay for many piano lessons.

I worried for a while and watched the news to make sure the hitchhiker hadn't assaulted some kind people who had offered a young man a ride. I also reasoned that, with the bent barrel, he wouldn't be able to hit whatever he was aiming at — but there could be some kind of collateral damage.

Despite his early challenges with school, Ron went on to get a master's degree and has held several senior manager jobs in both Canada and Australia. We have had a few chuckles over the elephant gun and our day at the Swap 'n Shop — a small piece of family lore.

The Wired Jaw Diet

It's worth explaining some further aspects of a dietitian's work, as many people have no idea what a dietitian actually does. I had a job at the Victoria General Hospital as a clinical dietitian, mostly working on diets for outpatients with heart disease, kidney disease and diabetes.

"Fay, you've got to help us," came the plaintive cry, one day, from one of the oral surgeons at the hospital.

"How can I do that, Mike?" I asked, somewhat warily.

"We need to find a way to feed our patients with broken jaws whose mouths must be wired shut for six weeks. In this time, they can lose twenty or thirty pounds."

At the time, I was dealing with various medical problems of obese patients, and I unkindly remarked that it probably would do most of them good, and jokingly asked if some of my patients could have their jaws wired shut.

"No, no," he said, "most of my patients are young and not over-weight, and losing 30 pounds is serious. We usually can find a hole between the teeth large enough to insert a straw, so whatever they eat must be able to go through a straw."

"Let me think about it," I said.

My life was busy, with a full-time job at the hospital, three children, a husband, a large house and garden and, at that time, a fairly busy social life. The prospect of taking on yet another job for the hospital with no time allowance for the hours of work required was not in the least appealing. I put the idea on the very back burner.

A few weeks later, I heard from Mike again. "How are you doing with the diet?" he asked.

"Not well," I replied. "I just haven't had time."

"We need it, Fay. Please do something!"

"Okay, I'll try," I said, as I hung up the phone, feeling a little defeated.

One of the other dietitians happened to be passing by and asked me what that was all about. I told her and she said, "Oh, I'll help you;

it sounds like an interesting project." She was young and unmarried, lived in a small apartment and needed something to fill her time. I did not realize at the time that she also had her eye on one of the handsome young oral surgeons.

Saturday mornings found me in my kitchen, devising ways of using a straw to get a person to consume their daily requirement of fibre, protein, iron, calories and nutrients. During these times, my dietitian friend was noticeably absent. She did make it one day to taste and assess what I had prepared.

Then came the real test. I invited all the oral surgeons and plastic surgeons who were involved in the surgeries, along with their wives, to the "Wired Jaw Party" at our house. All the food to be tasted was set up on a large table in the downstairs recreation room. Everything, of course, was puréed. We made bran muffins, mixed with enough milk to get it through the straw, and it tasted the same as eating bran muffins and milk. Meat was puréed and strained and mixed with various juices and broths; I added avocado to chicken soup to add calories; even salads were included in the diet. The flavour was more than acceptable, but the appearance was anything but appealing.

We all gathered around the table, straws and bowls in hand. They were somewhat appalled at what was in front of them, but I said, "This is what you require your patients to do, so now you'll know what they have to go through."

The young oral surgeon, who my friend was paying a great deal of attention to, kept saying, "Which one is the liver? I know you dietitians, and I know there is liver here somewhere!" I kept assuring him that there was no liver in any of the dishes, but with each new dish, he kept asking, "Is this one the liver?"

We finished tasting and evaluating about 15 dishes. They all agreed that it had gone well and approved everything, that is, as long as they did not have to eat it! We then went upstairs and had a real meal of roast beef, potatoes and vegetables, of which they were very happy to partake.

The recipes were taken to the hospital where they were typed up and printed with the Victoria General Hospital logo and given to the doctors. They could then give them to their patients.

Soon after, I was told that my dietitian friend was going on a speaking trip with the young oral surgeon to promote the new diet that he and she had developed. He even had the nerve to print it up, taking off the Victoria General name and logo and replacing it with his! They even took off the wired jaw name, which I thought had a little panache to it, and renamed it the "Blenderized Diet." How boring. In any case, I'm sure that they had a very nice time touring the province together.

A few years later, various pharmaceutical companies began producing products such as Ensure and Boost, complete meals in liquid form. This was much simpler for everyone as it reduced the preparation time and the delivery to patients to almost nothing.

But I use this story as an example of the kinds of things that dietitians do. I became involved in many aspects of a dietitian's work, from administrative (which I hated) to long-term care, juvenile diabetes (at the new hospital, I was head of the Juvenile Diabetes Section) and developing post-surgery and allergy diets. In the latter case, a woman came to me saying I was her last resort. Her nine-month-old baby was covered in scabs, and no one could figure out why. When I observed her nursing him, he turned red. I determined that he was allergic to some of the food she was eating. Until then, it was thought that allergens didn't pass through the placental barrier, so it wasn't common knowledge that foods consumed by the mother could, through her milk, affect the baby. So I started developing (on my own time, I might add) an allergy diet.

Pre-Occupied with Painting

When I was working at the hospital, we moved house. The one we had moved into when we left Qualicum was a 1960s split-level rectangular box with room to expand on the lower level — and we did.

Graham built two bedrooms and a bathroom to add to our other three bedrooms, and I was relieved of being on the other end of a heavy four-by-eight-foot plywood sheet, as Ken, now 13, was bigger and stronger than I. He helped his father with the building. I was relegated to mudding, sanding and painting the gyprock walls — and received failure marks from my perfectionist husband.

But something else was afoot. The house overlooked a small orchard and, beyond, glimpses of the ocean — a very acceptable outlook for us. However, with "progress" abounding, the owners sub-divided the property across from us and the lot was sold to an architect who proceeded to build one of the ugliest houses in Victoria. We had to move. By chance, I found a lovely older home on the ocean, on Beach Drive, and we moved in just before Christmas. It was indeed in need of some redecorating, and undaunted by my limited painting skills, I got right to work.

Our house at 607 Beach Drive

Our house on Beach Drive, as seen from the road, with Trial Island and the Olympic Mountains in the background

When I paint, everything gets painted: walls, trim, hinges and me. Somehow, my face has as much paint on it as the walls, my hair is either white, blue or green, and the baggy paint smock I wear is a kaleidoscope of colours.

We still had a Chinese vegetable man come to our house on Beach Drive in the 1980s who, I'm told, was the last in Canada — the end of an era

We had not been in our house long, and although we had had a few important upgrades done, like plumbing and carpeting, we had a long list of to-dos that we had inflicted upon ourselves. One of these was eliminating some of the more garish assaults on the house by sanding and painting most of the walls. The husband of the former owner was the proprietor of The House of Cards, a greeting card store, and it appeared as though he was trying to transfer some of the designs of his cards to the walls of the house. The sunroom was papered with orange and red wallpaper overlaid with black flocking. This was further enhanced by an orange free-standing enamel fireplace and a white carpet. Other rooms had been equally tormented. Graham had his work cut out for him with all the fix-it things necessary in a normal house, but this house, being old and on the water, required a great deal more care and attention than most.

I was on my usual third rung of the ladder with the usual amount of paint in my hair, on my face and my painting smock, when the doorbell rang. Should I bother to answer it? My hands were also wet with paint. It rang again so I decided that it must be something urgent. I opened the door to a respectable, nicely dressed woman in her fifties. "I'm Mrs. Bower," she said, "and I want to ask you what your stand is on the pump station." The pump station was to be a small pumping station to transfer the raw sewage that was being discharged at McMicking Point, essentially right on the shore adjacent to the golf course, to Clover Point, where it would be discharged into a long outfall that would run into the Strait of Juan de Fuca.

Graham and me, by our house on Beach Drive, with our children, from left, Shelley, Ron and Ken, and our dog, Haile — circa 1976

"Well," I said, "we have just recently moved in, and I haven't been following the situation closely, but I understand that it could go in under the bank in the park and be quite unobtrusive. Or," I continued, "perhaps the corner of the Victoria Golf Club under the bank; no one would even know it was there."

"The golf club would never allow that to happen," she countered.

Anxious to get rid of her and wanting to end the discussion, I made my fatal error. "I understand," I said, "that there is a house down the way that the district has offered to buy, at fair market value. It's in a good location and it might be the solution to the problem."

She became very angry, muttered something about my stupidity and stormed off. I wasn't sure what I had said to offend her but did find out later. Mrs. Bower was the wife of the publisher of the *Times Colonist* newspaper, and the house to which I was referring, was their house. Diplomacy was never my forte.

In any case, the house in question was not only non-conforming, it should never have had a permit to be built. There was not enough land to build it on, and even today, the real depth of the property is only about 18 feet. But it was built, by whom I don't know, and now owned by a very powerful man.

I did not involve myself further, thinking that the municipality had things in hand. I was working, still had two children in high school and one who had just announced that he was going to Papua New Guinea with CUSO. Not surprisingly, I heard nothing more from Mrs. Bower.

A night out — circa 1980

4

Travel Tales

PAPUA NEW GUINEA

A New World

"I'm going to New Guinea, Mom," said Ken. "I have joined CUSO [Canadian University Services Overseas] and that's where I'm being sent."

"Oh." I said, trying to mask my shock and surprise. "That's down near Borneo, isn't it?"

"Well, yes and no," he replied. "It is in the South Pacific, but it is quite a long way from Borneo."

He had just finished his science degree at the University of Victoria, and like so many other young people, he wasn't sure where he wanted to go next. This sounded like a good diversion and an opportunity to travel and perhaps help people in a developing country. And a developing country it was indeed, as we were to discover in the near future.

The Leahy brothers and Jim Taylor had fought their way through dense jungle infested with snakes, leaches and wild boars in 1930 to find that there were people living in the Highlands in primitive conditions. They had never seen white men before, and white men had never seen them. No one had even known of their existence. The coastal people were known, of course, but not the Highlanders, and Ken was going into the Highlands. Papua New Guinea had been ruled by various countries — Germany, Britain and, last of all, Australia — from which it had been granted independence in 1975. This was much too premature for a tribal country that had 850 languages, very few educated people and little, if any, business acumen.

In late August 1979, Ken left for Ottawa, where all the volunteers met for a week's briefing before heading out to their respective destinations. It was not easy saying goodbye to our oldest son, not knowing much about where he was going, what conditions he would find there and whether we would ever see him again. He had been assigned to a school in the Highlands in a place called Mendi, altitude about 1,600 metres, possibly near where the Leahy party had encountered the New Guinea Highlanders.

Word came back fairly quickly (the school had a telephone) that he had arrived safely, he had a house and was about to embark on his teaching career. The area, he said, was beautiful and spring-like, being only six degrees south of the equator and at that high altitude. He said they grew vegetables in the high country and their stable food was the sweet potato, which the women cultivated. In fact, the women did almost everything, including looking after the pigs, tending the garden, raising their children and almost any other work that was required. The men, on the other hand, dug the garden, a once-a-year job, and spent the rest of the time decorating themselves. They were called upon from time to time to engage in a bow-and-arrow war, which usually lasted about 20 minutes, until someone was killed or injured, or to take part in a *Sing Sing*, a ceremonial occasion where they dress in their finery, decorate themselves with bird of paradise feathers, each tribe using a particular bird of paradise, dance and sing and enjoy a luau, with the men receiving the choice parts of the meat and the women, if they are fortunate, receiving the ears or some other less succulent part. The women were little more than slaves. They either slept with the pigs or in a corner of the man's house. There was very little interaction between the two, and for the most part, only for sexual purposes. The children lived with the mother until the age of six, when the boys would move into their father's hut, and the mother most likely was left with the pigs. The women were frightened and in awe of the men and the men too were afraid of the women, particularly during the menses, when they felt that a drop of menstrual blood would destroy them.

And so, in a country with a culture so different to his own, Ken began to teach sewing and pig husbandry, neither of which he knew anything about. The headmaster, an Irishman, and another teacher, an Australian, were already teaching the core subjects at a very scaled down level, so Ken got the leftover courses and was not sure how to proceed. Working with the boys in the class, building pig pens and raising pigs, was not too difficult for Ken, but what would he do with the girls? Whenever he walked into the classroom, they would scurry off and hide, and besides, he couldn't possibly teach them anything they did not already know. In the end, he gave them a hammer and some nails and they merrily whacked away on the pigpens and, in fact, were better workers than the boys. Later in the year, one of the girls made him a *bilum* (a woven bag made from vines, which the people, particularly the women, used for carrying everything from babies to vegetables), which he used then and for many years after, and which he still has.

The pictures he sent home, the descriptions of all the activities and the unusual culture began to interest us, and we asked if it would be possible to visit him. "Yes," he said, "that would be wonderful, and I will come to the coast to meet you. We'll take some time in Rabaul and in Lae, and come back up on the Highlands Highway. I can probably find a vehicle to deliver to someone up here."

We prepared over the next few months. No travel agent had ever heard of Papua New Guinea, and when they did find it on the map, they had no way of knowing how to get there.

Finally, we received our routing. Victoria to Vancouver, to San Francisco, and to Sydney, Australia, where we would stop for a few days. Then on to Brisbane and then Port Moresby, the capital of Papua New Guinea, with a day there, and then to Rabaul where we would meet Ken. There would be three of us: Graham, me and Shelley, aged 15. Ron had gone to university in Toronto and was not able to take the time away.

It was December 1978. We arrived in Sydney two days before New Year's and found our way to a hotel that friends had told us was central, good, reasonable and had a wonderful free breakfast. It was all these things, but our friends had neglected to tell us that this particular hotel was right in the middle of the red light district! People on the airport bus were appalled at where we were getting off, and I do have to admit, we saw sights that we had never seen before or since. It was, in fact, rather fun. Those same friends also introduced us to friends of theirs who lived in Hunters Hill, an upscale part of the city. When Frank came to pick us up for a party at their home on New Year's Eve, he was quite disgusted with our accommodations and swore he would never drive his Mercedes to that area again.

It turned out to be a memorable evening, as they had three teen-aged boys all vying for the attention of my daughter, who could hardly understand a word of what they were saying due to their harsh Australian accent. Meanwhile, we were having our own problems with the dialect, and Graham, discovering that Frank liked to target shoot, spent a good part of the evening telling him about his rifle range in Parksville. Frank did not say a word, but later in the evening, his wife pulled out several large medals that Frank had won at Bisley, a prestigious shooting competition in England. Graham felt like a fool, and for the first time in his life, he remained almost speechless for the rest of the evening. Later, sitting on the deck overlooking Sydney Harbour, the bridge and the opera house, we were treated to a spectacular fireworks display to usher in the new year. Frank did take us back to the hotel later that evening, without incident.

The next day, I phoned to confirm our airline reservation to Port Moresby to find that we were not booked (our travel agent had made a mistake) and there were only two planes a week, both of which were fully booked. Eventually, the ticket agent managed to find one ticket, which I said to book in Graham's name, and Shelley and I would try to fly standby or follow at a later date. We arrived at the airport the next day to find a long standby queue. It did not look hopeful until, at the last minute, we were called. We had to fill out forms, pay departure tax and run as fast as we could to catch the plane, which was parked far out on the runway, halfway, it seemed, to Brisbane.

We boarded, the door slammed shut and we cast about for empty seats. Graham was already on, of course, and Shelley and I found the last two seats, mine beside a young Japanese man. Panting with exhaustion, I buckled my seat belt, the plane took off and I began to wonder who the pilot was. As we were flying on Air New Guinea, I silently hoped it was not someone straight out of the jungles of Papua New Guinea.

Then, from the cockpit, came one of the sweetest sounds I have ever heard: the voice of the pilot, in a slow Texas drawl: "Hello, y'all, how ya doin' back there? This is Capt'n Martin speakin', and I'm going to tell you a little about this place. That down there is the Coral Sea; we did a lot of fighting there in World War Two."

"What he say? What he say?" came a voice from beside me. I told him in clear English, and when I finished, he stood in front of his tour group and explained what the pilot had said. His group was suitably impressed that he could understand the captain so well, and the trip continued with the captain speaking, me repeating and the tour guide receiving many accolades for his proficiency in the language, Texas accent and all.

During the intervening time, I spoke to him slowly and carefully and asked where they had been. "Oh," he said, "one week tour. We do Australia and New Zealand."

"How can you possibly do all that in one week?" I asked.

"Oh, easy," he said. "We do Canada and USA in two weeks. Land Vancouver, go to Banff, Toronto, New York, Florida, Los Angeles, San Francisco and home. Two weeks, easy."

The Australia–New Zealand trip was really only five days as one night each way had to be spent in Port Moresby. Later in our travels to other parts of the world, we often encountered Japanese tourists sleeping on buses, planes and trains and missing almost all the scenery, and we understood.

We landed safely in Port Moresby and stepped out of the plane to face 42-degree-Celsius temperatures. Even Australia had not prepared us for this.

Port Moresby

It was not without research and preparation that we faced our new adventure. We had received instructions from Ken on some of the culture and mores of the country, most of which were directed to me. This was partly because of the male-female protocol that was very defined, and partly because Ken was a little concerned about his outspoken mother and what trouble she might cause. Most of all, I was not to point with my finger, a habit we all have in North America, when we want to show someone something or emphasize a point, and particularly, I was not to point at a man as it may cast a spell on him and he may die as a consequence.

We had gathered all the information we could, from books and documentaries, as well as from a young New Guinean we had by chance been introduced to, who was taking a master's degree at the University of Victoria. He had a good apartment in the lower part of a house close to the university, but the house was up for sale and he had to find new accommodations quickly. He should, in fact, have already completed his degree, but it was taking longer than it should have because of cultural differences and limitations of Papua New Guinea's education system. Graham, of course, came to the rescue by offering him a place to live … in our house, free of charge, for however long it took to finish his degree. It took a year! And even then, I'm not sure he really got the degree.

Sam was a good person and an ideal houseguest. It was interesting, though, to see how well he adapted to our country's affluent lifestyle. This young man, from a family of eight children, who had grown up in a mud hut on an island off Papua New Guinea and followed all the rituals and tribal requirements, arrived at our home with tennis racquets, Nike running shoes, all the right clothes and sports gear and enough bath gel and cologne to stock a small esthetician's salon. I do have to admit that the upstairs part of our house had never smelled better as he gave himself the full treatment of oils and colognes daily — perhaps an homage to the days at home where men spent most of their time combing, grooming and decorating themselves.

All of Sam's family had done well. His brother in Port Moresby had taken law, another brother in Rabaul was also a lawyer, a sister was in the medical profession and the others had attained some degree of higher education. The education system in Papua New Guinea was set up so that a village would pay for its brightest children to go to school. They had exams in Grade 6 (probably equivalent to Canada's Grade 3 or 4), and if they passed, they were sent to a middle school and boarded. They were tested again in Grade 9, and if they were found capable, the government took over the educational responsibility. If a student was deemed suitable, they could go as high on the academic ladder as they wished and be totally funded by the government. This had been the case with Sam and his siblings and explained how Sam had been able to travel halfway around the world to study in Victoria.

We did learn a little from Sam regarding customs and culture, but he, by this time, had become worldly and did not talk much about his background and primitive lifestyle. He was also from an island four degrees off the equator, which was a long way from the Highlands, both in distance and in customs. He did, however, put us in touch with his brothers, one of whom lived in Port Moresby. And here we were in Port Moresby, where our experiences in a country very different from our own were to begin.

As we stepped off the plane, we could see the hotel where we would spend our first two nights. Under normal circumstances, we would have walked, but the intense heat almost felled us and we took a taxi the 600 metres. Dinner that evening was interesting. We, the only diners in the dining room, were surrounded by 10 young men, all in various stages of learning how to serve. On the table was an array of cutlery that even I had no idea when to use. There was a boy to pour water, a boy to put your napkin on your lap, a boy to bring the bread, a boy to take your order and a boy to bring your meal. Then there was the dessert boy and the tea and coffee boy. I tried in vain to have a cup of tea served with my meal, as the tea and coffee boy had been trained in good British fashion to *never* serve tea until the meal was over. It was a somewhat comical but, at the same time, unnerving experience to go through, and we wondered how these young men would put all this training to use in the real world.

Tom, Sam's brother, picked us up the next day for a tour of the city and environs. The roads did not go far into the countryside, so it was possible to see most everything of note in a reasonable length of time. Tom was a very pleasant young man, a few years older than Sam, married to a white Australian and with three young children whom we would meet for dinner later that day. Tom showed us the town, which probably had a population of about 30,000, but with, unfortunately, a large number of "rascals." These were usually the young boys who had achieved some degree of education but had not been able to pass some of the required exams and had been dropped from the school system. They did not wish to return to their villages and were not educated enough to work in stores, banks or almost any other job. They then moved to the main city of the country, where they caused a great deal of havoc by breaking into homes, mugging people and generally being a disruptive element. The country was having a hard time dealing with these young men.

Tom also showed us many of the remnants of World War II, such as old guns, tanks, planes and embankments. In 1979, these people were still reliving the war. It had, of course, been the single most significant event that had ever happened there, and the people had been at the mercy of both the Americans and the Japanese. My understanding is that they had been treated rather badly by both. But it had been exciting, and it had made them more aware of all the other people in their own country, and that there were other countries with different-looking people.

Before going to Tom's house, we stopped at a grocery store so he could pick up some food for supper. Trying to be useful, I immediately grabbed a basket on wheels and began pushing it. A great grin broke out on Tom's face and he began to laugh. We weren't sure why, but when he regained his composure, he said, "This is a historical first. It is the first time in Papua New Guinea that a white woman has ever pushed a grocery basket for a Black man!" It had pleased him immensely.

We then went to his home, a standard oblong house built with aluminum siding to discourage termites and louvered windows to let the air through but protect against strong wind and rain and rascals. His wife was charming. He had met her when he was studying law in Australia, and they had come back to PNG to help with the administration of a newly independent country. He may also have been bound to return to work in the country as payment for his education. His children too were very appealing and we had a pleasant evening with them, free from the dining room circus at the hotel. Tom returned us to the hotel so that we could get ready for our early morning flight to Rabaul. We were anxious to see Ken.

Rabaul

Ken looked well and happy to see us, which is not always the case when it comes to young people and their parents and younger sister. Perhaps the 15-month absence from us or anyone else from home had made him mellower than usual. We were staying at a three- or four-star hotel in Rabaul, but it was surprisingly expensive. I mentioned this to the hotel manager as we were sitting on the patio having a drink before dinner, as I was curious how a place with so few tourists (I had expected them to be promoting tourism) could attract people to the area with such high prices. "Oh," he said, "we are not the least bit concerned about tourists. We fill the hotel every night with government people."

"What kind of government workers and what do they do?" I pressed on.

"They have meetings and seminars, sometimes an engineer will be brought out to discuss a project, and often they will spend a week or two at a time here."

I said no more but could see from this very small incident that the money received from other countries, particularly Australia, was not going to last long if this wasteful practice by government continued; and, indeed, we found, travelling by plane, we would be seated by some government official wearing a crisp shirt and neat shorts with a hole through the septum in his nose where a bone had originally been placed during a tribal ceremony. Still, it was pleasant sitting there with tropical flowers surrounding the patio, three caged sulfur-crested cockatoos making their very loud additions to the conversation and the warmth surrounding us like a heated blanket.

Our first sightseeing stop was the magnificent World War II memorial cemetery containing the remains of 3,000 Commonwealth soldiers — 2,000 Australians, the others British, Indian and Papua New Guinean. It is always sobering to attend these gravesites and read the names and ages of the young men who lie beneath the markers. The Australians were all young, 19 to 23, and we shed a tear for them and their families. The Indians were older, 35 to 40, no doubt from a special unit of longtime professional soldiers. I don't remember the British or Papua New Guinean graves; they may have been in another section of this magnificent cemetery surrounded by frangipanni trees, their petals softly drifting through the sunshine to land gently on the grass or the grave markers.

This part of Papua New Guinea was occupied by the Japanese from the spring of 1942 to September 1943, when it was reclaimed by the Allied Forces under General Douglas MacArthur.

The next day, we went to explore the area around Rabaul and investigate some of the WWII memorabilia, which abound in the area. The Japanese invaded Lae, farther up the coast, in 1942. Their intent was to use Papua New Guinea as a base to attack and invade Australia. They were stopped short just a few miles from Port Moresby. Fierce fighting occurred all along the coast and Rabaul still had, at the time we were there, many of the weapons of war in caves and tunnels throughout the area. One memorable spot was a huge cave entirely full of equipment, landing craft, tanks and guns. It was a strange feeling edging our way through the rusting and sinister-looking machinery and remembering the terrible battles that raged there not that many years prior. There was also a plethora of stories of Japanese soldiers who had remained hidden for many years after the war was over, afraid to come out, perhaps because of losing face, not knowing whether or not the war was over or for fear of punishment and disgrace. We knew we wouldn't come across one at this late date, yet there was that eerie feeling that we might find a skeleton or at least a few bones that would cause some revulsion or horror.

There is a huge volcano in Simpson Harbour in Rabaul, and it has belched and erupted many times over the years. That is why there are so many caves and tunnels in the area, which enabled the Japanese to hide their equipment. The last eruption occurred in 1994, laying waste to the town and covering it with a thick film of grey ash. Hotels have been rebuilt since then, and Rabaul is now something of a tourist area, and a particularly good one for diving among the many ships that have been resting at the bottom of the harbour since 1945.

Rabaul was a sleepy, somewhat idyllic place with lush vegetation, a few coconut and papaya plantations — not the small Hawaiian ones we know, but huge sweet orange ones — and many missions. It was the home of the Tolai people, a tall, elegant group that benefitted from an abundance of fruit and a variety of seafood from the nearby ocean. Of all the Papua New Guineans we encountered, these were certainly the best-looking and the most worldly. Several churches had schools and missions established there to "save the native population." Ken had no use for them at all as he felt that they took away much more than they gave.

We headed down to Simpson Harbour to see if we could rent an outrigger canoe to cross over to the volcano, now in a dormant state. We found an old man and his daughter on the shore and he agreed to let us have two canoes to get across the bay, probably a distance of about half a mile. Through sign language and Ken's fractured pidgin, we managed to negotiate a deal. Suddenly, Ken, Shelley and Graham were in one outrigger and I was left with the daughter in the other small canoe. I protested loudly but was told that his unmarried daughter could not be in a canoe with men! So three strong men and my strong young daughter flew across the harbour in minutes while I, the only power in the outrigger, took much longer to get across. The girl, who was steering the vessel, did not feel it was her job to put any effort into getting us to our destination. Furthermore, the outrigger was made of solid hollowed out wood and very heavy; luckily there was a small breeze on our stern helping me across, but I was still exhausted by the time we reached the volcano.

We climbed to the top of the cone, our feet warmed by the intense heat below the surface. We looked down into the crater belching smoke and fumes and spent some time investigating the rocks and debris thrown up by former eruptions. Then it was time to go.

By this time, the wind had stiffened and would be against us on our return trip. I knew that I was not strong enough to get the two of us back to the other shore by myself. Undiplomatically, I said, "Ken, I need you in my outrigger; I cannot take the thing back with the wind against me." Ken jumped into the canoe, but when we arrived back, there was a roar from the father. I just held up my hand (I didn't point my finger) and said, "Yes," very assertively. He had calmed down a little when we reached the other side, enough at least, to accept our money, but I'm still not sure whether he was protecting his daughter, or the all-important man, my son.

Lae and Travelling to the Highlands

Although I have a basic understanding of Bernoulli's principle, I can't really understand, from a practical point of view, how a huge piece of metal can fly high in the sky without any visible support. Therefore, I never can get totally relaxed in the passenger seat of an airplane; however, the flight between Rabaul and Lae was short and comfortable and capably flown by a blond, Australian pilot.

Lae, the second largest town in PNG was hot, humid, muddy and grey. Corrugated aluminum was widely used in construction for roofs, fences and the front of most buildings, which gave the place a dreary temporary or half-finished appearance. The heat was oppressive and seemed to come from every direction. I was relieved to see that our motel for the night had a swimming pool of sorts. It was a large, painted, concrete rectangle with little to recommend it, but at least it looked like somewhere we could cool off. Wrong! As we eased ourselves in, we discovered that it was the temperature of a very warm bath, unrefreshing and a little slimy. A quick cool shower erased our heat problems for the moment and we were ready to begin our exploration of Lae and its surrounding areas.

The one redeeming feature of Lei was a beautiful botanical garden, possibly one of the best in the world for tropical plants. We may have been very fortunate, or it may be like this all the time, but there were literally thousands of orchid plants with hundreds of different varieties, and almost all were in bloom. How can one begin to describe a garden such as this? It is impossible. We wandered about in awe and near silence as we went from one garden to the other, admiring their individual beauty.

Sadly, we had to tear ourselves away from this divine place and we left, feeling both humble and inspired.

The next morning was to be the beginning of the real test of our ability to cope with the many situations we would encounter on our trip to and in the Highlands. Ken had been breaking us in very carefully. Lae is the gateway to the Highlands, and Ken had assured us that he would be able to drive a truck up the only existing road to the interior of the country. Unfortunately, no one needed a truck driven up at that time, but he was not perturbed. "We'll get the Highlands bus," he said casually, and began making enquiries. "Needum Highlands bus go Goroka," he said to someone he thought should know.

"Highlands bus no got," came the answer.

"How come Highlands bus no got?" Ken asked.

"Bugger up true," was the reply.

After much discussion in pidgin, or *tok pisin* as it is called, it was decided to try to find a public motor vehicle, usually a van of some kind, driven by a Papua New Guinean and owned by who knows. Ken took off in search of one of these vehicles and about half an hour later we saw him running down the muddy street, yelling, "Get your stuff together, we're leaving now. We can't afford to lose this guy." Following along behind him was a half-decent looking van with three wooly-haired men in the front seat. We grabbed our belongings, threw them in the van and we were off ... we thought.

One of the reasons that the Highlands bus was "bugger up true" is that the society operates on a *wantok* system. There are 850 languages in the country and each tribe has its own language or dialect. Whoever speaks the same language is your *wantok* (or "one talk") and has all the privileges of your immediate family so if you own a store, whatever is in that store belongs to the whole tribe. Not many Papua New Guineans own stores for that reason, since they can't stay in business due to too many *wantoks*. The same was true of the Highlands bus: too many *wantoks* not paying their fares. Another reason is that the society, particularly in the Highlands, has come from a primitive existence to modern society with all its mechanization in less than 50 years. As we were to discover, there were some gaps in their advancement: while they had learned to drive the equipment, they had absolutely no idea how to repair it.

Shelley and I ended up sitting behind the driver and his two *wantoks*, with Ken and Graham farther back in the van, and our journey started. We made a series of stops en route: first, to pick up another *wantok*. The second stop was for betel nut, or *bui* as they call it. It is ground up seed of the *Areca catechu*, a type of palm tree, and they mix it with lime and eat it. It gives them some kind of high, but it also turns their gums blood red and causes their teeth to fall out. It is not grown in the Highlands, so this was an opportunity for them to make a little money on the side. Then the middle *wantok* decided that he was going to woo me. He turned around and gave me a wide, bloody, toothless smile. This surprised me as, considering the male-female protocol here, I didn't think I would rate, but maybe their perception of white women was different. Wasn't I lucky? The next stop was at some kind of a fruit stand where my wooer got out and procured a watermelon — for me — which he proceeded to cut up and hand me pieces of. Ken, in the back seat of the van, was laughing his head off.

Next, we stopped to pick up a small, very old lady with a bilum full of cabbages. Her load was so heavy, and she was so small, she could not make it up the step. Graham reached out and lifted her aboard. She sat down next to us with her load of cabbages. I learned later that this tiny, frail lady, who looked about 80 years old, was probably under 40. She reached over and grabbed Shelley on the bare part of her leg. Shelley froze; she didn't know what to do. I took out some bracelets I had brought and gave them to her and she released her hold, very pleased with her newfound wealth. All Papua New Guineans love to decorate themselves but usually only the men get the opportunity.

Meanwhile, the road was getting narrower, rougher and more precipitous. We bounced, bumped and rolled as we made our way higher, peering down at steep precipices. All the while, lover boy in the front seat was giving me frequent bold smiles and trying to entice me with more watermelon.

Next, we picked up three young girls who, when they saw Ken, headed to the back of the van, and as we jolted along, they would repeatedly peak at him from under dirty towels and giggle.

As if planned, the last passenger that we picked up was waiting where there was hardly room for him and the van between the mountain and the precipice. There stood a man in full regalia: bark belt, ass grass, rag down the front, painted face, a very sharp machete, an even sharper axe and a headdress. I assume he thought himself most handsome.

As we gained altitude, the air became fresher, the countryside became astoundingly beautiful and the road less precipitous. I was beginning to enjoy this little adventure. Suddenly, we were in Goroka, our destination for the night. Ken had arranged to use the house of one of the teachers, a young woman from Canada, who was away. While we were not expecting luxurious accommodation, we were not prepared for what we found awaiting us. She had given her key to two of her most trusted students to look after the place and they, in true *wantok* fashion, had moved in with most of the tribe. Not since the days of Genghis Khan has a house been more trashed. Ken roared in and yelled "PISS OFF!" and they were gone, leaving us to try to resurrect some semblance of order for the night. I will never forget the kitchen pots with hard, sticky rice clinging to the insides, three inches thick and harder than concrete, and trying to get just one pot clean enough to make enough food to sustain us.

Mount Hagen

The next leg of our trip was through the Chimbu province and on to Mount Hagen, the capital of the Eastern Highlands. This is a somewhat dangerous area as the tribes are quite warlike, and Ken wanted to be sure that we arrived in daylight. There was a bus, of sorts, that travelled between Goroka and Mount Hagen —sometimes — and we went down to the shed to see if it was running that day. It was, and we were to leave within the hour. The walk to the bus was fascinating. The people were wandering about, wearing their traditional dress: ass grass and a rag hanging from a bark belt for the men, and the women with ragged skirts and a top made out of whatever material they could find and always with their bilums full of food, babies or wood, with the straps across their forehead, and often coaxing a pig along the road on the end of a rope. Added to this scene was the backdrop of an airport with the loud roar of the planes taking off and landing. This huge dichotomy of cultures and mechanization did not seem strange to anyone but us.

There is, however, a wonderful story of when planes first began to arrive during the Second World War. They were U.S. planes loaded with large amounts of cargo. The people had never seen a bird like this before, nor had they seen so much wealth in the form of goods and food. They were amazed, they were intrigued and they were acquisitive. They wanted to know how to get one of these big and bountiful birds for themselves, so at night they were out with torches looking underneath the bird to see if it was male or female. They reasoned that if they could capture one of the opposite sex, they could mate them and there was a good chance they could obtain one of the offspring! This was the fascination of Papua New Guinea at that time. They were still living primitively, while wanting to quickly adapt to a modern lifestyle without quite understanding that "middle step," as we shall see.

Upon arriving at the bus shed, we were confronted with two Papua New Guineans and a very ancient (or at least it looked ancient) orange (I think it was orange under the dirt and the rust) bus. This was to be our transportation to Mount Hagen. We climbed aboard along with several locals in various arrays of clothing and carrying bundles of who knows what. Fortunately, no pigs were invited to come along for the ride. We rumbled out of the shed and onto a very rough road, a continuation of the Highlands Highway. To call it a highway would be to stretch the imagination to the utmost. It was a narrow dirt road with thousands of potholes and no work crews to maintain it. It rains heavily there at times, which only exacerbated the growth of the holes and made it very hard on any vehicle that used the road to transport goods or people.

We had not lurched along the road very far when Graham remarked, "This thing isn't going to get us to Mount Hagen in this condition; in fact, it isn't going to get us much farther." Within 100 metres of him saying this, the whole side of the bus sagged and there was much yelling and wringing of hands from the driver and his assistant. Finally, it was ascertained that we had to go back to the shed. We crept back and an hour later they began the repair. First they had to find a piece to replace the broken one. That took an hour, going through all the other wrecks of buses in and around the shed. Then they got out the jack, which they had no idea how to use. They finally got it working and began to jack up the bus. As they tried to make the repair, the bus continued to lift, and was getting farther and farther away from the replacement piece. I said to Graham, "Why don't you tell them how to use the jack so that we can get out of here?" His reply was terse: "Because I don't want a machete through my skull. If I start giving them instructions, they may take a very dim view of it and our trip will be over." An hour later, he decided to carefully make a suggestion or two on how it might work if they did this or that. Surprisingly, they were quite grateful for the help and within minutes we were on our way. The necessary middle step.

We jostled and jolted along through beautiful green countryside, with people coming out of the bush and getting on the bus, and others getting off the bus and disappearing into the bush. There seemed to be very few paying for the ride, so we had to assume that we were their only cash customers. We could see no sign of huts anywhere until the sun began to set and we noticed fires dotted all through the trees and realized that somewhere in there were some kinds of mud huts or shelters.

Well after dark, and not long before reaching Mount Hagen, it began to rain heavily. A torrential rain. The bus stopped in front of a large complex and Ken said, "Okay, Mom, you go in and see if they can accommodate us." I reached for my raincoat, one I had carefully chosen to wear in this climate — light, bright red, with a hood. It was gone. True to the what's-yours-is-mine culture, someone must have seen the corner of it sticking out of my packsack and had decided it was more useful to them than to me. I was furious, but Ken said, "That's the way it is here, Mom. You look after everything you don't want to lose."

"Well," I replied crustily, "I'm soaked to the skin, my hair is straight as a poker and I look like a tramp. No one is going to give me a room, so you'll have to come with me."

He laughed and said, "Look at me; I look far worse than you. I'll scare them to death." At that time, he had long, blond hair and looked like a wet, bedraggled yak. We went together and the Australian lady who owned and ran the place said yes, she could put us up for the night. We hauled ourselves and our packs up the stairs to minute rooms, some with one bed and some with two. There was nothing else in the room, but the beds were comfortable and the rooms were hospital clean. The walls were stark white, the floors battleship grey, and we were very happy to be off the bus and in a warm, dry building. When we asked about the bathrooms, we were shown the men's bathroom just down the hall.

"What about the women's washroom?" I asked.

"Oh," was the response, "it's down the stairs, and about 50 metres into the bush." An outhouse! In this country, where men are kings and women are slaves, I was prepared to make concessions, but Shelley and I were not prepared to head into the bush in the pouring rain at night to relieve ourselves. Graham was enjoying this immensely, but he finally said, "I'll go into the men's washroom, make sure there is no one inside and stand guard until you come out." Having said that, he marched into the men's washroom, did a quick look around and pronounced it all clear. I went in and got into one of the stalls and suddenly felt a presence in the room. I could hear breathing in the stall next to me and realized that a Papua New Guinean man was standing on the toilet to avoid being seen and was far more frightened than I was. I came out, washed my hands and brushed my teeth, all the while he was in the stall trying not to breathe, and I was having a good chuckle about the turn of events. A few minutes later we peeked out of our room and saw him nervously making his escape down the hall and into the night.

The next morning, we were given an Australian breakfast, complete with beans, tomatoes, bacon, eggs and coffee. The woman who ran the place was a tough Aussie; she had to be to deal with all the problems in this part of the country, from stealing, to tribal wars, to dealing with people who were very superstitious and, in some cases, not too civilized. We went to pay our bill. No, she didn't take Visa. We did not have enough cash and she did not take cheques. "Well," she said, "when you get home just send me a money order or bank draft, that will be fine."

"We won't be home for over a month. You will trust us that long?"

"I can read people pretty well," she answered. "You are trustworthy. I've been wrong only once."

With that, we thanked her and went in search of a car. Ken assured us that we could rent one here and drive it to Mendi, our destination. We did get a rental car in reasonable shape and with tires that looked like they may last long enough to carry us the next 70 kilometres.

Before leaving Mount Hagen, though, Ken had something to show us. We drove to a large dusty enclosure that had cages of every kind of bird of paradise found in Papua New Guinea. It was an awesome experience. There were blue ones, red ones and orange ones, and each bird's plumage was unique. Although the area in which they were kept was dusty and without lawn or trees, the birds themselves were in good condition. Obviously, whoever looked after them took their job seriously. It was a privilege to see them all and although perhaps they should have been released into the wild, there was little guarantee of their safety, as the men were always on the lookout for them to use in their *Sing Sing* or tribal festivities. Each tribe uses a different bird of paradise feather to distinguish themselves, and millions have been slaughtered for this reason. There are, in fact, very few birds of paradise left in New Guinea, the only place in the world where they live. We also saw cassowaries, as well as tree kangaroos, an animal I was unfamiliar with. They are small kangaroos with a coarse, hard fur that looks like fake fur and like it was made from Dacron. It seemed strange to see kangaroos climbing trees, but apparently they were originally tree animals, and when a few fell to the ground, they decided they liked it there and evolved into land animals.

We began the last leg of our journey with some trepidation in this somewhat dangerous part of the country. Ken was driving and relating to us the story of the American man who hit a young girl and made the mistake of getting out of the car. When the tribe appeared, they took a machete and sliced his head open. That is what they call "pay-back." An eye for an eye, so to speak. Then they looked at the girl, who was not dead, just stunned, and they put a machete to her head as well. The pay-back had already been paid, so they had to kill her too. He was watching the road carefully as he did not want to hit a child or a pig. Pigs could also be a major problem as they are the tribes' wealth. It was at this point that Shelley, who had been suffering from a stomach upset, announced that she had to go to the bathroom. Of course, there were no Motel 6s or gas stations along the way, and Ken did not want to stop. I said, "Well, you either stop and let her out, or there is going to be a very big mess in the car." He stopped and Shelley raced for the bush. At that moment, I noticed a wooly black head in the bush heading in the same direction as Shelley. I was concerned. Finally I asked Ken to go and see if there was a problem. Grudgingly, he got out of the car, and a few seconds later I heard the familiar loud refrain, "Piss off!" A young boy of about 15 or 16 was standing over a squatting Shelley, demanding 20 toya (their money) for the use of his land! The rest of the trip was relatively uneventful, and we arrived safely in Mendi.

Mendi

Ken had a decent house. It was a rectangle, mounted on metal stilts to keep the termites at bay. The exterior was aluminum and the windows were louvred. There were three bedrooms, a living room, dining area, kitchen and bathroom. The floors were made from a beautiful local wood, as were the walls, but what a mess they were, covered with a green mold. I was stunned. How could Ken allow this to happen, considering the excellent upbringing we had given him. "You can't do anything about it, Mom," he said, noticing that I was eyeing the green slime.

"Well," I answered, "I'm quite sure I can get rid of that with some bleach and some elbow grease. I'll get at it tomorrow."

He showed us the washing machine that more or less worked, and suggested to keep a watch on any clothes we hung on the line and to never leave them out overnight, as one of the *wantoks* would just help themselves.

Then we were off to the pig pens to see how his project was going. He showed us all the pens and troughs he and the students had made, as well as a number of very healthy-looking pigs. "That one is mine," he said. "We'll slaughter him and have a *mumu* on the weekend. Everyone will come to help and, of course, to eat." That meant all the students, the headmaster, an Irishman of about 40, and the expat teachers, a New Zealander and an Australian. The preparations were to begin the next day, and we were very much looking forward to it.

Mendi was, and still is, one of the more remote parts of the country and most people lived in mud huts or lean-to shacks. They wore their traditional dress and spoke their particular tribal language. The students, for the most part, wore old shorts and t-shirts and could speak English quite well. Their accent was soft and gentle, and I have always wondered how that could be when they were taught English by the Australians, whose accents, from my perspective, were neither soft nor gentle. They led a subsistence life, their gardens being their main source of food. In the Highlands, vegetables grow well but fruit does not, so their main foods were cabbage, sweet potato and pumpkin tips (a green). Protein was in very short supply, in fact, almost non-existent, and the people who owned a pig guarded it ferociously. And when they had to leave their huts, the pig came too, hobbled by a rope around its front leg to prevent escape and encouraged to move by a light switch to its buttocks. The women, of course, tended the pigs at all times, as they did the gardens. In fact, when a woman came of age, at 12 or 13 years old, she was gifted a digging stick, her sole tool, to be used for the rest of her life. And her life would not be a long one.

CUSO, or one of the other organizations trying to help the people, had introduced a new vegetable called a wing bean, which was supposed to be high in protein. It was interesting looking, an elongated box shape, with feathery projections from the corners. I took some home to cook one day and found them almost inedible, as did everyone else, even the poorly nourished natives.

The climate in Mendi was refreshing. After the oppressive heat of the coast, the cooler air (around the mid-twenties) imbued us with energy, and the following day, we were ready for all tasks at hand. We set off with buckets of water spiked with bleach and began our assault on the moldy walls and floors. It took all day, but we were pleased with our results. The floors sparkled, the walls shone and the wood revealed all its beautiful grain and colour. Ken was out with his students, slaughtering and de-bristling the pig. Feeling pleased with ourselves, we sat down to a dinner of cabbage, sweet potato and fish.

The fish had arrived at the back door about mid-afternoon, brought by a young boy who had caught it in the river (a rare event) and wanted plenty of money for "piss." I was happy to give him plenty money for the "piss."

Preparing for the Luau

The next day, they prepared for the big *mumu*, digging the pit, which was done by the male students, and getting the rocks ready. They gathered banana leaves, and the girls prepared the vegetables. It was an idyllic setting, with the sun shining on the slopes of the hills, which looked like enormous lawns decorated with large upswept trees. On the highest mountain peak, a little snow was visible. Ken and Graham were cutting the meat when I noticed that whenever Ken had an abrasion of any kind from a sharp bone or a nick from the knife, it would leave an angry looking mark. I also had noticed a rather nasty ulcer on his leg that he dismissed as "a common problem in these parts." I was not a bit convinced and asked him about his diet, and what protein he was eating. It turned out, almost none. "Why aren't you getting more protein food?" I asked.

I knew that the frozen meat and fish in the store looked and was substandard, but it was still protein. "Don't worry, Mom," he said, "the natives don't eat much meat and they get along okay. Besides, I needed some transportation, so I bought a small motorcycle and they don't give you enough money to do more than just barely get by. Besides, the stores rob you and no one can afford to buy food there." Then he dropped another little remark. "Next term, I will be going up to Koroba to help build a school and there is an abattoir. I'll have plenty of meat there."

"Where is Koroba?" I asked, as calmly as I could, knowing that we were as far as we could go by road.

"Oh, it's north and west of here, about eight hours away, but it's over very bad terrain. The Duna and Huli tribes live there. They are the ones who use human hair wigs as their headdresses."

"Have they ever seen white people there?" I asked tentatively.

"Don't think so. Not many, anyway. Dave [the Australian] is going to be the headmaster. He's a great guy, we'll have a good time."

With that, we went back to our respective jobs and I was left thinking that I had just one month to feed him some good high-protein meals and get him back to a healthier state.

The next day was interesting, watching the searing rocks covered by banana leaves and grass, then the pork added, then the leaves, followed by layers of vegetables, more leaves and grass, and finally covered to cook for several hours in the pit.

When it all came out, it was a festive occasion. Everyone was dressed as well as they could be, and the tables looked lovely, decorated with available leaves and flowers. The drinks were mostly fruit juices, except for the expats who had little stashes of various types of liquor (ourselves included) and who pretty much used up all of the reserve. The food was exquisite and eaten entirely by the approximately 35 people in attendance. Almost all the pork was consumed by the students who, in their entire lives, had never been given that much meat. By the time the festivities were over and the cleanup finished, we went back into the house, tired but very happy. Except, was I seeing correctly, or did I notice a faint green tinge to the walls? Had I had that much libation? I'd check again in the morning.

It was always a wonderful feeling to wake up in the Highlands of Papua New Guinea to the sounds of a type of yodelling that carried from mountaintop to mountaintop. They called to each other in this way, and it was transferred from area to area as they passed the communication along. I will never know what they were saying; maybe a baby was born or someone had broken a leg, or there was a new pig in the pen, but whatever it was, it was musical and reassuring. I missed hearing it when I got back to Victoria.

Out into the living room I went, and no, my eyes had not deceived me the previous night; the green mold was insidiously growing and advancing along the walls. It grew as I watched it. There was nothing to do but shrug my shoulders and apologize to Ken. He just laughed. "You can't beat it and it doesn't seem to bother anyone too much, but I'll show you what it has done to my camera lens." It too was covered in green mold, and we were going to have to find him a new lens so that he could continue to take the outstanding pictures and tapes that he would send back to us in Victoria.

Walking in the Highlands

Papua New Guineans have large, wide feet and what appear to be prehensile toes. They do not wear shoes. It often rains at night, leaving the hillsides coated with a slippery mud and they must walk up these greasy slopes to their gardens, which are scattered throughout the uneven mountain terrain. To do this, they must dig their toes into the hillside. It was on one of those clear rain-washed mornings that we decided to take a walk in the hills, led by one of Ken's students, Wari. It wasn't long before we were on the ascent and Shelley, wearing flip-flops, was down in the mud and arose looking more like a Gorokan mudman than my beautiful daughter. She was good-natured about it and we pressed on, our running shoes, by this time, coated with mud.

As we walked along, we became aware of a presence behind us and turned to see eight Papua New Guineans following us. A few minutes later there were 20, and shortly after that there were 30 bodies, mostly women and children. Wari shooed them away with a short rebuff and they all disappeared as quickly as they had come … for a while. But it wasn't long until we had another contingent following, and we went through the same procedure. "Why are they following us, Wari?" I asked. "Do they want something?"

"No," he replied, "they are just curious and want to know what is going on, where we are going and what we are doing. It will be some-thing for them to talk about for the next month."

We continued through the fresh countryside, watching the women at work in the gardens and admiring the beautiful vista we were afforded as we walked. Many were calling out to us, and Wari was answering them in their language, but I could always hear the word *Europa* being exchanged. "Why are you telling them that we are Europeans and not North Americans?" I wanted to know.

"Because they would not know anything about North America or any other part of the world. They know that there is a place where Australians come from, but they think that is Europe too. All white people are European." I thought about this for a while and began to realize that these people were right. All white people are of European descent.

Eventually we did a big loop and ended up back at the house, where we washed our shoes and hung them on the line to dry. We left them on the line all night. The next morning, when we went out to retrieve our shoes and get ready for the day's adventure, there were no shoes on the line, nor on the ground, nor anywhere else that we could see. Ken had warned us, and we had forgotten. We were now *wantoks*, since we were living there, and what was ours was theirs, or so they thought! In a way, it was amusing, but in a way, it was not, as we were travelling as light as possible and did not have a large choice of footwear. Ken thought we may see them walking around in the village later in the day, but that did not occur.

The previous day, we had been down to see the hospital, as we were interested in the medical services that were offered. Most of the patients were admitted for injuries, often caused by arrows during their tribal wars. Sometimes Ken assisted the Canadian doctor in the surgery although he had no experience in the medical field at that time. This is likely what planted the seed for Ken to eventually become a doctor. The hospital was a rectangular building that could house about 10 patients. It had a small surgery, a kitchen and two rooms containing bed frames and nothing else. There were no bedside tables, no basins or equipment of any kind and no mattresses on the beds. The bed frames were beautiful, made from local wood, criss-crossed to form a lattice. They were a work of art and very heavy. "Where are the mattresses?" I asked, "Well," said Ken, "by now you know the *wantok* philosophy — if there is anything that is moveable, the patients will take it when they are discharged. We did have mattresses once, but they all went on a walkabout, and there is no point in replacing them. The patients sleep on the bare bed." As beautiful as the beds were, I could not imagine myself sleeping on bare hardwood after having had surgery to put my intestines back inside my body, but that is what they did and their survival rate was excellent.

Two nights after our walk in the hills with Wari, I went out for a walk. It was early evening and the air was fresh and clean. Various flowers and plants were blooming along the road, including the lovely, deadly nightshade, its huge yellow trumpets reaching almost to the ground. As I walked along, I saw one of Ken's students approaching. "Hi, Lumph," I said. "Where are you off to this evening?"

"My uncle is getting out of the hospital tonight," he replied, "and I have brought him a change of clothes." I looked, and in his hand he was carrying a large bunch of "ti" leaves, the ass grass that they wore down the back of their bark belts, one of the most important parts of their wardrobes. I had to wish him goodnight and turn away quickly, in case he saw the laughter rising up my body to my face.

There were many more walks and wonderful experiences in Mendi, but one of the most memorable was the day we went to the Hum Gap a few miles away. Ken borrowed a Land Rover type of vehicle; it was very old with no springs and no proper seats. We took off on a road that was not really a road and jolted and pitched for about an hour until we arrived at our destination, sore and bruised. The view was lovely, but we had not come entirely for the view. One of Ken's students' family was starting a small coffee plantation, and we were going to see coffee grown, ripened and picked. The parents did not speak English, but Ken's student Towe was there and showed us around the area. They were indeed the most progressive Papuans that we had met.

After a while, Graham, Shelley and I decided to go a little farther afield and do a little walking to make sure our bones and other parts of our bodies were still intact after the ride up. We had not gone far when out of the bushes came three Papuan warriors in full dress. Their faces were painted bright yellow and blue, and their knives and axes were sharpened like razor blades. They were carrying large black bows with their arrows at the ready. We stood there, mouths agape, not knowing what to do next, while they stood there, staring at these strange-looking people with white skin and odd clothes, not sure what to do either. It was a very tense situation as we could not easily communicate and we did not dare move.

Finally, Graham very slowly and carefully began to try to communicate with sign language. He carefully showed them the Polaroid camera he had with him and convinced them to stand still as he pointed it at them. I was sure at this point they would attack, but they did not. Slowly, the picture began to emerge and Graham gave it to one of the men, showing him he must hold it between his thumb and forefinger and not let go. As the picture became more clear, they began dancing about like three little boys at a birthday party, the one hanging onto the corner of the picture so tightly you could see the red blood through his fingernails. The tension was broken, and we knew we were safe. They would have done anything we asked, but all Graham wanted was more pictures of them taken with his good camera. Papuan men are quite vain and spend a great deal of time sharpening their axes or decorating themselves, but they never get to see themselves or know how they look, so they complied willingly. We did get some wonderful pictures, but unfortunately every picture contains a very noticeable black and white Polaroid photograph being tightly held by one of the men. When people see this picture, it is a little hard to convince them that these men had never seen white people before. Towe told Ken that a week later, this same man was still wandering around the area with the picture still firmly between his thumb and forefinger, afraid to let go for fear the picture would disappear!

Goodbye

Our departure date from Papua New Guinea was imminent, and we were looking forward to it with very mixed feelings. In the short time we were there, we had learned so much about the different and difficult culture and about the giant leap the people had had to make from primitive to modern in the space of 40 years. True, most were still living in huts and shacks in villages throughout the jungle; they were still calling to one another by transmitting voice messages from mountain top to mountain top; they were still carrying out their tribal rituals, some of them quite brutal or deadly; and they were still locked into their *wantok* system of "shared ownership." But they were being brought into the modern world by use of machinery: cars, trucks and airplanes. The young, who were intellectually gifted, were being educated in provincial schools taught by Australians, New Zealanders, Canadians, Americans and Europeans. Some were studying to become teachers, doctors, dentists, nurses and lawyers. They had gained their independence and some were involved in the administration of their own new country. Admittedly, it was a some-what rocky beginning, but one that was under the close surveillance of the Australian government, a major contributor to their economy.

There were many things that had not gone well in this transition. Their diets, which had been marginal and lacking sufficient protein, were further compromised by their curtailment of peanut growing. At one time, peanuts, which were a staple food supplying protein, fat and other essential vitamins and minerals, were being supplanted by candy and lolly water (soft drinks) heavily promoted by Coca-Cola. The example of tall, strong Australians eating these foods and the enchantment of the sweet taste made them believe that it was not only good, but good for them. They did not realize that the "whites" were eating other things that gave them adequate nutrition. They could not afford the other things; thus their nutrition suffered and, consequently, their health.

Use of alcohol was also becoming a problem, brought in by the "whites" who, either naturally or by years of use, have a better tolerance for its effects. In a culture rooted in a male superiority belief, the already downtrodden and abused females suffered even more brutal attacks by their husbands.

Another major problem was caused by the failure of part of the education system. As the villages raised money to send one or two of their brightest children to school, it was important for these children to succeed. As described earlier, if they could reach Grade 9 and pass to the next level, the state educated them for as long and as far as they were able to go, but many did not make it that far. They may have made it to Grade 6, failed the next level of exams and were forced to leave. Either due to shame or to a small degree of sophistication they had received in school, they were unwilling to return to their villages. They were not educated enough to hold white-collar types of jobs, so they tended to migrate to major towns, especially Port Moresby, where they joined the gangs of "rascals." These gangs were a serious problem, as they were involved in muggings and robberies. We saw some evidence of this on our return trip.

It was going to be difficult to leave this idyllic landscape, the wonderful students and the other people we had met. We would also miss the excitement that evolved as each new day unfolded, but, as with any trip, one is prepared for a certain length of stay, and we had reached that point. After a month away, it was time to return to work and school. Also, Ken too was getting ready to move on to the new school to be built in Kordoba. He was up for the challenge and anxious to get going.

We had decided not to try to return down the Highlands Highway to Lei and then board a plane from there to Port Moresby. Instead, we would fly from Mendi to Tari and then on to Port Moresby. The flight to Tari with one Australian pilot — no co-pilot — and one Papua New

Guinean flight attendant, who I'm sure could not have helped anyone had the need arisen, was brief and uneventful until we approached a landing strip that was not only short, but on a 10 to 15 degree incline. I could not see how we were going to do anything but crash onto the runway but, miraculously, the pilot pulled up at the last moment and we landed with reasonable delicacy.

Shortly thereafter, we took off on the last leg of this journey. We were flying between jagged mountains, breathtaking in their beauty but terrifying in their closeness and irregularity. I was thinking how relieved I was to have a competent pilot on this trip and one who knew his way through the tortuous route, when I chanced to look through the open cockpit door to see our competent pilot with his feet up on the dashboard and reading the funny papers! Having seen the muddy rivers winding through the dense jungle below and knowing that if we went down and survived the crash, we would not survive the snakes, crocodiles and mosquitoes, I wanted to go forward and tell him to get his feet down and pay attention to his flying but was restrained by my husband who assured me all would be well. I was not appeased or amused but, a short time later, we were safely on the ground at the Port Moresby airport.

This time, although the temperature remains much the same year round, we did not notice the intense heat we had felt on our arrival a month previously. It was very warm, to be sure, but we did not feel that our skin was being fried or that we were not capable of walking more than a few steps. As the airport hotel was fully booked (probably with government representatives), it was necessary to stay in a hotel in town. We thought we might go to dinner, see a movie and have a look through some of the stores. I also thought that I could have my hair done — a luxury unavailable in the Highlands.

On arrival at the hotel, we were greeted, shown to our rooms and given many warnings: don't go to a movie, don't go out to dinner and don't go out on the streets more than a few doors from the hotel, because the "rascals" are causing a great deal of trouble right now. There is a hairdresser three doors down; it is safe to go there. The hairdresser, an Australian lady, welcomed me, and then I noticed that she was flanked by two large Doberman pinschers. "They won't bother you," she said. "Sit down and make yourself comfortable. I have them with me at all times to protect me from the "raskals." Never one to be intimidated by dogs, I felt quite at ease as she did my hair and put me under the dryer. She then picked up some papers and said, "I have to go to the bank. I won't be long. The dogs will look after you." With that, she was gone. After a few minutes, the dryer was a bit hot, so I pushed it back and began to get out of the chair to pick up a magazine. That's when I heard the growls and looked up to see two sets of very large, bared teeth attached to two dogs who looked twice the size of the two I saw upon entering the shop. I eased back into my chair, trying hard not to breathe. The dogs relaxed to a sitting position, still with their eyes fixed upon me and watching for any untoward movement. I sat there frozen, almost hoping for a few rascals to appear to create some diversion for the dogs. Finally, the lady returned with assurances that they would not have harmed me unless I had tried to leave the premises! I happily paid her and scuttled down the street, without further incident, to the hotel where we all stayed for the rest of the afternoon, evening and night.

The next morning, we were off to the airport. We had accumulated a number of treasures on our travels, among which was a large black palm bow, a hand-carved spear and some arrows with exquisitely woven decorations on the shafts. Graham had lashed them together carefully and was hopeful that we could get them on the plane.

The airport building was basic and square with few amenities. There was no air conditioning, only large fans that hung from the ceiling. As we walked in, I noticed a fellow tourist holding a beautifully carved spear upright. And I saw the fans. Before I could warn him of the inevitable demise of his valuable artifact, he stepped forward. The fan, with a loud thump, clipped off the first foot of the spear and sent the rest clattering to the floor. He stood there in dismay as we slid our precious bundle along the floor towards the check-in counter. Graham, with his great power of persuasion and a big smile, managed to get it loaded on the plane.

We left Papua New Guinea with a feeling of wonder, humility and accomplishment. We were grateful for all the new experiences we had had and all the knowledge we had gained of this country and its different, rich culture.

5

Challenges on the Homefront

BATTLES FOR THE COMMUNITY AND FOR LIFE

Local Battles

On returning home from Papua New Guinea, and after my initial encounter with Mrs. Bower about the pump station two months prior, I read in the newspaper that there were some negotiations going on regarding the purchase of the Bower house, which would be demolished and used as the site of the pump station. This house, a poorly built structure, had at some point received a building permit that never should have been granted. It was a mistake by a municipal clerk but, once given, it could not be revoked. It was park property, and the depth of the land was only 18 feet. A concrete footing was placed well down the bank and a house was erected on top of it.

Mr. Bower would not sell. He enlisted some vocal neighbours who did not want a pump station near their house, although few people knew how the station would look or how it would function.

The only solution would be expropriation and no one on Oak Bay Council, including the mayor, Brian Smith, wanted to antagonize Mr. Bower, the publisher of the *Times Colonist*. This was particularly true for Mr. Smith, as he had aspirations to continue on in politics to at least the provincial level. He later became the Attorney General of British Columbia and subsequently the chairman of the Canadian National Railway and BC Hydro, and was inept at both.

The issue became quiescent, and I became complacent. I thought, foolishly, that solutions were in hand and a new location for the pump station would be found. It did not matter much to me whether it was in close proximity to me or not, it just had to be done. The beaches were completely fouled by the debris from the spillage of raw sewage from several outfalls along our shores. Within the space of half an hour, one could pick up enough condoms and tampon applicators to fill two shoeboxes. I know because I did it. There was raw faeces littering the beaches, some human, some canine.

The plan was to strain and comminute (grind) the sewage and pump it to Clover Point where a new and long outfall was being built. At least it would concentrate the sewage in one place with a view to treatment at some time in the future. It is interesting to note that the Pollution Control Board demands that when an outfall is created, land must be made available for a treatment plant to be built, if and when required. This does not seem to be the case in Victoria.

I noticed that something was happening on Kitty Islet, which is a park. A major excavation was in progress. Puzzled, I phoned the municipal office to be told that they were doing studies on an old Indian midden. As I hung up the phone, I realized that something was amiss; archeological studies are seldom done with a large bulldozer!

With some difficulty, I was able to learn that this excavation was in preparation for a new outfall and comminuter. It would be difficult to put in, due to tidal currents, so it would require a great deal of blasting and land disruption, possible damage to surrounding homes. It would cost $3 million, and it was doomed to failure.

Naïvely, I made an appointment with the mayor, Brian Smith, to discuss the project and the fact that the engineering study done by a well-respected firm in Texas clearly stated that the effluent would be cleaned up on the golf course side of the Bay, but Shoal Bay and Kitty Bay (Rattenbury Bay) would still be polluted.

Mr. Smith was not interested in my concerns. In fact, he was not only rude, but also so verbally abusive I was physically shaking when I left his office. His wife, who was in the waiting room as I left, had obviously heard the conversation and she too looked shocked and shaken. Of course, at that time, I had not realized that his political aspirations were to rise to higher levels than mayor.

Undaunted and sure of my facts, I began to mount a campaign.

My husband drew a map of where the new outfall was to go, and I wrote the explanation and cited the studies I had read. I left the pamphlets on the street near Kitty Islet and soon the phone calls began. A committee was formed. One of the committee members, a gentleman and longtime resident of Oak Bay, Ed Flanagan, became my most staunch supporter and later an alderman on Oak Bay Council.

This committee was not a group of professional protesters, but a committee of doctors, lawyers, university professors, teachers and nurses as well as others whose background I did not know. But they were all educated, articulate, concerned citizens of Oak Bay, as well as some from Victoria and Saanich. Unfortunately, I did not get much support from my neighbours. The ones down the street, Mr. Bowers' anti-pump crew, were not able see further than their NIMBY (not in my backyard) approach to the pump station, the ones up the hill were, in one way or another, required to be silent on the problem, including Dr. Arneil, the Medical Health Officer for the Capital Regional District (CRD).

In the meantime, I read every report I could find. I read the Daniel, Mann, Johnson & Mendenhall report, which clearly stated that this outfall would not free the area of pollution.

This report, commissioned by the CRD, at a cost of $300,000 (at that time, a very considerable amount of money), looked at all factors involved and concluded that this outfall, even if the effluent was ground (or comminuted), would not free the beaches from contamination. It would be less visible, but the coliform (bacteria) count would remain unacceptable.

I knew every coliform count on all the outfalls in Saanich, Oak Bay, Victoria and Esquimalt, and I knew where all the outfalls were. There were 20 of them. I knew how much mercury, copper, silver, gold and lead they were spewing into the ocean. I also knew that a large part of Saanich, all of Oak Bay, and some of Victoria, including all the effluent from the Jubilee Hospital, were sending us their sewage.

In a community where liquor stores and gas stations were not allowed, we seemed to be overly willing to pour sewage from our and other communities into the ocean, 300 hundred feet from shore.

I also read studies on bacteria and viruses being encapsulated in the fresh water and rising to the surface within minutes of being poured into the sea. With the winds in Victoria, all this could be blown up to five miles inland, perhaps causing health problems throughout the city. Some bacteria may not survive the cold, but viruses can. Were there going to be more studies on this?

The more our ad hoc committee learned, the more we realized that few people had been doing their homework.

On one trip to an Oak Bay council meeting, I asked the council if they knew exactly where this outfall was to go. Only one member, Susan Brice, who had been down to see me knew the exact location, yet they were going to vote on this expensive experiment without even knowing its location or design.

In retrospect, I realize that some amusing incidents occurred as well, although, I admit I did not find it all that entertaining at the time. One such incident occurred in the summer of 1979. One Sunday, I went to the Oak Bay Tennis Club and arrived just before tea. Tea, at our little club, was quite a social event, with most of the players stopping for tea and conversation. The building itself was a dilapidated green wooden structure, held together by the ivy that clung to the foundations and walls. It also housed a mostly non-functioning toilet. But there was an electrical outlet, a Ping-Pong sized table and a freestanding old wooden bookcase. Nevertheless, tea was the highlight of the afternoon, and everyone partook. Also, everyone took turns making and serving the tea and supplying the cookies and cake.

That day, our mayor and his wife, Barbara, were on tea duty. I said nothing to Mr. Smith but remarked to everyone that I would be leaving a few pamphlets on the proposed sewage outfall for anyone interested. I then went out for a game.

When I returned, I noticed that all the pamphlets were gone. "Oh," I commented, "has all the information been picked up?" I was dubious, as most people had been outside or playing tennis during this short interval. A few minutes later, Barbara reached behind the bookcase and brought out the pamphlets. "These must be what you are looking for," she said, as Brian scowled in the corner. I thanked her but realized that she was risking his wrath. They later divorced, not due to her witnessing the two incidents with me, I'm sure, but perhaps, in part, to his somewhat childish reaction to controversy.

Not long after this, Mr. Smith resigned from his municipal job to run for a seat in the British Columbia Legislature, which he won.

Enter the next Oak Bay mayor: Douglas Watts, an engineer with the B.C. government's Ministry of Environment. I was delighted, as he seemed to be an ideal spokesman for both Oak Bay and the environment; unfortunately, that was not the case. In fact, it seemed to me and others that the last thing Mr. Watts was concerned about was the environment.

One of his first statements was, "We should be putting something back into the food chain by use of long outfalls." No mention of chemical pollutants, bacteria, viruses or floatable material, of which there were many. But the proposed outfall was only 700 feet from Beach Drive and only 300 feet from Kitty Islet, a much-used park. Many children played on the Islet year-round, and in the water during the summer months. This was not going to be a long outfall, and it was not going to achieve the desired effect of pollution-free beaches.

I invited Mr. Watts to my house to observe for himself the water flow on a rising tide. He agreed to come. That evening, on a full flood tide, there was a good amount of debris in the water — driftwood, small logs and seaweed. As we watched the flotsam and jetsam flow to the location of where the proposed outfall would discharge, it began to flow sideways and become caught in the back eddies, which form on a flood tide. The scene before us couldn't have been more graphic.

"You see," I said, "when the effluent surfaces, it will follow the same pattern and become caught in the back eddies and land on our beaches, just as the debris is doing."

He glanced out the window, shrugged his shoulders and said, "I have a gut feeling this is going to work." I was horrified and disgusted.

I said, "It is totally irresponsible, for you, an engineer, to deny what you see before you: to close your eyes and ears to engineering reports that say that this outfall will not work, and to subject your constituents to a large amount of unnecessary construction and expense. I'm appalled!"

With that, he shrugged and stated, "I have to go now; I have a son graduating from the University of Toronto tomorrow, and I have to catch an early plane in the morning."

"I too have a son graduating from the University of Toronto tomorrow," I said, "but I do not have salaries from the government, from the Capital Regional District and from Oak Bay, which would allow me to attend his graduation. Goodbye, Mr. Watts."

In the meantime, volumes were written in the newspaper regarding the condition of the water surrounding greater Victoria, Saanich, Oak Bay, Victoria, Esquimalt and extending to Sooke, which were all serviced by short outfalls. Our ad hoc committee attended many Oak Bay Council meetings, hoping to get commitments from the councillors as to where they stood on the question of the new outfall. We also made presentations on various areas of concern, such as aerosol contamination and the possibility of the Finnerty Cove effluent being diverted to the northeast sewer line and discharging into McNeil Bay.

We had a large meeting attended by Oak Bay Council members, Mr. Bob Wright (chairman of CRD's waste management committee) and 300 concerned residents. At this meeting, the ad hoc committee and residents voiced their concerns regarding the proposed outfall and requested the CRD and the province to look towards a sewage treatment facility.

Mr. Wright rejected these concerns out of hand, saying, "A treatment plant would cost at least $60 million." I countered with, "Ten years ago it would have cost $6 million and ten years hence it might be $600 million." A short time later, he revised his opinion and began to propose a plan, including receiving funding from all three levels of government, to build a treatment facility.

After the meeting, there were a few negative letters in the *Oak Bay Star*, such as the one from the original anti-pump group (Mr. Bower's followers). This letter was several columns long, but the essence of it was that she trusted the experts who wanted the short outfall (as long as it was not near her house) and who assured her that she was not going to get tangled up in coliforms or bacteria or viruses. It was beyond her scope to discuss about two-thirds of what the ad hoc committee had to say and that she couldn't understand why the "Pettapiece Group" did not launch its campaign two years earlier instead of washing Victoria's dirty linen during the tourist season. She also had the location of Kitty Islet and McMicking Point mixed up.

I couldn't let this one go, as she had taken up so much space in the paper, so I answered her in the paper the following week, pointing out her lack of knowledge of the geography in front of her own house. There were also phone calls; I remember one, in particular, as I had stated at a meeting that I felt we were losing a great deal of valuable water in our dry climate and, facing an expanding population, it might be an idea to try to reclaim some of the wastewater to be used on parks and golf courses. The caller began: "You stupid woman. Don't you realize that if you put all that water on Beacon Hill Park it would wash the whole bank away?" And another, who said: "I work for the Pollution Control Board. You are absolutely right. Keep going with your campaign."

"Will you come to court with me?" I asked.

"No," he said. "You are absolutely right, but I can't afford to lose my job."

We then went on to another large meeting, this one convened by the Victoria Chamber of Commerce. I was spokesperson for our group and voiced our concerns that the new outfall would fail to eliminate the pollution problem and that it was an unnecessary and expensive experiment, the cost of which the taxpayers would have to bear.

Frank White, owner of White's dive shop, a spokesperson for the Vancouver Island Professional and Amateur Divers Association, and a diver himself, noted that he has seen the waterfront around Victoria gradually close down due to pollution. Dr. Derek Ellis, a biology professor at the University of Victoria, was basically neutral, saying that although sewage may provide nutrients, we may be over-fertilizing. "A bigger worry," he said, "is the number of other contaminants like pesticides going into the sea through the sewer system." Dr. Paul Broome, president of the Victoria Medical Association, expressed concern about the number of diseases that might be spread by improper sewage disposal. Dr. Allan Arneil, regional health officer, also expressed concern, although he stressed that he was more concerned about what might happen in the future. Bob Ferguson, director of the Ministry of Environment's waste management branch, defended his department's policy of using long outfalls before treatment plants. Dr. Antione Koers, Nanaimo manager for Associated Engineering Services Ltd., recommended sewage treatment on the Saanich Peninsula and long outfalls on the South Coast, the elimination of private outfalls in Oak Bay and Saanich and the sewering of the Western Community.

And then the Right Honourable Stephen Rogers, environment minister, began his speech — and blamed everyone but his own government for lack of action on Greater Victoria's sewage problems. "I say it's time to get off your butts and get on the move. And I say it is time that the Regional District follows the advice of their costly engineering studies and gets on with the job. Because of inaction by local governments, Victoria is paying a high price, including fouled beaches, a contaminated marine resource, a threatened tourist industry and a great many irate citizens groups."

He also said that the CRD should get on with the short McMicking outfall! Rogers saved his strongest blasts for Oak Bay. "I'm told there are several overflows from combined storm and sanitary sewer manholes discharging directly to the foreshore along Beach Drive. Despite the public outcry against their foul beaches, there are still 20 major raw sewage discharges between Gordon Head and Clover Point, plus an estimated 70 or more private households discharging raw sewage to the same beaches. At Shoal (McNeil Bay), a community septic tank discharges directly onto the beach. Some of the people using this septic tank may well be the ones that objected to a pump house, which would have eliminated the problem."

I couldn't help but wonder, why didn't the municipality, the CRD and the environment ministry not have the courage to counter Mr. Bower and his group and get on with the pump house? Was it his power as a newspaper publisher, was it Brian Smith, attorney general, or was it the ministry itself having more politically important places to put their money? We'll never know, but I do know that at this point, and from then on, I became a much less trusting and naïve person.

Rogers then went on to justify why other regions in the province needed more provincial government funding than Victoria, but that he would make available any and all the expertise in his ministry to work with the engineering departments in the districts and the CRD — experts such as Mr. Watts with a "gut feeling" that the short outfall at Kitty Islet would work?

As we learned at the meeting, no matter what the public said and wanted, Mr. Rogers was not going to support a sewage treatment concept. He obviously had other areas where he wished to spend the department's money. Mayor Watts, being in the environment ministry, may or may not have been in a conflict of interest. In any case, at no time did he remove himself from discussions or voting privileges on Oak Bay Council and, of course, sided with (or succumbed to) the wishes of the environment minister. He also appointed himself to the committee on intergovernmental affairs, as well as the Oak Bay representative on the CRD.

It was apparent that our only recourse was court action.

With the help of our two volunteer lawyers, one, a government lawyer, the other a prosecuting attorney, a petition to halt the Kitty Islet Outfall was filed with the Supreme Court of British Columbia, February 20, 1981. We were seeking a court order to have the existing discharge of effluent through the McMicking Point outfall declared unlawful. This outfall, built in 1913, had never had a permit issued for dumping as was required by the Pollution Control Board Act. Furthermore, the new outfall was not an extension of McMicking Point and required a permit under the Act. A certificate had been issued to build the outfall but no permit was issued to use the outfall after it was built. We asked that the certificate be declared null and void because persons affected by the discharge should have been given an opportunity to register objections as per the PCA. As well, the contract between Dillingham Corporation (winners of the contract to build the outfall) and the CRD should be declared null and void because the CRD had no authority to enter into the contract. It had a certificate to build the outfall but not to discharge. It had no authority to spend public funds without first obtaining a permit for the outfall's use. An application for a permit might be refused and thus the proposed outfall could never legally be used. Another misuse of public funds.

As the proposed construction start time was slated for June 1981, our time frame was short. We were relieved to be able to obtain a court date for March 1981. We worked diligently on our petition with enormous input from our two lawyers. We had a large contingent of citizens willing to come to the courtroom with us, and Mr. Ron MacIsaak, who was one of the two volunteer lawyers, was to be the lawyer representing us.

We knew that there would be highly paid lawyers from at least two levels of government, the CRD and the provincial government, against us. A David and Goliath situation.

I was asked to speak at schools, teachers hoping that this may prove that sometimes the small voice can be heard. We were also on radio stations explaining why this outfall, in particular, should be stopped, and why our beaches were in such a shameful state. We were ready for the court challenge.

I should also mention that while all this was going on, I was still working full-time at the hospital, in addition to being president of the Dietitians' Association of B.C. Needless to say, my stress level was rather high.

Two days before our court date, Mr. MacIsaak called to say that he could not attend, as his father had died and he was called back to Saskatchewan. He said we could either apply for a later date or his young law assistant, David, who was conversant with the case, having done much of the research, could represent us. What a dilemma! If I postponed it, with our short time frame, we may lose the opportunity altogether. On the other hand, this young man had had very little courtroom experience. Mr. MacIsaak assured me that he thought he would do well. I accepted that and we went to court on the assigned date.

It was a disaster. The young lawyer did not put forth the petition properly or in its entirety. When the judge asked him to clarify his statements, he could not. The three experienced lawyers made short work of him, arguing that the municipality of Oak Bay had registered the outfall prior to 1979 but had never been required to obtain a permit.

Even though it was conceded that the CRD did not hold a pollution control permit, as required, the judge ruled that by not applying for or obtaining a permit, the CRD had acquired and preserved immunity. His last comment was that it was all political anyway.

David had lost! We all sat there in shock, trying to understand what had occurred, how it had occurred, and why.

When Mr. MacIsaak returned, he came to see me and suggested that we appeal the decision.

I would gladly have done so, even in my exhausted and somewhat depressed state, but I had been warned that if I lost the appeal, I could be liable for all court costs and lawyers' fees. As our only real asset was our house (which was not fully paid for), it would have to be sold to pay whatever fees were required. I did not feel that I could subject my family to this loss and perhaps even more expense. I had to abandon the fight, feeling guilty that I had disappointed the school children and all the others who had given me so much support.

And it still galls me that my and the committee members' tax dollars were spent to fight ourselves.

The Final Chapter

And so the blasting and digging began. Our dog, a placid and gentle black Labrador retriever, became jumpy and nervous. His usual place was in the kitchen family area and he never crossed into the rest of the house. In fact, when we wanted a family picture, dog and cat included, he had to be carried into the sunroom where he felt anxious and uncomfortable. But this all changed when he heard the whistle that preceded the blast. He would run to me no matter where I was in the house and stand by me, shivering, as we awaited the explosion.

A cursory inspection of the house had been done prior to the construction of the outfall to identify any existing cracks in the walls and foundation. The blasting went on and on, and the dog and the house shivered and shook with each detonation.

When it was over, it was deemed that our house had suffered no damage, but the house across the street and up the hill, built on solid rock (a house owned by one of the principals in the law firm that had defeated us in court) had sustained enough damage to warrant a full redecoration of the living room, dining room and bedrooms. A few months later, when the rain began, we had a severe leak in our bedroom. No responsibility for that crack was recognized, and we repaired it ourselves.

The entire summer wore on with dredges in the bay, trucks parked on our boulevard, the crashing of machinery on the hard rock and the continuum of earth-shaking blasts.

As we were on the scenic route, we erected a sign that read: "A new CRD outfall will dump raw sewage 300 feet from this shore." The mayor and council and the CRD were not pleased, but they could do nothing to make us remove it. Residents and tourists alike were beginning to realize that our city was not as unsoiled and pristine as it appeared on the surface.

Newspaper photo showing the sign we erected warning about raw sewage to be dumped close to shore

In May 1982, the new outfall began pumping raw sewage from Saanich, Victoria and Oak Bay into the waters of Enterprise Channel. It was 300 feet from the shore and 50 feet deep. The seagulls were ecstatic as was evidenced by their excited screams of appreciation for such a feast — and so close to the shore!

The coliform counts soared, reaching over 5,000 times the safe swimming standards in some areas. Some of the pollution was caused by storm drains connected directly to residences (our committee had also referred to the appalling state of our infrastructure).

Dr. Arneil, our regional health officer, decided to do a small survey of the airborne bacteria coming off the water. Our committee had pointed out the likelihood of viruses and bacteria being blown around the district, possibly to a distance of five miles. He placed Petri dishes on three nearby houses (ours being one of them) and one on his property on the top of a steep hill above Beach Drive to be used as a control. The state of the tide, faecal coliforms in the water and wind speed and direction were also noted.

The results were predictable. All the dishes had a significant density of coliforms, some more than others, depending on the velocity and direction of the wind. Dr. Arneil did tell me that when he presented this information to the CRD, one ore two comments were made to the effect that I was tampering with the Petri dishes. I think it gave him some pleasure in reporting to them that I had the least contamination on my dish and his carried the most.

It was evident that the situation was far worse than before the outfall went in. Mercifully, a new CRD engineer, Craig Sommerville, was brought in, replacing the old incapable engineer who was under the thumb of the CRD, with Mayor Watts at the helm, and not wanting to lose his pension. Wearily I made an appointment to see him, by this time expecting no support and possibly some abuse. I could not have been more wrong. I cannot remember the exact conversation, but he spoke for at least 15 minutes, disgusted at what had been allowed to happen and reiterating every argument we had used in our campaign: the embayment of the area, the tidal currents, the proximity to shore, the possible air contamination and more. "Don't worry," he said, "this outfall will not be dumping raw sewage on the beach in the near future. This should never have been allowed."

Meanwhile, Mr. Bower, the instigator of the "ban the pump house" campaign had quietly slipped away to take up residence in New Zealand. And our "I've-got-a-gut-feeling" mayor was now crying a different wail, like Chicken Little, "Something must be done, something must be done," unapologetic about the part he had played in the expensive fiasco.

Fortunately, the something that had to be done was not left in the hands of our environment ministry employee and non-environmental mayor. Mr. Sommerville was allotted $40,000 to study the beaches from Ogden Point to Gonzales Point. The results shocked everyone. Coliform counts were being measured from 41,000 per 100 millilitres to 1.3 million in McNeil Bay. Acceptable levels are less than 200 faecal coliforms per 100 millilitres. Wildwood Avenue reached 3.3 million.

He formulated a plan to install an east coast interceptor line that would intercept the Saanich and Victoria sewage at Fort and Foul Bays and divert it to Clover Point. All the Oak Bay sewage would then be stopped in the Windsor Park area, where a larger pump house would be required to divert it to the east coast interceptor and on to Clover Point. All the other outfalls would be closed and the sewage diverted to the main line. The main pump station would pump the sewage a short distance, where it would flow by gravity to its destination. It should be noted here that Oak Bay was paying 38 percent of the cost of the Clover Point outfall and only one small outfall at Harling Point had been diverted there.

Mr. Sommerville was given permission to go ahead with this diversion plan. Work proceeded and appeared to go well for a few years until the exact site for the pump station had to be decided. Windsor Park was the prime location. Typically, the uninformed NIMBY group rose again. How could anyone allow the desecration of Windsor Park? A pump station — unthinkable! So that idea was quashed. Two houses across the street on Currie Road were bought by the CRD as a possible location. This again brought about the nay-sayers.

I began to see where this was going and enlisted my neighbour Tony Gooch to help us get pump-house approval. Tony had recently moved from Toronto. He was an eloquent speaker, with an acceptable Australian accent, and he quickly grasped the situation. We also enlisted most of the people from our former ad hoc committee, born again as the Committee to Stop Pollution.

We put an ad in the paper, clearly explaining the problem, how the east coast interceptor would work and the funding of the project while also reminding readers that a pump house is not an evil, noisy, smelly edifice. Rather, most of it would be underground, using about 2,600 square feet above ground. The building would be about eight feet high and designed as a tasteful house with fences and proper landscaping.

Of course, there was the usual wringing of hands and weeping about the location. One man said he would have to move in order to protect his son from the stigma of living near a pump station.

At one meeting, Tony remarked, "The pump house has to go somewhere in the triangle between Windsor Park, the Marina and Glenlyon School. Wherever it goes, people are going to go up the wall, so someone has to bite the bullet and decide." He added, "We have two alternatives: we either allow the pump house to go through or people in Oak Bay will have to stop shitting."

This drew deep gasps from the genteel folk of Oak Bay, but he had made his point. The new mayor, Susan Brice — the only former alderman who had grasped the situation in the earlier outfall days and had voted against it — along with a new and more informed council voted to use the Currie Road site. Work commenced almost immediately.

The house atop the pump station is odourless, quiet and beautiful, in fact — the nicest one on the street. It is also a perfect neighbour — no barking dogs, no screaming children and no heavy traffic. Too bad the gentleman who was so concerned with the stigma of living nearby sold his house. The result is, of course, that our beaches and air are cleaner.

In retrospect, I have to say that the whole exercise was exhausting, gut-wrenching and frustrating, particularly when we had done the scientific research and presented it in a logical way to people we had voted in to make wise decisions. It was shameful that one powerful man, as well as a group of uninformed zealots and some civil servants with political ambitions could incur so much cost, so much anguish and so much disruption to the citizens of Oak Bay.

No longer naïve, but not a cynic, I like to think that our little committee helped lead the way to a better solution to a very large problem. We lost the battle but, in the end, we won the war.

A New Project ... and a New Discovery

With the sewer project behind us for now (Victoria did eventually get a tertiary treatment facility), we decided that it was time to make some upgrades to the house. It needed, among other things, a new roof, improved drainage, a new garage and a great deal of landscaping, particularly on the ocean side. We also decided to make a proper suite in the downstairs area and rent it to university students in the winter. In the summer, we would have the place to ourselves — a good plan that didn't quite work out that way, but turned out better! We rented the suite to a wonderful young couple, Rob and Lesley Termuende, who took turns going to university and working. When they finished, they got married at the house and they, particularly Rob, were an enormous help to us both during the time they lived in the suite — 21 years, to be exact.

We were fortunate to find an experienced and brilliant architect, Pam Charlesworth, who was able to upgrade older homes without losing their charm or identity. She also had a talented sister who was a landscape architect, who did an exceptional job of restoring the derelict grounds.

The work began and it occurred to me that while we were in the midst of destruction and construction, we should re-do the kitchen. I suggested it to Graham, who turned pale at the idea and the ensuing costs. With serious persuasion and a bit of whining, I finally convinced him that this was an appropriate time since it was necessary to take out one of the kitchen walls anyway. Work progressed; we were fortunate to have a good builder and wonderful Italian carpenter cabinet-maker. Even so, the job took quite a long time and, of course, money.

Finally, when it was all finished, I suggested that we should find a painter to do the kitchen. Graham balked. "No. No painter," he pronounced.

"Who is going to do it?" I asked.

"You are," he replied.

I was astounded. First of all, I was usually not allowed to paint because I was too messy. Secondly, I had a full-time job and still had to do the cooking, laundry and all the other household work. And thirdly, there were 50 deep cupboards in the kitchen, which had ten-foot ceilings, and furthermore, I'm afraid of heights. I couldn't even reach the back of the cupboards without crawling inside. Although this was very out of character for Graham, he was adamant.

Shortly after this discussion, he went on his annual hunting trip to the interior of the province, which he very much enjoyed. At the same time, I fervently hoped that he would not bring home a dead animal. Not that he wasn't a great game hunter, but usually I didn't have to worry about his bringing anything home. By then, I had eaten enough wild duck, venison and moose in my youth that I did not particularly enjoy.

He got back about 11 p.m. Sunday night, while I was on the top rung of the ladder, head in one of the high cupboards. "It was a good trip," he said. "But I found I was having some trouble breathing at the higher altitude."

I replied, not at all kindly, "Well, I'm having trouble breathing too, with my head stuck in the cupboard and inhaling paint fumes!"

Nothing more was said, but over the next few months, he found that he was a little out of breath climbing stairs and he couldn't run as easily as before. His doctor sent him to the cardiologist where he was pronounced clear of heart problems. He went to the respirologist, who told him, somewhat roughly, that he didn't have asthma and he didn't want to see him again.

His symptoms did not improve and we decided that maybe he should retire. We planned a 65th birthday and retirement party to take place in August. It was a gala affair with a Dixieland band, roasted lamb on a spit on the beach, Queen Elizabeth II (a very good imposter), an open bar and tables set up on the patios for the feast. It was great fun, and Graham was pleased.

He still had some lecturing to do in Banff, and since he had always wanted to see the canyons in Utah and Arizona, we decided to combine the trips, going to Banff first, then dropping down through

Montana, where he had a cousin, and then on to the Grand Canyon. It was a beautiful drive. The aspen trees were at their shimmering best and we were happy with our newfound freedom.

We carried on to Bryce Canyon and were truly in awe. It is a spectacular place, and no amount of description can do it justice. Graham could hardly wait to start taking pictures, a serious hobby of his. The next day, loaded up with heavy camera equipment (I was the grip), we took off to explore. We headed down a steep, winding, narrow trail, the mountain at our backs and a precipice in front. Partway down, he turned and looked at me, as I stood frozen against the mountain. Knowing my fear of heights, he said, "Please go back. I know you are not enjoying this. I can handle all the camera equipment and I won't be long." I went back to the top and waited and waited. Finally, he appeared, looking white and drained, with his heart fibrillating wildly. We were at 8,000 feet. We decided to leave for Zion National Park, which is at a much lower altitude and where you could view the mountains from the bottom, not the top.

The fibrillation would not stop. We phoned his doctor, who said, "Come home and I'll set up a series of tests and we'll find out what is going on." We decided we'd leave the next day, and I would do all the driving. Shortly after our journey began, I realized that I did not have my driver's licence with me but I didn't say a word; I just drove the 2,000 kilometres, hoping I would not be stopped for a misdemeanour or at the border crossing.

At home, the tests were done, this time by a different respirologist, who asked Graham, "How long have you had this?"

"Had what?"

"Pulmonary fibrosis."

I had a pretty good idea of what it was, due to my time working in hospitals, but said nothing. A few days later, after, I suspect, doing some research, Graham said, "Do you know what this is?"

"Yes," I said. We hugged and we cried.

Pulmonary fibrosis is a lung disease that is idiopathic, meaning it has no known cause. It is when the lung tissue becomes stiff, making it difficult for the lungs to work. The person becomes progressively short of breath, and the prognosis is three to five years. The only solution is a lung transplant. Not only is this a difficult operation, but there is also an insufficient supply of lungs.

Australia

We knew our time together was limited, so we decided to make the best use of it. Graham's mother had left him an inheritance that we invested in Microsoft, at that time (September 1994) an emerging company. It increased in value quickly, and on the basis of this, we planned a trip to Perth, Australia, where our son Ron now lived with his partner, Rick. I suggested a three-month trip, after which Graham said two weeks. Once again, I insisted on three months (after all, Australia is a very large country). He said one month. Again, I countered with three months and all he said was, "I like the way you compromise!"

We began in Sydney, then carried on to Brisbane and Townsville where we boarded a catamaran, snorkelled on the Great Barrier Reef and arrived in Cairns five days later. After exploring the northern area, we flew to Darwin, from which we could visit the Kakadu area and observe some of the Aboriginal life. We carried on to Alice Springs, where a boat race is run every year. I say "run" advisedly, because most years there is no water, so they cut holes in the bottoms of the boats and ran. We took two days to explore Ayers Rock (now named Uluru) and environs, and then flew to Perth to meet Ron and Rick.

Perth is a modern city between the Swan River and the Indian Ocean. The port for Perth is Freemantle, about 20 kilometres south. It is an intriguing, small city, with an abundance of sandstone buildings erected by the "convicts" who were sent over by Britain for major and minor crimes and used as labourers in the late 1800s. Most were sent to prisons where they lived in appalling conditions.

The boys toured us through most of the southern corner of Western Australia, showing us everything from dairy farms to stands of large timber, which yielded beautiful wood for furniture and decorative items. Unfortunately, in the early days, some of the valuable wood was wasted on utilitarian things such as bridges and railroad ties. After this, we had time to experience Perth and the surrounding areas, absorbing some of the customs and mores of Australia and its inhabitants.

Three weeks later, we boarded the Union Pacific train to cross the Nullarbor Desert, and on to Adelaide. From there, we picked up a car and drove along the southern coast to Melbourne. We then flew to Tasmania for a two-week investigation of the island. After returning to Melbourne, we drove to Sydney and then flew home. Three months well spent.

A Search for Life

Once home from Australia, we focused on searching for a cure or some way to keep this dreaded and insidious pulmonary fibrosis in abeyance. We found that a group at the University of Washington Medical Center in Seattle did lung transplants and was also working with a pharmaceutical company to test a medication that could stop or slow down the progression of the disease.

This entailed many trips to Seattle for tests, consultations and meetings. Graham was enrolled in a double-blind study (we did not know if he was on the drug or placebo). As Victoria is on an island, this involved many ferry trips, and we were never sure whether our appointment would take a day or if it would involve an overnight stay.

After a few months, the pharmaceutical company abruptly stopped the tests. I assumed that either it was not effective, it was becoming too expensive or it was not a good prospect for wide distribution. Whatever the reason, we were faced with trying to get him on a list for a lung transplant. We knew it would not be an easy task as organs are scarce, particularly lungs, as they are often reserved for young people with cystic fibrosis, a procedure for which both lungs are required. Other procedures usually need only one lung, which means one donor can save two lives.

We tried at the Vancouver General Hospital as it was closer to home and all medical expenses would be paid, but they would not accept him due to his age. He was creeping up to 70 and the Vancouver General had a strict age policy that recipients must be under 60.

We were hopeful the Seattle University Hospital might accept him, pending results of his medical viability. Tests of every type ensued: heart, liver, kidney, blood type and psychological. He was a healthy man and passed all the required tests easily. Finally, he was put on the list for a lung transplant.

By this time, he was on oxygen 24 hours per day, and our trips to Seattle became more difficult as I had to carry the heavy oxygen canisters to the car and into the hotels or hospital. This disturbed him a lot, as he had always been the big "strong" man.

As fall approached, I began to worry about the trips to Seattle, as sometimes the ferries would not run in rough weather and flights would also be curtailed.

I found a pleasant, furnished condo I could sublet in White Rock, on the mainland and close to the American border. I could get to Seattle in two and a half hours if the traffic would allow. I was told by the owners to pay the rent to the building manager, as did a few other sublets in the complex, and she would deposit the funds to their account, which I dutifully did on the first of each month. With Rob's help, we moved into the apartment and waited for the call for an available organ. We would have three hours to arrive at the hospital.

A call came in one morning saying there might be a lung available. I got Graham down to the parking garage, while carrying two oxygen tanks, and we got to Seattle in the prescribed two and a half hours. When we arrived, we were told that the lungs were not suitable to him nor to the man who would receive the other lung. There were no cell phones at that time to warn me that it was a no-go. I turned the car around and made it back to White Rock before dark.

The second call came, and we repeated the same procedure. Then we waited. After about four hours, we were told that the lungs had gone to Idaho where a young cystic fibrosis patient had been waiting for a double lung transplant.

This time, our return trip was more daunting. It was November, and it was already dark when I drove out of the hospital parking garage. It was a raining and I was on a fast-moving freeway with huge trucks passing by, spraying large amounts of water across my windshield and reducing my visibility. I was also worried that there might not be enough oxygen in the one remaining tank to get him home. He, of course, desperately wanted to help with the driving, but could not. By some miracle, we made it back to the apartment safely, and I said, "I just want a hot bowl of soup, a hot bath, a hot rum and to sleep for 12 hours." And I did.

When the next call came in, on December 1, I asked, "Is this a real possibility?"

The answer came, "Yes, definitely." We got into the car and, once again, we were off to Seattle.

When we arrived, everything proceeded quickly, although he did not get to the operating room until about 9 p.m. I sat in the OR waiting room until 1 a.m., when the surgeon came out. It was not the experienced, competent surgeon that I had expected, but rather a young, much less experienced doctor. Because Graham was stronger and healthier than another patient receiving a lung, the surgeons were switched. Despite some minor complications, he said it should be all right. Then he walked off and I never saw him again.

The next day, Graham was sitting up in bed, smiling and happy. He could breathe! The day after that, he felt well and said, "Why don't you go home? I'm fine."

"No," I said, "I'll stay to be sure you're okay." The other recipient survived the surgery, but had a stroke shortly after. Fortunately, as he was in the hospital, they were able to administer the proper drugs and stave off any major damage.

I was feeling almost guilty that Graham was doing so well. But when I returned to his room, he was fibrillating. He had been taken off the anti-fibrillation drugs to do the surgery. He was put on monitors, which I watched almost constantly. More drugs were administered and more machines were hooked up, with no improvement. A tracheotomy was done, he was put on a respirator and tubes were inserted to drain fluids.

Sitting in the hospital lobby, somewhat depressed, an angel appeared in the form of the wife of a well-respected endocrinologist that Graham had known at McGill and a close friend of a cardiologist friend in Victoria. Cathy, who lived in Seattle, was volunteering at the hospital when she saw me and asked why I was there. I told her about Graham, and she asked, "Where are you staying?"

"I have a nice room in a small hotel nearby," I replied.

"You're coming home with me."

Not wanting to impose, I said, "No, no. The hotel is close, and I don't want to interrupt your lives."

"We are ten minutes away, we have a big house, and you will have your own bedroom and bathroom."

Their large house was beautiful, and it looked out over Lake Washington. On the opposite shore, Bill Gates lived in his mansion. Kathy and her husband were a huge moral support and her husband, John, helped with any medical information that I required.

Ken came down to Seattle to offer whatever assistance he could, and Shelley arrived with her husband and baby to visit her father and to help out. I was fortunate to have the support of people around me, as well as receive phone calls from people in Montreal, the U.S. and Victoria.

Finally, things began to improve. The tubes and respirator were removed and the tracheotomy closed; however, the costs had been rising exponentially, and although they would not do the surgery in Vancouver, I hoped they might take him for his recovery period. With some difficulty, I got in touch with the head of the lung transplant department who had turned down Graham's surgery in Vancouver. He said there was nothing he could do at that time, as it was getting close to Christmas but to call him again sometime in the New Year. I contacted his respirologist in Victoria, who said, "I'm sure we can manage him here."

Christmas was upon us and another friend in Seattle said to me, "You need a break. Why don't you go to Shelley's for Christmas?"

"Oh no," I said. "I couldn't leave Graham."

"He's stable right now," he replied, "and I will pick you up tomorrow and drive you to the bus. You'll be in Vancouver in three hours." I did go, and it was a relief to have a break from spending all day in a hospital room. We had a lovely Christmas, but as I was leaving the next day, Shelley said, "I don't want to tell you this, Mom, but I went out to your White Rock apartment and there was an eviction notice on your door."

Upon further investigation, it turned out that the manager, after collecting all the money from several sublets over several months, cashed all the cheques and put the money in her own account. She left town, leaving no trace. Fortunately, I had all the cancelled cheques and was able to contact the owners who were understanding but quite upset about the turn of events, and I did not need further stress in my life.

On my return to Seattle, I began to search for a place to move Graham into, to continue his recovery. Costs that would otherwise have been covered in Canada were mounting. At that time, I made a decision to transfer him to Victoria. Then I would be at home and only minutes from the hospital. I arranged for an ambulance and attendants to bring him to the border and another from the Canadian side to take him to the Jubilee Hospital in Victoria. He was placed in an isolation room where all attendants were required to gown and mask while in the room, in order to avoid infection.

He appeared to improve a little but had to be on a feeding tube and given high doses of prednisone, which caused his blood sugars to increase.

Then, one evening, something was not right. I called the nurses, who tried to allay my fears. It was the weekend, and they did not want to call the doctor. The next day, Graham was worse. He had gone into full organ rejection. By the time the doctor saw him, it was too late, and he was beginning to fade. Shelley came over. Ken, a doctor himself, came over when he could, and Ron, in Australia, was notified. He caught a plane immediately and we told Graham that Ron would be there soon. He kept asking Shelley, "When will Ron be here?" She assured Graham that Ron would be here within hours.

Ron arrived and was able to speak to him, knowing that Graham was listening and could understand what Ron was telling him. The family stayed with him around the clock, often taking turns so that others could sleep.

Miguel, Shelley's husband, was with him at six in the morning on Valentine's Day, in 2000, when he left us, with a sigh. He had wanted so much to live.

AND LIFE GOES ON

A Road Trip with the Postman of Cape Leveque

Life goes on. It's never the same, but it does go on.

In 2002, two years after Graham died, I decided to travel to Perth, Australia, to visit Ron and Rick. Ron and I flew to Broome and, using it as our base, did two adventurous and exciting trips.

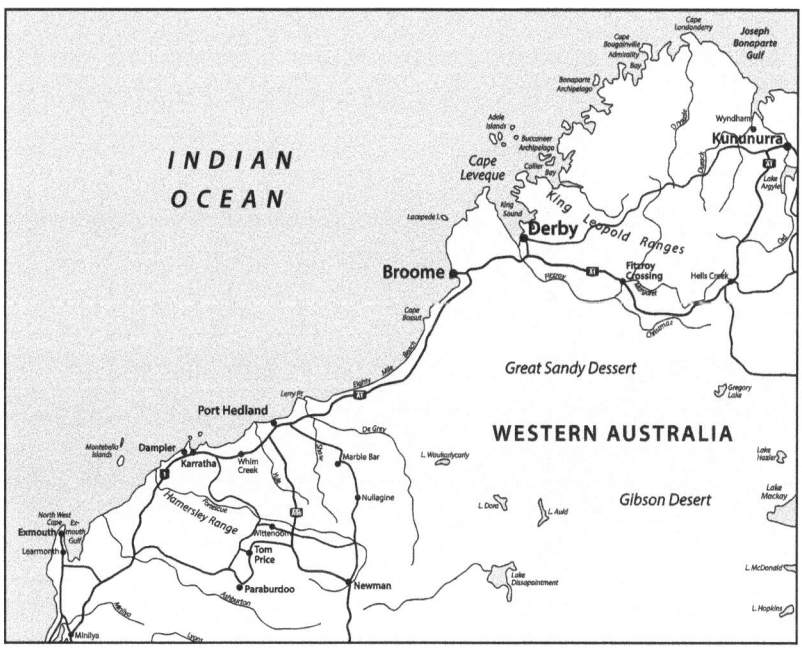

After two days in Broome, we flew to Kununurra in the northern Kimberley region of Australia. There, we had a cabin on stilts, due to the abundance of snakes in the area. We had a friendly one living under the cabin that would come out to sunbathe on a slab of concrete at the foot of the steps every morning. For some reason, even though I described its distinctive features to locals, no one could tell me what kind of snake it was. It was only when I got back to Perth and went to the museum to check it out that I realized that it was a death adder, which is extremely venomous.

Leaving the Kimberly region, and goodbye to our very worn-out shoes

One of the many lizards who were our front door pals

We were fascinated by the large lizards (about two metres long but apparently harmless) and fruit bats by the thousands, which darkened the sky at pre-dusk.

From here, we were flown into the Bungle Bungle mountains by a 13-year-old pilot (well, maybe not 13, but no more than 17). We arrived in the Bungle Bungles to be met by 40-degree-Celsius temperatures and an army of flies. We were shown our individual tents and instructed to zip our closures tightly as a passing snake may wish to become a roommate. Nights in the canvas tent were even hotter than the days, as there was no air flow through the small mesh openings on the sides. We did two hikes a day, mornings and afternoons, and were fed in a large outdoor edifice constructed of corrugated metal siding topped with mesh.

Our plane to the Bungle Bungles

The Bungle Bungles

The mountain landscape is unusual, with orange and dark grey banding on the conical rock formations, which is caused by differences in the layers of sandstone. The ground is mostly sand that's broken by a row of these huge rocks that jut out of it.

We returned to Kununurra, flying over Lake Argyle, a 25-mile-long man-made lake that was a result of damming the Ord River. The lake replenishes itself very quickly in the wet season.

We stayed in our cabin another day and then embarked on the second leg of this part of the trip, to visit some of the deep gorges that abound in the northwest of the country. On the way, we drove through several streams until we reached Ivanhoe Crossing. We looked at it dubiously, as it looked more like a waterfall than a stream, and driving on its edge could easily result in us sliding into the hungry crocodile-infested water below.

Ivanhoe Crossing where the water was at least three feet deep

We watched a utility truck coming towards us cross successfully. However, it was a much larger and sturdier vehicle than ours, and the water was even coming over its hood. We asked the driver how it was looking, and he quite dismissively said it was okay and quickly continued on his way. Ron and I looked at each other and wisely decided to try to find a route around instead of crossing. We did manage to find a way, which took us though several farms. I was the gate-opener, often finding myself face-to-face with a Brahma bull.

We visited several beautiful gorges, such huge bodies of water with high cliffs on either side. We hiked up (a tough hike, with Ron having to help me due to my weakening lungs) to a place that had a large circular area with a waterfall and pool. It was absolutely spellbinding.

On the next leg of the trip from Broome, which was the most memorable in a different way, we rode the mail truck to Cape Leveque.

Cape Leveque is at the northernmost tip of the Dampier Peninsula in the Kimberley region of Western Australia. It sits 208 kilometres north of Broome and is surrounded by the transparent blue waters of the Indian Ocean. The local population is principally the Bardi group of First Nations people.

Due to the remote conditions and sandy terrain on the peninsula, it was essential that we find transportation that wouldn't get bogged down. Apparently, this is considered the worst road in Australia. It is seemingly endless kilometres of corrugated red dirt, potholes, creeks and streams and leads to the First Nations community of Beagle Bay. In fact, I have been on worse roads ... in Costa Rica, New Guinea and even Canada. When we looked into the renting a four-wheel-drive car in Broome, we found that the cost was astronomical, at over $400 per day.

At the time, Ron was director of community services for the West Australian Red Cross. Through his connections at work, he obtained the name of a man who would drive us up the Dampier Peninsula from Broome to Cape Leveque. His name was John. And he was the postman who delivered the mail on that route a few times each week.

At 4 a.m., Ron and I waited outside the Mangrove Hotel, and when the door of the postal van opened, we were greeted by John, the "postie," who turned out to be one of the most colourful characters I have ever met. To say that some of his language on that trip does not bear repeating — in any company — is an understatement. We also had on board a pearling captain and one of his Japanese crew, and both were as dumbfounded as we were with John's tall tales and abominable language.

As we lurched along, it was clear that John liked having an audience. He used an array of foul language, the least of which being the "F" word. All the while, Ron sat behind me on top of the mail packages, cringing that I should be hearing such language. As soon as we alighted at Cape Leveque, Ron started to express his embarrassment at what I had been forced to endure. Before he had finished speaking, I butted in with "so what the *eff* do you want to do right now?" Greatly relieved, Ron laughed himself silly, realizing that this was not the first time I had ever heard someone swear. In fact, John had been very informative, even though his description of First Nations people and culture was wildly racist, sexist, derogatory and, most probably, highly distorted.

As John drove away, back down the sandy roadway, we suddenly saw the overwhelmingly beautiful place we were in. There were miles of white sandy beaches surrounded by red rocks, some of which were carved into shapes one would find in USA's Bryce Canyon, and a turquoise ocean for as far as you could see. We only had time to stash our gear in the elegant safari tents that sat on top of huge wooden platforms before heading out for our day on the ocean.

The boat was owned and operated by a blended Aboriginal family. Joining Ron and me was a young French couple and an Australian couple. It was a truly magical day. First of all, I fished, got a huge strike and began pulling it in. But after five minutes, the line went slack and when I pulled it in, everything was gone — lure, weights and fish. It could have been anything from a shark to a barramundi that did it. Disappointing, because we will never know. Happily, we caught six kinds of colourful fish that day, all big enough to be edible, and we brought them back to the safari tents to cook on the barbecue. These were caught by jigging and using squid as bait.

Then a humpback whale and calf came by and gave us a show, after which we found a little bay and went snorkelling — seeing some of the same kinds of fish we had in our catch bucket. We had lunch on a pristine beach, hiked into a former missionary homestead and then headed back. On the way, we encountered the same pair of humpback whales, who had decided that they had not performed well enough when we passed earlier. So they proceeded to give us the show of a lifetime. They breached, they dived, they leaped and they blew, all within 150 metres of the boat.

We arrived back at camp at dusk to find that the very basic restaurant-cum-mini-store was not open that particular evening, and there was no other store anywhere near this very isolated location. So we took our two fresh fish and put them on the $2,000 barbecue on our deck, poured water over some dry noodles we had packed, and that was dinner. Our only other consumables were a bottle of gin and some tonic water. We proceeded to have one, and then another, gin and tonic as we looked over the beautiful view, absorbing the tropical night heat while the fish cooked.

The next day, we wanted to go to One Arm Point, about 15 kilometres to the south, but we had no transportation. We wandered down to the little café/store and ran into the Australian couple we had met on the boat. They told us they'd be happy to go to One Arm Point and bring us back if we couldn't find a lift.

One Arm Point is an Aboriginal community — as are all the communities on the peninsula. We were told that white people (called "*Wetjala*" or "white guys" by the Western Australian Aboriginal groups) may not be welcome. But Ron had a contact through his work with the Australian Red Cross, so we set off. As it turned out, Ron did not find his contact. Happily, we ran into our boat captain of the day before, who is one of the head men in the community. He gave us carte blanche to go wherever we wished, as long as we stayed away from their sacred areas.

The following day, our postman, John, took us back to Broome via small Aboriginal villages along the way. Before we left, Ron and I noticed a putrid smell in our safari tent. We searched everywhere and were baffled by the overwhelming stench. Eventually, when exploring under the tent platform, we found the source: our rotting fish carcasses from our first night of barbecuing, combined with the gin and tonics. Raw fish that has sat in a hot metal garbage can in the North Australian sun, we discovered, goes "off" much faster than it would in Canada. Having skinned and cooked fish our whole lives, Ron and I again laughed ourselves to tears, contemplating our stupidity. Clearly the gin and tonics had something to do with the fact that we'd completely forgotten about the off-cuts of our dinner.

The trip back to Broome, especially Beagle Bay, was fascinating. The missionaries were in evidence here again. One church was quite a work of art, with the altar, picture frames, part of the floor and various tables and chairs all decorated with pearl shells, mother of pearl, abalone and trochus shell.

It was a subdued and much more polite postman John that brought us back, as he was wearing his gentlemanly hat and using much more polite language. Clearly, he'd had time to reflect on the impression he left a few days previously. He took pleasure and pride in telling us stories of the places we were visiting — not all accurately, but close enough!

My main job on the last part of the trip was to keep John awake. After 10 hours on a less-than-perfect road, he was getting weary, and his eyes often dropped shut. I wasn't overly worried, as I was watching him carefully and, in any case, there was no place to go except into the soft piled-up earth on the sides of the road. When we got back to Broome, he drove us around and showed us the all the sights, including the cemetery for the Japanese pearl divers, many of whom perished doing their work. It seemed that he didn't want to let us go. So, in the end, he turned out to be a fairly decent fellow. And it turned out to be a trip full of great laughter and learning.

Norwegian Impressions

It surrounds you for 24 hours every day. You can't escape it. You are almost tired of it — but you don't really want it to end. Sunshine, or at least daylight, all day, all night. You are standing on the ship's deck at midnight, enveloped in magnificent scenery, with the sun still shining, glancing off the mountaintops that are forming a halo around you.

As you ease out of the fjord and head towards a break between the islands, you see the sun struggling towards the horizon. It dips through a few wispy clouds and you look for a sunset — but there is none. The sun is on the rise again and you are cheated out of both sunrise and sunset.

Of course, there is no dark to usher you to bed for a night's sleep; no, you must remain awake to watch the ever-changing scenes that appear before and around you. No one sleeps, no one wants to sleep, but finally at 3 a.m., with the sun reaching ever further into the sky, you go to bed, as day continues to block the darkness.

The experience cannot be imagined. It must be lived.

It was July 2008. I had invited my daughter Shelley to accompany me on a trip up the Norwegian Coast from Bergen to Kirkenes, near the Russian border, aboard the *Trollfjord*, a small local passenger freighter, or coastal boat, as they are called, from the Hertigruten line, which stopped at many towns on our voyage north and different ones on the way back. Sometimes we stopped for two or three minutes, sometimes for two or three hours, with people, dogs and cargo being loaded on and off, 24 hours a day.

It was brave of her to come, as her youngest son, Sasha, was not quite two years old, and Gabriel, his older brother, was nine. Both were left with Shelley's husband, Miguel, for two weeks. He was a good father but had never had the full responsibility of looking after the boys. As it turned out, they were all alive and well when we returned. They probably didn't eat the allotted meals Shelley had prepared for them, nor attended many of the activities she had planned (and paid for), but they were healthy and happy and delighted to see her when we returned.

We arrived in Bergen a day before our journey was set to begin. One of the old jokes about Bergen is that a woman asked a local boy, "Young man, does it always rain in Bergen?"

"I don't know ma'am," came the reply. "I'm only thirteen."

But we were lucky. The sun shone brightly, and we walked the cobblestone streets, took the tram up the mountain and sampled some of the delicious ocean delicacies that abounded in the kiosks around the harbour. We were, however, shocked at the price of food and ate sparingly.

The next day, we boarded our freighter.

Some of the Norwegian fjords are wide, deep and curving, with waterfalls cascading down the sides. Farms and the remnants of farms cling to the steep terrain, still picture-perfect and manicured, although some have been abandoned as people have relocated to larger towns. It is said that in the past, ladders were used to gain access from the fjord to the farm, and when it was time for the tax collector to make his calls, the ladders were pulled up.

A few fjords, like the Geiranger, are large enough to allow some cruise ships to reach the end and turn to repeat their spectacular journey back. Other fjords, like the Trollfjord, are so narrow that there was little water on either side of our small coastal steamer, and the captain had to focus so as not to scrape the sides of the boat on the steep and unforgiving rock wall that juts up 200 metres from the sides of the fjord. No cruise ship down this one!

It widens a little at the end and the captain was able to swing the ship 180 degrees, inching by the rocks at both bow and stern and sending us on our return journey, accompanied by the powerful sound of Edvard Grieg's "In the Hall of the Mountain King" from his Peer Gynt Suite. One could almost see the trolls smiling wickedly as we passed by.

The midnight sun and the fjords are magical and mystical but not all of Norway acquiesces to this dreamy ambience. Most of it is hard and real. The strength and tenacity of the Norwegians along this difficult island's strewn and rocky coast demand respect. While the women are home, looking after the children, the animals and the gardens, which yield only the few vegetables and berries that can grow in the short six weeks of 24-hour daylight (which, incidentally, must be paid for by 24-hour nights in the winter), the men are fishing, summer and winter, for the various types of fish and mollusks available in their areas.

The Norwegian economy was founded on the fishing industry. Cod and pollack are dried for a three-month period and reconstituted into various delicacies. Most of the fishing occurs in the northern part of the country and fishermen ply the waters year round, due to the warming effect of the Gulf Stream. The waters never freeze, allowing fishermen to fish and the coastal steamers to follow their routes throughout the year.

Seafood is the mainstay of the Norwegian diet and the variety is impressive: herring, Atlantic halibut, Arctic char, salmon, sea trout (steelhead), cod, pollack, flounder, mussels, crab, Norwegian lobster and shrimp. About 60 percent of this is exported and 40 percent remains for home consumption.

The sea was, and to a large extent still is, the main mode of transport for both goods and people. In the late 1800s, a young steamship company took up the challenge of providing a regular service between Trondheim and Hammerfest. This began a communication revolution, which gave coastal inhabitants and industry better access to each other and the rest of the world. Letters, which sometimes took five months to be delivered, reached their destination in five days. The coastal steamship company expanded its reach, and now, every day, a boat such as the one we were on runs from Bergen to Kirkenes, near the Russian border, at the 71st parallel north, carrying mail, cargo, coastal inhabitants and tourists. The entire trip takes 12 days.

It is interesting to note that in these isolated places where the coastal steamer serves much of their need for transportation in this sparsely populated country of 4.5 million, there is now a train that runs from Oslo to Bodo, a distance of almost 1,200 kilometres. There is also a road system that connects the southernmost part of the country to the north. This system includes many of the islands with only a few homes, all connected by hundreds of bridges, tunnels and small ferries and all perfectly functional and well maintained.

There is also power in remote villages. Even homes that appear to be well beyond the town limits have power. One wonders how this is all maintained in some of the most challenging weather conditions, 400 kilometres north of the Arctic Circle. In addition, almost everywhere you look there are communication towers, which allow internet and phone access to anywhere in the world.

Although Norway has been ruled at various times by the Danes and the Swedes, they have never been subjugated. They have maintained their identity and their borders. This long, narrow country abuts Sweden, Finland and Russia. Crossing into Sweden and Finland poses no problem, but the feeling at the Russian border is one of tension and unease. Going up the Pasvik River on a cloudy, rainy day, in a motor-powered dug-out like boat, a sombre mood engulfs you.

When we were taken ashore, we could see a line of yellow posts planted across the river and up the hill. Beyond that, and three metres back, is a parallel line of red markers. In the middle, a metre and a half from either side, is the Russian-Norwegian border and you are cautioned not to cross the invisible line. Apparently, last year, a tourist held her camera over the line to take a picture. She was incarcerated and fined heavily. She also missed her boat back to Bergen.

The entire area is carefully guarded by outlook posts and ground sensors. This is not necessarily considered a hostile border, just a carefully controlled one, and most problems are dealt with locally and efficiently.

There are, however, a few concerns with the Sami people (Laplanders) and their reindeer. They too must respect the border, but the Samis are spread between Norway, Sweden, Finland and Russia, and their reindeer do not understand borders. Usually, if one or two of the animals cross the line, the owners are allowed to retrieve them without penalty.

The Sami people live mainly above the Arctic Circle and the estimated population is something over 100,000, with 35,000 to 60,000 living in Norway. There are also about 10 different dialects, so that a Norwegian Sami cannot necessarily communicate with a Russian Sami. And in Norway, at least, they do not always look similar. Some have the swarthy round faces of the Inuit population but with somewhat finer features, and some have blond hair and fair skin, indicative of the intermarriage with the Norwegians.

Not all Laps are reindeer herders. In fact, only about 10 percent still farm the animals, but the ones who do live in wooden houses in winter, with all the amenities, and in summer, when their animals are taken to their summer range, they'll live in large tents as they did in the old days. They will often take the reindeer by truck to their summer grazing area, sometimes on an island, and then, in the fall when the young are grown and strong, they will swim them across a two-kilometre channel back to the mainland and their winter range.

We visited a "show home" of their original winter homes, similar to a yurt, covered in birch bark and sod. Inside, in the centre of the large room, there was a fire pit and a hole in the roof to allow the smoke to escape. It must have been difficult to find sufficient wood for building and burning, as the land is mostly tundra and trees do not grow tall or in large numbers at this latitude. On top of the sod-covered floor was a layer of reindeer skins. It was warm and comfortable when we visited on a dreary rainy day and, supposedly, it is the same at -50 degrees Celsius.

Another surprising feature about these people is their education. They speak Sami, a language akin to Finnish and Hungarian. They also speak Norwegian and English. Schooling for them is the same as for all other Norwegian children, and when they enter adulthood they live and work in jobs the same as the rest of the population. They are no longer the mysterious snow encrusted people living among the reindeer herds and cut off from the rest of the world; most of them are, in fact, well integrated into the Norwegian culture, economy and work force.

But how does this small country afford all the social and educational programs, as well as the infrastructure, communication and transportation systems? Two words tell it all: oil and gas.

In 1970, a commercially viable oil field was discovered adjacent to the demarcation line between Norway, Denmark and Britain. Exploration continued, oilfields were developed, and now Norway is the world's third largest oil exporter. It also supplies 10 percent of Europe's gas consumption.

A complicated system of pipelines runs down the outer coast. Oil and gas are transported through these lines to the Norwegian coast and to other European destinations. All of this brings in revenue of 200 billion kroner (about $40 billion) annually.

There is much more to say about this beautiful and fascinating small country, such as their occupation and involvement in WWII, their medical system and their social programs, but each one could be its own book, so you will have to wait for the sequel.

Trollfjord at midnight

Shelley and me at the Russian border

Shelley at the Trondelag Folk Museum

A Sami couple

The trip up the mountain on the Floibanen tram in Bergen

Epilogue

As I look back at my life, having recounted it through anecdotal samples, I realize how fortunate I was to have lived in this period of time. I have tried to illustrate the difference in the customs and mores of the times from the start of the twentieth century until now, and thereby show how much the world has changed in a relatively short time. The rapid growth, in many ways, has been beneficial. I would not like to give up electricity, running water or any of the medical advances we have benefitted from, but have we gone a little too fast or sacrificed a little too much in doing so? What with the advances in technology, the plight of worldwide pollution and so many other consequences of our rapid progress, is it time to slow down a little, value what we have and become a more caring society?

As I contemplate all this, I look around at my life now. In 2020, I sold my beloved Beach Drive house and moved into a very nice apartment in the area. I admit it was wrenching, but the time had come.

I'm lucky that my children have stayed in B.C. Ken and his wife, Kathleen, and their daughter, Rhianna, live in Ladysmith (south of Nanaimo) and their son, Graham, is in England. Shelley and her husband, Miguel, and their children, Gabriel and Sasha, live in Port Moody, while Ron and his partner, Rick, live near me in Victoria.

As I said earlier, life goes on.

Family Album

Christmas with the family — 1986

Standing, from left: Karen Smart (daughter of Graham's brother Ken Pettapiece), Karen's husband Ron Smart, Eva Ulman (sister to Graham's mother, Grandma Pettapiece), Trish Pettapiece (daughter of Ken), Mary "Grandma" Pettapiece, Ken's wife Shirley Pettapiece, me, Ken's son Bruce Pettapiece, Ken Pettapiece, my mother, "Grammy" Dobson, Graham, our son Ken's wife Kathleen, our son Ken. Sitting: Our son Ron and Graham's dad Wallace "Granddad" Pettapiece. They're holding a sign that says "Thinking of you Shelley" as our daughter was away at university in Japan on a UBC scholarship.

Ken and Kathleen in our sunroom with their children, Rhianna and Graham — circa 2008

Shelley and Miguel with their sons, Gabriel and Sasha, and their mastiff, Archie, as a puppy — 2015

Ron and his partner, Rick, with me in Shanghai — 2011

Celebrating a birthday dinner in the dining room of our old Qualicum house that we rented for a week in July 2021. Clockwise, from left: my grandson Gabriel, Ron, me, Shelley's husband Miguel, Shelley, my grandson Sasha. Ron's partner, Rick, took the picture.

Dinner at the Crown Mansion in Qualicum. Clockwise, from left: Gabriel, me, Miguel, Ron, Shelley, Sasha and Rick.

Appendix 1

Bella Coola — A Historical Narrative[3]

In my story about my trip on the SS *Cardena* I describe some of the history of Bella Coola. I've expanded on that in this appendix, with some repeated information as well as more details.

Bella Coola, B.C., a beautiful, mystical valley, lies 450 kilometres north of Vancouver, at the end of a long fjord that runs inland 100 kilometres from the Pacific Ocean. The mountains rise up 3,500 metres on either side of the narrow valley and stand as sentinels, protecting it from the inclement weather of the North Coast. It has an interior climate rather than a coastal one.

The first known settlers were the Indigenous Peoples but even their history is a mystery. The present Bella Coola First Nations are Salish, as are the Okanagan and those of the Fraser River Delta. No one is sure how they became isolated 400 kilometres away from the others of their tribe and it is thought that this present group has only been in the valley for the past 600 years.

Norwegian adventurer Thor Heyerdahl spent several months in Bella Coola. He was intrigued by the rock carvings in the Marquesas Islands of French Polynesia and their similarities to the ones in Bella Coola. There were other similarities as well, such as their methods of cooking and their dialect. Heyerdahl surmised that the original Bella Coola First Nations, due to their easy lifestyle, abundant food and the security of their protected valley became indolent and were not prepared for the enemies that came overland through the mountains.

---

3 I have taken information from the book *Bella Coola*, by Cliff Kopas, published by Tenas Tiktik Publishing, Vancouver, B.C., sometimes reproducing the narrative here verbatim, and in other instances, as text summary.

He believes that the rock carvers were driven from the valley, escaping their invaders and settling on the outer islands of the coast. Heyerdahl proposes some even travelled far enough offshore for the strong southerly current to carry them to the Islands of the South Pacific and a new paradise. This, of course, is speculation, but carvings as far away as New Zealand bear a definite resemblance to the ones in the Valley.

The later First Nations built their own new civilization and culture. The abundant cedar bark was woven into hats, cloaks and baskets, and braided for fishing lines or ropes. The trunks of large trees were made into river and sea canoes. They wove stinging nettles into fishnets. They caught eulachon in large numbers, rendering them for their cooking oil and candles. They developed a complex society and social structure with aristocracy, commoners and slaves. They held potlatches and carved great totem poles, making paint from grinding colourful rocks and mixing the powder with fish oil.

To my sorrow, on a trip to San Diego a number of years ago, I found dozens of Bella Coola totems residing in one of the buildings in Balboa Park — many more, I think, than there are in the Smithsonian. At some time during the 1920s or 1930s, people from U.S. museums arrived in the Valley. Chainsaws in hand, they cut down and removed these totems. Perhaps, they felt, they were preserving them, but was it right?

In the late 18th century, the quest for the Northwest Passage was on. It was thought that there was a strait called the Strait of Anion, which split the continent in two, from the Atlantic to Pacific, south of the Arctic Circle. Some Spaniards declared they had sailed it from the Pacific Coast to Hudson Bay in 27 days!

The Spanish and the Russians were involved in exploration and trade with the Indians of the North Coast, but it was the English, with Captain Cook as the naval commander and two illustrious naval men aboard, George Vancouver and William Bligh, who did most to explore and chart the West Coast. Captain Cook did not find the Strait of Anion and did not believe it existed.

A second expedition saw Captain Vancouver, in 1792, on his ship *Discovery*, circumnavigating Vancouver Island and meeting with the

Spaniards (Juan Francisco de la Bodega y Quadra) and the Indian Chief Maquinna at Nootka.

In 1793, Captain Vancouver worked his way up Burke Channel and Bentinck Arm, the longest inland channel of the Pacific Coast, and on June 3, he visited the Indian Village of Bella Coola. In the middle of June, the *Discovery* and the *Chatham* headed north, unaware that an expedition, led by an intrepid Scotsman, was making its way over-land to the head of North Bentinck Arm to discover the first land route from Canada to the Pacific. He was Alexander MacKenzie and he arrived, after a gruelling trip fraught with danger and stark terror, on July 19, 1793, just one month after Vancouver had departed. This small group of voyageurs also carried with them proof that no Strait of Anion existed.

In the mid-1800s, the Caribou Gold Rush waxed and waned and white men found their way from the Caribou to Bella Coola, following MacKenzie's path. They came, bringing whiskey and smallpox, which decimated many of the villages. Towards the end of the century, the missionaries arrived, robbing the people of their beliefs, their gods and their potlatches.

In 1885, B. Filip Jacobsen arrived in Bella Coola from Norway. He had been there the year prior, visiting Indian villages and collecting artifacts to sell to German museums. He was a lean, bright and indus-trious man, and he saw the possibility of building a settlement in the Bella Coola Valley. He had been born on a small island 14 miles from the city of Tromso. He liked the Indians and managed to convince a group of men, actors and artists in the tribe, including the Chief, to accompany him to Germany. They boarded a steamer to San Francisco, rode the train to New York (the first they had ever seen) and continued, by steamer, to Germany. They arrived three weeks after leaving Bella Coola and stayed in Germany 13 months, putting on shows and telling people of their homeland. The German girls liked the men, but the Chief discouraged them from marrying. The Chief himself had a proposal from a wealthy lady, but he told her that he had a wife at home and that he was retuning to her. One man learned to speak fluent German and claimed it was much easier than the Bella Coola language. They all returned safely to Bella Coola.

On his frequent trips to Victoria, Jacobsen tried to convince government officials that Bella Coola was a good place to establish a settlement. He was laughed at. Who would want to go to the remote North Coast with weekly (if they were lucky) ferry service as the only mode of transportation south? He persisted, and with the help of the Indians, made maps of the amount of arable land in the Valley. Because of this, the following year, the B.C. government officially surveyed the land for settlement.

Jacobsen also wrote articles for Norwegian language newspapers in Canada and the United States. One of the articles was picked up by Reverend Saugstad, a Lutheran clergyman in Minnesota who was looking for a pristine place where he could take his flock away from the vagaries and vices of populated areas. Also, at this time, there was a severe depression in the U.S. and Canada, and his people were on the verge of starvation in Minnesota. Since the writings of Jacobsen were still fresh in his mind, he decided to investigate the Bella Coola Valley. He liked what he saw: the gentle climate and huge fjords reminiscent of his home in Norway. And it was isolated from the world. He also spoke to a fellow Norwegian, Thor Thorsen, who had recently settled there with his family.

Rev. Saugstad went to Victoria and visited the government minister of immigration, who told him the Valley was reserved for settlement. If they could establish a colony of 30 families, a wagon road would be built and each settler would be granted 160 acres of free land as a homestead. He returned to Minnesota to tell his parishioners of the beautiful area, with its fjords, the majestic mountains leaping from the sea to a height of 3,500 metres and streams gleaming with salmon.

On October 30, 1894, the *Princess Louise* (a side wheeler) pulled into Bentinck Arm and dropped anchor. Aboard were 84 men, women and children from Norway via Minnesota. They must have been apprehensive as they looked at the dark forest before them, a river discharging to the east of them and huge brooding mountains. They must have been terrified when an armada of canoes manned by swarthy men burst forth from the river mouth and the shadows of the forest. As they stood frozen on the ship's deck, one canoe gained the lead and they could see a slender girl with blond hair in the bow, calling out in Norwegian, "Welcome to Bella Coola." It was Bertha Thorsen, Thor Thorsen's daughter. This must have allayed their fears somewhat.

By nightfall, the last canoe load of passengers and cargo had been landed in a field a mile up the river and opposite the Indian Village, and the *Princess Louise* departed.

When they arrived, it became apparent to them that this valley was not the idyllic Shangri-La that Rev. Saugstad had led them to believe. October was a poor month to arrive on the North Coast, as there was no time to clear land and plant crops. True, there were huge trees, fish in the ocean and an abundance of game, but time was of the essence to get shelter (sheds) built and wood for the winter. The first winter was a hard one, with floods, rain and snow — the worst the North Coast had seen for years. But most of them endured and grubbed out their little parcels of land with axes, saws and peeves. There were no horses or ploughs.

The homesteads allotted to them were 160 acres and numbered, and whatever number you drew was your lot, be it good or bad. It could be close to the only store or 40 kilometres up the valley. The boat bringing supplies came infrequently, so their orders may or may not arrive. Since there were no phones, one couldn't be sure whether their order had arrived or not, possibly making the 80-kilometre hike unnecessary. They carried everything on their backs, be it 40 kilograms of flour or a 100-kilogram stove.

Rev. Saugstad received the $10,000 allotted for the road and bridges, and most of the colonists built the 20-mile road up the valley, receiving one dollar a day in wages.

Thus began the most successful and enduring colony of immigrants on the North Coast. Anyone travelling to the region will find the descendants of the original Norwegians still there, vigorous, kind and welcoming.

Appendix 2

Brother XII[4]

The small house on the lagoon, in which Margaret, my sullen neighbour from my time at the Portage had lived, had a story of its own to tell.

Legend has it that it had been a hideaway for Madam Zee, the infamous and cruel consort of Brother XII. In May 1927, a man who called himself Brother XII arrived in Cedar-by-the-Sea with a small following of devotees. They were to begin an organization, calling themselves the Aquarian Foundation. They were to divest themselves of all worldly goods, and their money was funnelled into the coffers of the Aquarian Foundation. Brother XII was a small, fragile-looking man of about 55, but he looked much older. He wore black clothes and a tall black hat, and he had a black pointed beard and piercing blue eyes that seemed to cast a spell over anyone he encountered and certainly anyone he wished to entice into his sect.

They worked hard to build a self-sufficient community without benefit of machinery or even beasts of burden. Instead, they were the beasts of burden, pulling ploughs, hauling logs, water and rocks and building their own accommodations — which were sparse. There was no electricity, no running water, little, if any, heat and little communication with the outside world. They were forced to work long hours, driven by Brother XII himself. All forms of entertainment were forbidden. Still, they were content in the knowledge that their work and sacrifice were for a greater good.

---

4   I have taken information from the book *Brother XII — the Strange Odyssey of a 20th Century Prophet*, by John Oliphant, published by Twelfth House Press, Halifax, NS, sometimes reproducing the narrative here verbatim, and in other instances, as text summary.

The beginning of the period appeared to be a rather happy time. At the end of a day's work, they would congregate under a large maple tree and discuss their role in establishing an evolved race of humanity. The premise was that the world was entering a period of rapid decline and this new foundation of superior beings would form a sixth sub-race. Work was one form of preparation for this evolved form of humanity. It was also preparation for a divine being, who was to come to earth within the century and lead the sixth sub-race. In July 1928, Brother XII boarded a train bound for Chicago. On this train, he met and charmed an attractive lady, Myrtle Baumgartner, a doctor's wife. The doctor had been a vigorous athlete, but due to an injury on the football field he had become an invalid, and the lady had become weary of nursing him and weary too of his bitterness in what had befallen him. She was looking for a greater meaning to life, and who was there to help her find this greater meaning but Brother XII? After much sharing of souls, the lady ended up in Brother XII's sleeper. He had convinced her that he had had a revelation that she was the goddess Isis and he the god Osiris and that they would have a son, the reincarnation of the god Horus, who would become a world teacher and lead humanity into a new spiritual age.

Myrtle did not question any of these revelations and seemed quite happy to be the mother of such an important god.

Brother XII attended a political meeting in Chicago and carried on to Toronto, where he had arranged to meet Mary Connally, a wealthy member of the Aquarian Foundation. She was the daughter of one of America's oldest and most prominent families, her ancestors having arrived in America in 1608, 12 years before the arrival of the Mayflower. She lived in a 50-room mansion in Asheville, North Carolina, and at age 60, discovered Brother XII's teachings. As a student of religion and philosophy, his teachings were in tune with her own ideas on how the world could and should change.

Their meeting was harmonious, as she was in accord with his visions and plans, including his desire to build a new settlement on Valdez Island. Mary Connally then donated a further $23,000 to the $2,000 she had already given.

Brother XII returned to Cedar at the end of August, and with him was Myrtle Baumgartner, or Isis. They arrived at night, and by early morning, he had moved her to a sparsely furnished two-room cabin on Valdez Island, where she remained for some time. After she spent some months living alone on the island, he brought her back to Cedar so they could meditate together in the House of Mystery and fuse their souls. This was a house he had built for his own meditations so that he could elevate to a higher plane and receive inspiration and instruction from the masters of wisdom to carry on his works.

To have the sacred ground used for the purposes of sex was abhorrent to the followers of the Aquarian Foundation. Brother XII attempted to explain it all away by writing an article about three types of marriage: sexual, companionship and spiritual. His association with Myrtle was, of course, the latter, on a very high level.

Some of the followers believed and others did not. Unrest was fomenting. Brother XII himself was becoming less stable, and there were questions about the state of his sanity. He would fly into a rage on the slightest provocation and then withdraw from the rest of the group for days at a time. Various meetings of founding members ensued, and it was established that they wished to dissolve the foundation. Brother XII summoned Mary Connally.

When the foundation was dissolved, court cases followed regarding the distribution of the monies. In the end, Mary Connally appeared in court and declared that she had given her money to Brother XII without restrictions of any kind. Based on this evidence, he was acquitted of confiscation of funds. The judge, Beaver Potts, however, referred the case to go to the fall assizes (inquests). The judgement was accepted to mean that the provincial government intended to fully investigate the activities of Brother XII and the Aquarian Foundation. Once again, in November, at the assizes, charges were dropped, due in large part to the disappearance of a key witness. Speculation still abounds on what happened to this witness, but foul play is definitely suspected.

Meanwhile, work on Valdez continued, and Mary was taken there to be shown the development of the community and plans for the future. Everyone living there would surrender all personal possessions, all interests and activities and live the life of service and devotion. They also travelled to the DeCourcy Islands where, on one of the islands, there was a deserted farm, which, with a great deal of work, would be able to supply the colony with all the vegetable produce required to feed the community. He explained that he wished this new sanctuary to be the new headquarters of the colony. Mary Connally then purchased Ruxton and DeCourcy Islands and put the title in the name of Brother XII's secretary.

By this time, Myrtle (Isis) had been banished from the group. She, apparently, had had two miscarriages and was of no further use to him. Word has it that she went insane, but what really happened to her remains is yet another mystery of this strange sect spawned on the idyllic shores of Cedar, Valdez and the DeCourcy Islands.

In 1929, Mabel Skottowe and Roger Painter arrived from Florida. Mabel, a Canadian, had divorced her husband, and Roger had been married five times. They had entered into a passionate love affair. They had both been secretaries for the Aquarian Foundation in Florida and had come by invitation to the headquarters in Cedar. Painter, known as the "Poultry King of Florida," had contributed thousands of dollars to the foundation, had sold his business and arrived with $90,000 in hand to give to the Brother.

Recognizing the need for more governors, and happy for the money, Brother XII immediately made both Mabel and Roger fellow brothers. He claimed to have worked with Roger in a past life and conjured up an association with the Knights Templar of Malta through Painter and announced that the Knights were being reincarnated and assembling again.

Meanwhile, Brother XII was having his way with Mabel. At night, he would crawl into her tent and leave early in the morning. One night, screams were heard from Mabel's tent and when some of the colonists arrived, they saw Roger Painter running from the tent and Mabel beaten and bloodied. Roger was banished from the colony and returned to Florida — waiting to be summoned back to the fold. Mabel moved in with Brother XII and what followed was a strong and sinister alliance between the two of them. She became his personal secretary and was made foreman of the colony. Her new official name was Madam Zee. Some say she was tall, red-headed and unpleasant looking; others say she was feminine and clever. Whatever her physical attributes were, she was cruel and short-tempered and carried with her a whip that she used without restraint when she felt the followers were not working hard enough or following instructions implicitly. She was particularly hard on Mary Connally who, in her sixties, was frail and unused to work of any kind. She put her in a cabin without heat and with holes in the walls and put her to work cutting and carrying wood, scrubbing floors and windows and carrying food and supplies to other parts of the island. This took a serious toll on the frail lady, but she felt she was being tested for her work to come when she achieved a higher plane.

In early 1930, Brother XII and Madam Zee took a trip to England. While there, he did some writing, but it appeared to be just a holiday, as the two of them enjoyed luxury accommodations in some of the finer hotels and mansions of the country. He then bought a 62-foot sailing vessel, renamed her *The Lady Royal* and proceeded to sail her — not without incident — all the way back to Cedar, via the Panama Canal. The boat was unloaded under mysterious circumstances, secretly and at night. Many in the colony suspected drugs, due to the clandestine nature of the operation and his increasingly bizarre behaviour. But he was not as deranged as many began to believe. He was taking the money from the foundation, changing it into gold coins, placing them into specially made boxes and burying them around the island.

It was apparent that the colonists were becoming disgruntled, and they mounted another court case. This time they had Mary Connally on their side. All voiced their concerns and their accusations of fraud, but when the accused, Brother XII, was called to the witness box, no one responded. No one is sure where he and the infamous Madam Zee found sanctuary. There is evidence that they spent a year in Britain before they left for Switzerland, where he was admitted to a hospital in Neuchâtel and where he died. One tangible clue to his demise is a death certificate for Edward Arthur Wilson (his real name) in Neuchâtel, Switzerland, dated November 7, 1934. He was 54 years of age. But even this was suspect as there is some credible evidence that he was seen in San Francisco some years later.

Madam Zee's eventual circumstances also remain a mystery. There have been reports of people having seen her in a luxury hotel in Switzerland, in Montreal and in Seattle. The last sighting was in Nanaimo in the 1940s, where a workman recognized her under her elegant clothes and furs. Obviously, she was not living in poverty — as most of Brother XII's followers were.

Was he an evil man, a misguided man, a deranged man or a charlatan? Or did he just get overburdened by his responsibility and his own self-importance? Charles Lillard and associates have also written a book on the Brother, in which he disclaims that he was as evil as he is depicted. Lillard has done extensive research and has not found evidence to uphold all the stories and tales of Brother XII. Did the little house on the lagoon really house Madam Zee for her retreats or other activities she may have indulged in? Did they get away with all the boxes of gold? No one knows for certain.

But I do know that by the time we reached Cedar in 1942, stories were still being told and people were still digging all over DeCourcy Island, looking for the glass jars of gold sealed in wax and buried. None was ever found, and the mystery lives on.

Acknowledgment

My thanks to my editor, Eloise Lewis, for her patience and encouragement in this endeavour.

www.ingramcontent.com/pod-product-compliance
Lightning Source LLC
Chambersburg PA
CBHW051510120626
46551CB00012B/865